Always in Trouble

Music:Interview

A SERIES FROM WESLEYAN UNIVERSITY PRESS
Edited by Daniel Cavicchi

Always in Trouble: An Oral History of ESP-Disk',
the Most Outrageous Record Label in America
by Jason Weiss

Forthcoming titles in the series include books by Michael Veal on
Wayne Shorter and Harriet Alonso on Yip Harburg. For updates
and more information on the series please visit our website www.
wesleyan.edu/wespress.

Always in Trouble

An Oral History of ESP-Disk',
the Most Outrageous Record Label
in America

Jason Weiss

WESLEYAN UNIVERSITY PRESS

Middletown, Connecticut

Wesleyan University Press

Middletown CT 06459

www.wesleyan.edu/wespress

Manufactured in the United States of America

Designed by Katerine B. Kimball

Typeset in Minion by Integrated Publishing Solutions

Wesleyan University Press is a member of the Green Press
Initiative. The paper used in this book meets their minimum
requirement for recycled paper.

Library of Congress Cataloging-in-Publication Data

Weiss, Jason, 1955–

Always in trouble : an oral history of ESP-Disk', the most outrageous record label in America / by
Jason Weiss.

p. cm. — (Music/interview)

Includes index.

ISBN 978-0-8195-7158-8 (cloth : alk. paper) — ISBN 978-0-8195-7159-5 (pbk. : alk. paper) —
ISBN 978-0-8195-7160-1 (ebook)

1. ESP-Disk' (Firm) 2. Jazz musicians—United States—Interviews. I. Title.

ML405.W45 2011

781.65092'273—dc23   2011046333

5 4 3 2 1

Contents

Photographs follow pages 77 and 184.

Acknowledgments

This work began its own circuitous life in mid-July 2008, when Bernard Stollman called me up one day, out of the blue, and asked if I would like to write a book with him about the ESP label. Although I eventually came to understand that I was the one writing the book, he made himself readily available from the start and provided whatever support he could. So, I must first of all thank him for his good humor and patience, as well as his generosity of spirit.

In my frequent visits to the ESP office, I inevitably found any number of small details, favors, and questions to ask of the incredibly devoted staff, who have each in turn since moved on to new challenges: general manager Tom Abbs, director of promotions Adam Downey and his predecessor Fumi Tomita, and chief financial officer Douglas McGregor (their duties stretched well beyond what the titles indicate). I extend my sincere appreciation to them for their constant cooperation.

Of course, there would be no book without the candor and willingness of everyone I interviewed, so I am indeed grateful to them all. Their names you will know by turning the pages. The photographers as well proved remarkably kind in allowing me to use their work, and I hope that even within the present limits I have done them some measure of justice.

I would also like to thank Alan Sondheim for his ongoing advice and reflections in the development of this book; Gérard Terronès, for the time and music he so freely offered me at his home in Paris, which reconfirmed for me his lifelong dedication to the music and musicians' rights; Ken Wissoker, editorial director at another press, for his early enthusiasm, which helped propel the project further; and for assorted gestures of assistance and answering of questions: Pierre Crépon, Philippe Carles, Pete Gershon, Marshall Reese, Ali Alizadeh, David Stoelting, Franck Médioni, Matt Lavelle, Steven Joerg, Byron Coley, Filippo Salvadori, Christian Gauffre, Antoine Prum, Richard Meltzer, Kurt Gottschalk, Bruno Guermonprez, Guy Klucevsek, Fumiko Wellington, and Suzannah B. Troy.

Finally, but not least, I must thank my editor at Wesleyan, Parker Smathers, as well as the Music/Interview series editor, Daniel Cavicchi, and my fine-eyed copyeditor, Susan Silver, for their helpful guidance along the way.

A Note on the Photographers

While doing a bit of research on ESP at the Institute of Jazz Studies in Newark, I came across an interview that had appeared in *Jazz Hot* during the label's heyday ("Qui êtes-vous, Bernard Stollman?" *Jazz Hot* 33, no. 230 [1967]). Among the more informative pieces on ESP from that time, it was written by Daniel Berger, a young Frenchman who also included half a dozen photos that he himself had shot in New York. I was lucky enough to find him, via the phonebook, still alive and well and thriving in Paris. We maintained an intermittent e-mail correspondence over the next ten months about the possibility of using some of his photos for my book. At last, in July 2009, we met while I was visiting Paris. He suggested I count on at least a few hours to go through his various boxes of negatives and prints from forty-three years earlier. How much could there be, I wondered. In the end, we spent over five hours together, and in his great generosity he not only gave me whatever prints I chose but also lent me the negatives for other shots I wanted to have printed.

As it happened, Daniel never became a professional photographer. Through the 1960s and '70s, he worked as a journalist and in the music industry and as a producer for French television, before becoming a business consultant, most recently to the wine industry; he recently directed a documentary on wine and Europe for European television. But from February to May 1966, in his mid-twenties, he had gone off to New York with his friend Alain Corneau, the future film director (who recounted these efforts in his 2007 memoir *Projection privée*), to do initial research for a documentary on free jazz. Though subsequently abandoned, it was to have been produced by Claude Lelouch, who won the grand prize at Cannes that May for *A Man and a Woman* and thus went on to bigger projects. Diligent in their task, every day for three months the two visitors went out to meet the new musicians at their homes, at clubs, wherever they could, while getting acquainted with the Lower East Side and other neighborhoods. Daniel took well over a thousand photos along the way. As the reader can see by my selection, I appreciated especially the casual moments captured with the musicians. Some of these photos have never been published; others have appeared over the years in books, museum exhibits, and films.

During that same visit to Paris, I also looked up Guy Kopelowicz, a professional photographer for the Associated Press for forty years and now retired. His photos had graced covers in the original ESP catalog, and he was also present at Albert Ayler's *Spirits Rejoice* session. What I hadn't realized was how active he had been in documenting free jazz and a lot of other music, as a passionate sideline (with a record collection to match). He sent me a long list of the people he had photographed just through the latter half of the 1960s, mostly around Paris and in two visits to New York: few notable jazz musicians had escaped his lens. On our first meeting, I set aside a number of shots from the boxes of prints that he found readily at hand. But much more of his archives lay in storage in his basement, and he had to search around there to find what other prints might be available. Within days, he had located another batch of photos, and when I saw him again I marveled that such a trove lay quietly among his shelves, mostly unseen by the greater public. As with Daniel, Guy was utterly generous in letting me use whatever I wanted for my book.

Subsequently, I located another small archive of period photos. Sandra Stollman, youngest sibling of Bernard by fifteen years, had taken many shots of ESP artists in the 1960s. Her work was featured on nine album covers, including records by Byron Allen, Noah Howard, Frank Wright, the Godz, and the iconic photo of Sonny Simmons in Central Park for his debut *Staying on the Watch*; when Ayler saw her double-image portrait of him at a concert, he insisted that would be the cover for *Spirits Rejoice*. Though a substantial portion of her photos has been lost over the years, she knew just where the folder was that contained what did remain. From her home in Florida, where she moved in the late 1990s to care for her mother, she scanned and sent me copies of some prints and a number of contact sheets, the negatives in many cases no longer available. Again, I was honored to count on her participation.

I should also briefly mention the provenance of a few other photos to be found in these pages. Piotr Siatkowski, a jazz photographer in Krakow, Poland, had first contacted me about my book on Steve Lacy. When I told him of the ESP project, he responded enthusiastically, and so I mentioned a few musicians of whom I still did not have photos. Before long, he sent me the shots of Sonny Simmons and William Parker, each taken during performances in Krakow. And then, wondering where I might find a worthy shot of the determined survivor that is Giuseppi Logan, reemerged from decades of oblivion, I discovered on the Internet an incredible dossier of photos taken by Margo Ducharme, in which Giuseppi had been hired to model the debut line of clothing designed by her boyfriend, Greg Armas, for Assembly New York, his shop on the Lower East Side. The photos were taken on East 9th Street in New York, near Tompkins Square Park, where Giuseppi goes nearly every day to play his horn. Like the other photographers in this book, Margo did not hesitate when I asked to use her work. As the reader can see, I have been most fortunate in that regard.

Introduction

The history of independent record labels, in the United States and abroad, has run like a fleet-footed spirit alongside the larger, more commercial enterprises since the beginning of the industry. Less burdened by grand designs, and keeping a sharper focus and certainly a tighter margin of operations, the independents managed paradoxically to court greater risk; having almost nothing to lose, they could afford to produce art for art's sake, or simply for the invigorating sake of provocation. Of course, labels that started out small, as they grew and proved their singular worth, often were gobbled up by more robust companies. Yet even today, with the greatest concentration of media conglomerates, as the technology mutates into ever newer forms, and when it seems impossible for any company to survive by actually selling records, new independents still emerge in every corner of music and in every region.

Jazz, as an evolving laboratory for musical innovation, has always thrived on the daring of independent labels. Writer and record-store owner Ross Russell launched Dial Records in 1946, and for three years he produced crucial dates in Charlie Parker's career as well as in those of other bebop artists. The musician-owned Debut Records, led by Charles Mingus and Max Roach in the late '40s to the mid-'50s, provided the opportunity to hear not only their own early work but also that of various associates, including Paul Bley's first outing. In 1960 the farsighted Candid Records, briefly directed by jazz critic and civil libertarian Nat Hentoff, carried Roach and Mingus into a new era with more overtly political work, besides offering distinctive early sessions by younger musicians such as Cecil Taylor, Eric Dolphy, and Steve Lacy. In the wake of such adventurous small labels came Bernard Stollman with ESP-Disk', at the moment when a radical shift was taking hold: free improvisation as a dominant aesthetic in the new music.

Even today, some fifty years later, the unaccustomed listener will find most of ESP's initial releases startling, an assault on traditional notions of form and content in music. And indeed, they were. The advances pioneered in jazz throughout the 1960s were arguably the most far-reaching in the history of the music, then or since; subsequent generations are still harvesting, and grappling with, that legacy. The vanguard artists were exploding open the dances and popular song forms (the blues, Tin Pan Alley, show tunes) that served as the bedrock of jazz structures, to reconfigure what was once a familiar framework in ways that focused on all that was happening inside, to highlight the playing itself. In effect, for certain practitioners, this tendency toward greater abstraction, a kind of pure expression as it were, brought jazz in line with comparable developments in visual art, literature, and even contemporary composed music.

As in previous decades, New York was the primary forge for the newest experiments in jazz. Nearly all the major innovators were based there at the time, including John Coltrane, Ornette Coleman, Cecil Taylor, Albert Ayler, and Sun Ra. It was there too that the short-lived Jazz Composers Guild, a noble attempt to establish a self-sustaining musicians' collective, produced several historic festivals and series of new music concerts. But the force, as well as the rage, that characterized free jazz in its original period of growth was also bound up, often enough, with the political issues of the day, notably the civil rights movement and the massive protests against the Vietnam War. This context, ultimately, provided an inherent continuity to some of ESP's ventures further afield as it recorded provocative folk-rock groups such as the Fugs, along with other mind-expanding projects. The label thus articulated an identity, and when it came onto the scene, for those musicians it was really the only game in town. Stollman's discovery of the new music, therefore, was a direct result not just of his presence in New York but also of his innate sympathy for a community of artists whose instincts matched his own: their independent do-it-yourself approach, a bemused irreverence for established procedure, the need to question received wisdom both historical and social, and above all, a principled integrity that was about far more than mere commercial success. In short, all these wild-sounding individuals had their reasons, however mysterious, for sounding the way they did, and to Stollman it was a blessing that they did not in fact sound like all the rest.

Prior to founding his label, Stollman was not exactly a longtime jazz aficionado. But he liked the people and the new music suited his temperament, perhaps more than he realized at first. Trained as a lawyer, a profession he adopted by default as the eldest child of immigrant parents, he had gravitated toward working with musicians, intrigued by their particular problems. He was in his midthirties when the idea first occurred to him, in 1963, that starting a record company might be not only possible but a worthwhile and necessary endeavor.

However, not then or since did he learn to really treat the undertaking as a business; if he had, the label would not be what it was, or is today.

The 1950s and '60s were a particularly rich period in American vernacular music. Jazz musicians were carrying the harmonic and rhythmic discoveries of bebop into a wealth of new directions such as cool jazz, hard bop, and Third Stream, but also into far more open-ended forms. Folk music and blues idioms were being revived, revalorized, and taken up by urban sophisticates who wrought their own inevitable transformations. Rock and roll drew fresh impetus from the British invasion (and the British, of course, had developed their styles in part by borrowing from American song forms) and soon became a phenomenon of mass audiences. The popular growth of rock, in turn, accentuated the divide that had emerged ever since bebop began to veer away from dance and turn to art music. In effect, the jazz artists had freed themselves—often at the cost of their own economic survival—to pursue the highest realms of musical thinking, much like their classical counterparts but without the institutional infrastructures of support. Audiences grew smaller where the music became most unfamiliar and demanding, and yet a devoted public remained eager to partake of the adventure. What galvanized Stollman in his commitment to the label, as he explains in his part of this book, was first hearing tenor saxophonist Albert Ayler and then, nine-plus months later at a crowded café in his own neighborhood, attending the October Revolution in Jazz. Produced by Bill Dixon and the Jazz Composers Guild in an effort to generate their own working conditions, the October Revolution's several days of concerts featured many artists who would soon record for ESP.

So, how did Stollman decide on the name of his label? After settling back in New York at the end of the 1950s, amid attempts to establish himself in business or law, he also became involved in the Esperanto movement, which he helped to promote as a universal language. In recent years, he has even been a partner in the development of Unikom, an automated software system using Esperanto as an interlingual stage to assist in the rapid translation between languages over computer networks. In the early '60s, he produced his first record, *Ni Kantu en Esperanto* (Let's Sing in Esperanto), with that same idea of advocacy, showing the language in action using poetry, humor, and song. The label that issued the record was to be called Esperanto Disko (the Esperanto word for "records"), which became shortened to ESP-Disk'. That the name also suggests a special kind of intuition proved fortuitous when the label subsequently found its true direction. In the 1960s free improvisation became a sort of holy grail for jazz musicians who were pushing the limits, or rather a lingua franca, like Esperanto itself.

By reaching past the tradition of harmonic structures and chord progressions, improvising musicians found new points of contact, new approaches to making music together. A vast array of sound elements was increasingly put into play, in the ongoing search for whatever forms of music might evolve from the exchange. This was by no means a development limited to the United States: throughout Europe and beyond, a growing community of free improvisers was staking out undiscovered territories of music, and in their searches they sometimes joined forces with musicians schooled in other traditions (for example, Musica Elettronica Viva, the improvising electronic music collective founded by classically trained American composers in Rome in the 1960s, or Henry Cow, the British avant-rock improvisers in the 1970s).

From its inception, ESP-Disk' remained unpredictable both in the music it offered and in its defiance of industry conventions. The new music based on free improvisation was its core identity, but the label soon diversified into rock and folk, protopunk and protest music, as well as an occasional spoken-word document reflecting the historical moment—there was little discernible pattern or design. Stollman functioned more by instinct, circumstance, opportunity, and by following his own eclectic curiosities and taste. The label quickly became known—often by word of mouth—for its challenging and eye-opening productions, as well as for its singular cover art; stories abound about how it served as the measure of hip record collections. "You never heard such sounds in your life," was the banner it lived by. Just as important, printed across the bottom of every back cover, was the phrase that defined its attitude toward the people it recorded: "The artists alone decide."

For all its underground renown, in the spirit of independent record labels it survived for barely a decade, issuing some 125 titles; more precisely, as Stollman recounts, the company was pretty much out of business after barely four years, but somehow he stubbornly kept on producing records until it folded completely. Over the next three decades, however, a curious thing happened: ESP led a series of shadow lives through foreign licensing deals as well as bootlegs. What had originally been a catalog of quite modest press runs proved attractive enough that its titles kept resurfacing in Europe and Japan. These, in turn, found their way back into the United States. Stollman, meanwhile, had mostly left the label behind after its demise, eventually taking a real job as a government lawyer. He felt he had failed the artists he recorded—for not promoting them adequately, for deficient bookkeeping, for being unable to prevent the company from going under. At last, on reaching retirement age, he happily left government work as well. But it was not until more than a decade later, in 2005, that he took control again and relaunched ESP, bringing the label fully back to life.

Behind an unassuming and nearly unmarked storefront in the Bed-Stuy neighborhood of Brooklyn, occupying the entire ground floor in what was once a laundromat, Stollman and a few full- and part-time employees and interns stay busy, on any given day, keeping to their ambitious schedule. Through 2008 and 2009, ESP-Disk' released CDs and some vinyl five times a year, totaling more than fifty titles; these included reissues from the original catalog—remastered from the analog tapes and sometimes with additional material—alongside productions of new bands and previously unreleased archival recordings. This practice is a departure from ESP's quite irregular release schedule back in the 1960s. The label has also come to offer most of its catalog as digital downloads for sale through its active website, a source as well for video and radio features on ESP-related artists. As a community outreach initiative, since the fall of 2008 the label has sponsored a monthly concert of ESP artists at the Bowery Poetry Club in Manhattan, and more recently a similar series in Brooklyn at the Jazz Lounge, around the corner from its offices. The label has also sponsored or co-sponsored occasional marathon concerts, such as the November 2009 benefit for the Jazz Foundation of America held at the Bowery Poetry Club and the first annual Albert Ayler Festival held on Roosevelt Island in July 2010. Additionally, every week an ongoing project of restitution is quietly carried out, in which the sales and royalty calculations for one more artist in the catalog are comprehensively brought up to date as part of its Royalty Share program; where a debt is found to be owed, the company makes payment. Perhaps age does bring a bit of wisdom, after all, or at least experience counts for something when taking up an old enterprise again: never has the label been more organized, even if it hardly resembles a normal operation.

The revived company has occupied the Brooklyn offices since 2007. The not-quite-finished remodeling of the front half of the floor, where a small record store opens onto the street and taped drywalls mark off a distinct storage room, leads past several mixed-use corners into a central area with a cluster of separate desks where the staff performs various tasks of production, promotion, layout, accounting, and research. The patchwork repair of the place grows more ragged still in the ample room at the back, with its several patterns of old tin ceiling and a motley assortment of hanging lamps; the bathroom and a small kitchen are located in the rear, while along one wall stands a row of file cabinets stacked with big boxes and a TV. Across from these, Stollman's long desk, reflecting constant activity, is piled with CDs, papers, a computer, and a phone.

That phone is steadily occupied throughout the day. Besides representing several musicians and the estates of Eric Dolphy, Bud Powell, Art Tatum, Sun Ra, Albert Ayler, and others in the global administration of their recording and publishing rights, he is also pursuing a number of far-flung possibilities for release on ESP or a subsidiary imprint. Recently, these have included a trove of unreleased performances by Jimi Hendrix; recordings from Soviet archives of concerts in Moscow by Paul Robeson and Yves Montand in the 1950s; a recent stand-up comedy performance in an L.A. club by Mort Sahl; new archival projects of music by Horace Tapscott, Phineas Newborn Jr., and Eric Dolphy; and, surely the most unexpected, rare performances by Kate Smith. Stollman does not worry too much about diluting or confusing the label's identity. Even as it continues to offer sounds that may never have been heard before, he clearly enjoys unearthing little-known finds, the rare jewels that deserve to be made available. Unpredictable in genre and direction, the label maintains its ability to challenge expectations, including those built by its own practices.

In light of these multiple projects, the time seems ripe to tell the story of the label, from before its beginnings right up to the ever-moving present. After meeting with Bernard Stollman for a few hours, I became convinced that the only way to present that story was straight from the source. Complaints have circulated since the original releases about royalties not paid beyond the small advance; Stollman recognizes where proper accounting was lacking and to make up for that lapse is one reason he plunged back into the fray. But he also acknowledges that most of the records never sold very much when the company previously existed. What seems certain is that he never got rich off of anyone, far from it.

As an oral history, then, this book is divided into two main parts. In the first, based on many hours of interviews through the latter half of 2008 and regular visits over the following year, Stollman gets to tell his story, the only comprehensive account possible, despite its gaps. Edited to follow a more or less chronological order, it incorporates certain thematic chapters to focus on specific areas of activity. I retain some scaled-down version of my questions to him (except in a few chapters) to help direct the narrative through its many turns but also to keep a space open for interstitial remarks. At eighty-one, Stollman stands tall, straight-backed, and strong. Though longevity runs in the family, the fact is he was always inclined toward clean living. His memory still seems remarkably clear, and his outlook remains curiously upbeat. No question, this is what he wants to be doing more than anything, running the record label that he founded long ago, before he knew better.

Inasmuch as the label is largely the story of one man's instincts and eccentricities, it also belongs to all the musicians and others who have had a role in its history, and even to those far away in place and time, for whom ESP-Disk' served as an example or inspiration (a full discography can be found online at the ESP website, www.espdisk.com). Therefore, the second part of the book accommodates their varied perspectives, comprising more than three dozen interviews. These are meant to recount not only their own individual share in the story but also the artistic ideas and tendencies that animated them; moreover, these interviews reflect, whether briefly or at some length, the remarkable lives that converged for a time in the singular course of ESP's trajectory, while offering a glimpse in many instances of how those lives carried through to the present.

Brooklyn, September 2010

1

What Got into His Head

BERNARD STOLLMAN, FOUNDER OF THE LABEL

1 Who, Where, When

Beginnings and Departures

As the founder of a label unlike any other, Bernard Stollman shared the Jewish immigrant background of certain Hollywood moguls and also a few jazz impresarios, yet with many distinct turns. How he ended up in music, running a business that was hardly a business, seemed anything but a likely outcome. He recounts his own circuitous path along the way.

My father, David, was born at the turn of the century, in the small Polish market town of Krynki [Krinik]. He was the third youngest of nine children whose father, a devout Orthodox Jew, labored for long hours as the foreman of a local tannery owned by his brothers. The rafters of their one-story house held stacks of curing hides, which gave off a terrible stench. My father attended yeshiva as a child, until he was apprenticed to a tailor at the age of twelve. One day, his closest friend came running to the shop to tell him excitedly that a traveling cantor had arrived in town and was auditioning boy singers to accompany him on his tour of the great synagogues of Poland and Russia. My father's sweet voice won him employment, and the two boys found themselves celebrities, warmly applauded by congregations whose women showered them with attention and fine food.

When a year had elapsed, his voice began to change with the onset of puberty. The First World War had begun and the cantor abruptly fled to America, abandoning him in a distant city without funds. Desperate, the boy approached a well-dressed stranger on the train platform and told him of his plight. He asked to borrow the train fare, requesting the man's name and address, and insisted that he would repay the loan when he reached his home. The man gave him the fare and refused my father's offer. This generous gesture left an indelible impression on him, and he recounted it with wonderment to me half a century later.

My mother, Julia Friedman, lived in Jurewicz, a small town on the border of Lithuania and Poland. She had four sisters and a brother. Her father had attended university to study accounting, and he was the town scribe as well as a *schochet* [kosher butcher]. She and her brother, Boris, were raised by their grandmother, a strong woman who owned the town's livery stable, which housed the coaches that the czar would use when visiting the region. My mother attended the local grade school for three years under the new communist regime. Her father had left his family to go to the United States in 1913, in order to earn enough money to bring them over. When the war broke out in 1914, he could not return. His family was stranded without funds, so their living conditions were very harsh. The money that he accumulated was lost to a swindler. He was finally able to return in 1920. When she saw him, my mother angrily accused him of abandoning them.

When she arrived in the United States at the age of thirteen, she attended high school at night and worked in a department store during the day. She learned English and eventually spoke impeccably. My father was twenty-two when he arrived. He learned to speak reasonably well, with almost no accent. Both had come to the United States in 1920, the last year the doors were open to immigration. They met for the first time two years later, in the balcony of a Yiddish theater on the Lower East Side. She was not interested in him, but she had three older unmarried sisters she thought he might consider. He was not to be deterred and, after two years, they married. His three older brothers had come to America earlier in the century and peddled fruits and vegetables from horse-drawn carts in New Brunswick, New Jersey. He acquired his own horse and wagon, and among his customers was the Johnson family, founders of Johnson & Johnson. My mother decided they should open a dry goods store in Rahway, New Jersey, where they initially settled.

In the fall of 1929, four months after my birth in New Brunswick, we moved to Plattsburgh, New York, where my mother's parents and sisters had settled. A city of seventeen thousand, Plattsburgh is, like much of upstate New York, scenically beautiful, with a long history of economic distress. On the shores of Lake Champlain, thirty miles south of the Canadian border, it has one of the finest sand beaches in North America. It housed the barracks of the Twenty-Sixth Infantry Division and a paper mill, a teachers college, and little else of note. My parents opened a dress shop there in 1930, just a few months after the great crash on Wall Street, at the beginning of the Depression. Plattsburgh was composed largely of two population groups, both Catholic: the descendants of

French Canadians, many of whom spoke French at home, and the Irish. Each group had its own bishop, church, and parochial schools. There was little mixing between the two communities.

Was there an Old World orientation in the family when you were growing up?

My parents thought America was paradise. They never talked about the old country. They had dark, negative feelings about their early years and never expressed an interest in returning.

They were very progressive, and not at all religious, but they were honest and ethical. Mother's father combined the roles of rabbi and schochet. Before making their home in Plattsburgh, they had lived in towns up and down the East Coast. Wherever they went, they lasted about a year. To survive, her father surreptitiously became a conventional butcher. So he'd be butchering hogs, and it didn't take long for the Jewish community to become upset. He would lose his position, and they would move to another town.

My parents developed few social ties in the Plattsburgh community. They worked around the clock, spending much of their time traveling to small towns in northern New York and Vermont, where they opened six additional stores to form a small chain. My mother had good business sense, and my father's training as a tailor proved invaluable. He was an excellent window draper. His window displays were successful in drawing customers, which gave them an edge over the competition. He was a superb salesman who charmed the local farm women, to whom they supplied inexpensive and tasteful garments for their difficult figures. The stores became magnets for Canadian tourists, including prostitutes, for whom the Plattsburgh store stocked gaudy, vividly decorated dresses that resembled the Parisian bordello attire depicted by Toulouse-Lautrec in his paintings.

When they traveled to their stores, my father would drape the windows and teach the managers to display garments. While the name of most of the shops was Stollman's, in Burlington and St. Albans, Vermont, my brother Solomon, who had earned an industrial design degree from Pratt, installed modern stores for them, with my assistance, and those were called Bernsol's. My parents were astute merchandisers. Dad used a unit control system on flip cards that I had designed for him, which showed every item in every store, and he loved to sit at home and observe what sold in which stores. If a store manager or a saleswoman liked a particular item, and it was selling well, they would transfer these garments there from their other stores.

Where were they buying the clothes?

New York had a flourishing garment district in the West 30s. On the avenues were the higher-priced manufacturers, and my parents bought coats and suits from them. They stocked well-made, inexpensive garments. For a number of years, my parents used a resident buyer in the garment district who knew all the manufacturers. They made seasonal buying trips to New York, driving down Route 9, an eight-hour trip, and they would stay at the Hotel New Yorker, adjacent to the garment district. The manufacturers had great respect for them—my mother was a lovely woman; my dad was a gregarious, dapper individual. They were a striking couple. One day I said to them, "You've just become resident buyers. Print up your order book; you're going to become the AAA Buying Service." They did that and began to get the 6 percent commission that the resident buyer had obtained from the manufacturers. The manufacturers didn't mind, as it was factored into their prices.

As a youth I would travel down with them once a year, making the rounds of the showrooms with them. I knew nothing about women's fashions. But I reacted instinctively to colors and designs. Besides, the raincoat showrooms had models wearing black slips to make it easier to don and remove the coats, and they were beautiful girls. I was thirteen or fourteen, and it was mind-boggling for me.

What sort of perspective came with being the oldest of seven kids?

My parents were away a lot. Our French-Irish live-in housekeeper cooked for us and looked after the younger ones, but she had two children of her own. She was divorced, and her children were being raised by her parents. I felt a responsibility to my siblings. I was the surrogate father. The youngest was about fourteen years younger than me. I'm told that the oldest child in a family often does not marry. I had many opportunities, but I just let them go by—until I was in my forties, which is late.

As the firstborn son, did you feel particular expectations from your parents or within yourself?

Both. During the years I was growing up, I had to get a hundred in my exams. My parents never raised this subject, but somehow it was implicit that I would have to excel. I was totally absorbed in school and in every extracurricular activity. Throughout high school I did little socializing.

Were you raised with much of a Jewish orientation in the family? Did you hear Yiddish around the house?

My parents spoke Yiddish occasionally, but only to exchange their thoughts privately. The Reform synagogue had a congregation of upper-class, educated, second- and third-generation German Jews. And there was a second congregation, in the Orthodox synagogue. It was a conventional Orthodox shul, with a *bimah* [altar] at its eastern end and a *mikvah* [ritual bath] in its basement. I had my bar mitzvah service in that synagogue. These were two distinct communities: the merchant community that went to the Reform synagogue and the Orthodox Eastern European Jewish immigrants. As a twelve-year-old, I became the organist in the Reform synagogue. I wasn't trained, and I didn't know how to work the pedals, but I could play the keyboard. The rabbi was a gnome-like man of advanced age; he would cue me and I would play the hymn. Once, during a sermon, I mischievously pressed a pedal that emitted a squawking sound.

What kind of musical education did you have in Plattsburgh?

I had weekly piano lessons from the age of seven until I was thirteen. My teacher was one of three daughters and a son of the late Charles Hudson, a sea captain who had married a Chinese woman on one of his voyages. The Hudsons were tall, handsome, distinguished individuals, none of whom married, living during their later years in the shadow of the father whose memory they detested and suffering the racism that characterized popular attitudes during that era. They lived together throughout their lives in a stately, white frame house on Court Street, in which they ran the Hudson School of Music. All were highly accomplished musicians. They taught string instruments and provided cultural life to the town. They created a string ensemble that would rehearse there. The smell of rosin was pungent in the living room when I came for my piano lessons. Their parlor was full of Chinese screens and art objects, which their father had collected in his travels. The environment had a profound influence on my outlook regarding music.

How old were you when the family moved to New York? Did the change affect you much?

When I was sixteen, my parents bought a house in Forest Hills, Queens, but couldn't occupy it yet. I rented an apartment with my next younger brother, and for eight months we attended Forest Hills High School, living on our own. The year was 1945.

While I was a high school student in Plattsburgh, trains would come up from New York City with two daily newspapers: the *New York Post*, which was a very different *New York Post* from the Rupert Murdoch one of today, and *PM*, the radical left newspaper. I observed the Second World War through the lens of these publications. I read Max Lerner and I. F. Stone. They prepared me for the move to New York City.

How did you fare in college? Did you remain a diligent student?

When I attended Columbia, on a scholarship, the teachers were highly rated, but I was bored with sitting in the classroom. I lived in the dorm and then in rooming houses off campus. I would show up regularly to work in my parents' business, now based in a loft on West 36th Street in the garment district, from which they shipped merchandise to their stores. At Columbia, all around me were veterans of World War II, who were very serious about obtaining a professional education. The only courses I enjoyed were French literature of the nineteenth century, anthropology, sociology, psychology, and Chaucer. I tried campus radio, and then found a berth at the campus humor magazine, the *Jester*. In the spring of my third year, I was suspended from school in midterm for flunking Soviet Economics, poor grades, and cutting classes. I went west and found a job as a laborer in a Wyoming tunnel construction project, surrounded by strong silent men, and lived in a tiny cell with a slatted wooden door. At the end of two weeks, it was clear to me and the foreman that I was not strong enough to maintain the pace. I went on to Los Angeles, where I worked briefly at various jobs, including as a stock clerk in a drug store and as a gas station attendant. In the fall, I returned to Columbia, where I was readmitted. I took the law aptitude exam and scored in the top 2 percentile. My faculty adviser suggested that I enter Columbia Law School on professional option, which meant I would not have to finish college.

Was there anything in particular that made you think of law school?

It was the prospect of being drafted for the Korean War. I don't know if I ever would have chosen medicine as a career. A Jewish youth is expected to choose law or medicine or commerce. I was comfortable with law, assuming that the training would be useful in whatever career I undertook. Cutting classes, I would digest three texts for each course prior to the exam. This required a periodic frenzy of reading, but it freed me to continue my self-indulgent practices. As graduation day approached, the dean called me in. He said, "Bernard, we can't let you loose on an unsuspecting society. Your professors have no idea what you look like." He insisted that I take an extra term and attend class diligently. I graduated in January 1954 and then in March I was drafted. The Korean War was now in an armistice phase.

Were you ever tempted to enter the family business?

No.

So then you allowed yourself to be drafted. . . .

I could have avoided it. At my physical, the examining doctor offered me an out and said, in effect, "Do you want this?" Being drafted, I didn't have to take the bar. I didn't mind that at all. Also, I was curious about the world. The war was over, and I hadn't traveled outside the United States, except to Montreal.

I was assigned to Camp Gordon in Augusta, Georgia, to learn teletype operator skills and spent much of the hot summer in the base swimming pools. Visiting a large barbershop on the base for my first haircut, I studied the barbers and noted that one young black barber clearly took pride in his work. When his chair was free, I sat in it. The barber quietly informed me that he could not cut my hair. I asked him to identify the shop owner. The barber pointed to a short, elderly white man who was unloading barber supplies from his van. "Hold the chair," I said. "I'll be back."

I approached the proprietor. "I care about my appearance, and that barber is good. I would like him to cut my hair." He adopted a confidential manner. "Look, son, in our shops, white barbers cut white boys' hair and black barbers cut black boys' hair. You wouldn't want to catch a disease, would you?" I ignored the comment and reiterated my request. The owner, sensing an impasse, changed his tone. "You will have to sign a paper, releasing the barbershop from responsibility for anything that might happen to you." I stated that I would sign the release, returned to the chair, and directed the barber to proceed. I noticed that all of the eight barbers, white and black, were staring. The barber's hand trembled slightly from nervousness. When the haircut was finished, I signed the statement in a notebook that was proffered to me by the proprietor.

Recognizing that this practice was in violation of Defense Department regulations, I visited several base barbershops the following Saturday and interrogated the barbers. I learned that the white barbers would cut the hair of black soldiers if directed to do so, using a shaver attachment for this purpose. A white barber informed me that the preceding year there had been three days of rioting at a Virginia military base over barbershop segregation, and one man had been killed.

I collected statements from barbers and also from my black teletype instructor. He had been refused service by two white barbers, and they told him to wait for the black barber, who did not materialize. He had to return to his classes without a haircut.

Visiting the base recreation center on Saturday, I prepared a report titled "Integration of Camp Gordon Barbershops: Report and Recommendations." I attached the various statements, plus my own statement decrying this breach of law and policy. I made multiple copies and on Sunday delivered one to the office of the commanding general, and others to those of his subordinates in the chain of command.

On Monday morning I marched off to class. At noon I was called into the office of my company commander. "You do not follow the chain of command by what you have just done. You are supposed to bring it to me, and I refer it up the line." Laughing, he added, "I have just delivered a lecture to you on the chain of command. You have an appointment with the base IG [inspector general]."

I was interrogated intensively by the IG, a captain, who concluded that I was acting from conviction. I was given an assignment as an Information and Education instructor and relieved of all normal duties. After learning that my unit was to be assigned to Korean occupation duty, I visited the instructor who had provided me with his statement. He told me that all of the units on the base had been summoned to a formation to hear an announcement from the commanding general that the base would not tolerate discrimination in the barbershops and that the soldiers were to report any infractions immediately. In response to my expression of concern regarding my probable assignment to Korea, he directed me to visit the officer in charge of the assignment section and to request compassionate leave, ostensibly to visit my girlfriend in Europe. Following his instructions, I was greeted by a black warrant officer who smiled broadly and ushered me into the office of the captain in charge. He listened to my story and then proposed to assign me to European duty, so that I would not have to use up precious leave time for a visit.

In Germany I was assigned to an artillery unit. While on maneuvers in the Black Forest, I shared Thanksgiving dinner with a small group of soldiers. Seated across from me, a corporal commented that I appeared downhearted. I said that I was just thinking I would rather be in Paris. The corporal said he was being assigned to Paris. I remarked on his good fortune. "Don't sweat it, man. I am the chauffeur of Senator Harry Flood Byrd. I just wrote to him that my buddy was being sent to Paris, and so I wanted to be sent there too. You just write to the senator and tell him the same thing. I will give you his private mailing address."

I thanked him for his kindness and rushed off to write a letter to the senator. The following Monday, having returned from maneuvers, I had a reply from the senator—the chairman of the Senate Armed Services Committee, one of the most powerful politicians in Washington—acknowledging my request and stating that he would follow my progress with great interest. I obtained a pass to visit Heidelberg, where I called on the general in charge of legal matters for the U.S. Army in Europe. I asked to be assigned to Paris, where I proposed to study Civil Law, since I spoke French. The general granted the request. I was assigned to the Claims Office Team in Paris, a NATO liaison office that dealt with claims by French civilians against the U.S. Army.

On New Year's Eve, I was on a train to Paris. Arriving the morning of New Year's Day, I walked down the Champs-Elysées, oblivious to the cold. For seven months, I lived on the French economy, wearing civilian clothes and with a generous cost of living allowance for rent and food. I worked closely with a staff of French civilian women in the glass pavilion of the former Rothschild mansion in the Bois de Boulogne. I lived on the Left Bank and frequented the cafés, where I once observed tiny, white-maned Bertrand Russell swoop into La Coupole with a retinue of admirers.

Through mutual acquaintances, I met Henry Miller and Richard Wright. I went to Miller's small apartment on the Left Bank, which was cramped and filled with books. A man of advanced years, he was brusque but civil. Wright received me in his classic high-ceilinged Paris apartment. He was cordial, and we had a brief conversation. I was just curious to meet this celebrated and controversial expatriate.

I also attended performances by the Red Army Choir, the Beijing Opera, and Yehudi Menuhin, and the Russian opera *Boris Godunov*. In mid-August I was transferred back to Germany for the remainder of my tour of duty, until January 1956.

After your military service, what did you do?

Upon discharge I returned to New York and was admitted to the state and federal bar. I returned to my hometown, Plattsburgh, and hung out there for several months, trying to figure out what I wanted to do with my life. The town had become foreign. Thomas Wolfe was right: you can't go home again.

After that, I went to Tucson, Arizona, to check out the region. I found the desert magnetically attractive, but the local culture felt alien, except for a small community of artists who welcomed me.

Returning to New York, I met a young woman at a modern dance performance and was captivated by her. She was a designer of woven fabrics. I leased a large sunny loft at 329 East 47th Street—what is now United Nations Plaza—as a design studio and installed her in it. The rent was modest because the building was to be demolished in a few years. I bought hand looms and hired weavers. The enterprise attracted the interest of chemical companies that had developed synthetic yarns. We created demonstration fabrics for various applications, utilizing the considerable colorization skills of one of the weavers, Elsa Rush. The National Council of Negro Women rented space from me to hold meetings. After a year my partner started turning out designs that were purple-and-black combinations, and walked out. I realized this would not be my career of choice, so I dissolved the business.

2 Music and Law

Into the Deep End Fast

In 1960 you worked as an unpaid assistant for Florynce Kennedy, the attorney and activist. How did you meet her?

As a law student I attended huge parties that Flo Kennedy and her two statuesque sisters threw in their large Harlem apartment for law students. Later, when I found that she was practicing law in midtown Manhattan, I approached her directly and offered her my services as an unpaid gofer.

In Flo's office I met Doris Parker, who claimed to be the widow of Charlie Parker, and Louis McKay, the widower of Billie Holiday. I had never heard of these artists. Flo obtained the representation of the Parker and Holiday estates through the efforts of Maely Dufty, a Rumanian-born publicist in New York who had managed Billie Holiday and been married to William Dufty, the co-author with her of *Lady Sings the Blues*.

Two months after joining her office, I found out that Flo had scheduled a press conference in which she identified me as her associate counsel. I had no such formal standing. More importantly, Maely Dufty came to me and urged me to leave Flo, as "something is about to blow up." Maxwell T. Cohen, Esq., a prominent Manhattan entertainment lawyer, had been retained by Chan Parker, the actual widow of Charlie Parker, to enforce her rights to the estate. I left abruptly. Flo lost the representation of the estate.

Where did you go from there?

I rented a room in the law offices of Bruce McM. Wright, who later became a state supreme court justice, and Harold Lovette, Miles Davis's manager—a small suite at 120 East 56th Street. I was there for a year trying to form a practice. I had little interest in dealing with the typical problems and challenges of a conventional law practice. Prominent black musicians, clients of Bruce and

Harold, came by and I met them. I found these artists interesting people of depth and dignity, more sympathetic than the average run of humanity.

My first victory, while I shared the offices, was on behalf of three jazz bassists: Art Davis and Reggie Workman, and a third whose name escapes me. All of them had sent their basses to Chicago to be repaired, and the instruments had been damaged in transport by TWA. C. C. Tillinghast was its president, and his employees refused to respond to our claims. I hit on a stratagem: I called TWA and asked for Tillinghast, saying that it was a personal and confidential matter. They put me through to him in his home, as he was having dinner. He got on the phone, and he said, "What is this?!" I said, "Mr. Tillinghast, I'm a lawyer. Basses were damaged, and we're being brushed off by your staff." He hit the roof! "How dare you call me at my home?" He was incensed! I apologized, and he settled our claim.

Composer and pianist Mary Lou Williams—brilliant, saintly, and influential—paid little attention to her recording and publishing interests. I engaged in extensive research for her in these areas, compiled an inventory of her songs and recordings, and presented it to her. She then proceeded to contact the labels and publishers, from whom she collected long-overdue royalties. I chided her for disregarding my entitlement to compensation for my work, and she was clearly ashamed. I didn't press the matter, because I knew her to be charitable and supportive of her fellow musicians.

Did these early associations help you in subsequent relations with musicians?

While I was working for Flo Kennedy, Dizzy Gillespie was in touch with her, and it occurred to me that I might do some work for him, since I was then engaged in research regarding the copyrights of the Parker and Holiday estates. I called Lorraine Gillespie, his wife, and introduced myself, suggesting that perhaps I could be helpful to him in this area. She replied, "Dizzy will want to speak with you." She set up a meeting, and I visited him at his home in Corona, Queens. I worked for him for about two years, attending his performances in New York City, and succeeded in recovering his copyrights from Norman Granz, the producer and record label owner.

After you left the offices of Lovette and Wright, you then had a new round of musical adventures.

I migrated over to Broadway and became acquainted with black R&B writers who were starting to write for white rock-and-roll artists. They hung out in the bars on 52nd Street. There was Charlie Singleton, one of the most prolific and successful figures. "Horse" was a large, soft-spoken, dignified, and congenial individual. Otis Blackwell wrote Presley's biggest hits. We three formed a publishing company, whose songs included "Breathless" and "Hey, Little Girl," but it was short-lived. The songwriters were streetwise and engaged in monumental battles with publishers. They would sell a song to one publisher, get an advance, then sell it again to another publisher. It was too fast a crowd for me, so I left the scene, after winning my first court case for a songwriter.

David Curlee Williams, a Kentuckian, had written a hit song, "Whole Lotta Shakin' Goin' On," and the publisher had left town with the earnings and could not be found. Curlee was broke, and I agreed to represent him. I sued the publisher in Supreme Court, New York County, and won a default judgment. When I gave Curlee the good news, he said nothing, but went to Lee Eastman, a prominent publisher, and published the song with him. I phoned Eastman, who had earlier interviewed me for a job, and informed him that I had just won the suit and had a contingent retainer agreement with Curlee that would entitle me to a 25 percent interest in the publishing rights. Eastman replied matter of factly, "I guess you'll have to sue me." Disheartened by the experience, I decided that I did not wish to be a lawyer in popular music.

Given your contacts in the jazz world, were you going out much to hear live music?

Sporadically. I was naive, and my responses were totally spontaneous. I was just providing legal services for people in that sector of music.

So, if you were not an aficionado, what kept you going in that realm of music and law?

The artists I encountered in the so-called jazz sector were serious composers and performers. They conducted themselves with dignity, reserve, and integrity. They were profound philosophers and articulate; I had and still have great respect for them.

Around 1963 Stollman persuaded his parents to buy a large co-op apartment at 180 Riverside Drive on the Upper West Side. The apartment included a tiny maid's room (and bath) on the top floor of the building, where he lived for the next few years. He continued to provide legal services, usually without charge, for composers and performers of the new music.

I was visited by a young woman choreographer. I welcomed her to my parents' apartment, where I conducted my practice. She said, "Why aren't you helping Ornette and Cecil?" I said, "Ornette and Cecil who?" She was clearly taken aback. "You don't know who Ornette and Cecil are? They're the princes of the new music. I've talked with both of them, and they want you to manage them." I met both of them to discuss their concerns.

I didn't do very much for Cecil, except to get his pianos fixed. He had a loft on Chambers Street, and his two Steinway grands had been damaged by rain from the skylight. I contacted Steinway, and they repaired both pianos without charge. Gil Evans had made *Into the Hot* [Impulse, 1961], and half of it was written by Cecil Taylor, who also performed on it, but they called it a Gil Evans record. I contacted the label, and they surrendered their claim to the publishing rights to Cecil for his publishing company, whose catalog I now represent globally. The percussionist Sunny Murray, who toured for years with Cecil, reminded me recently that I was instrumental in getting them booked in Europe for the first time. In 1965 Cecil asked me to manage him. I surmised that others could do a better job for him and declined his offer. We hadn't been in touch for many years, when I invited him to dinner at his favorite restaurant recently. As we ate, I said to Cecil, "The answer is yes." He said, "The answer to what?" I said, "The question you asked me in 1965 was whether I would manage you. I'm sure you could use some help." I negotiated a booking for him into the Iridium, the midtown Manhattan club. He was pleased with it. And they were pleased with my participation.

When I met Ornette, he was already famous, having been featured on a *Time* magazine cover with his plastic horn. But he was in a protracted depression. He had already done all those records on Atlantic. They were about to release a new one, for which they had not made a contract with him. At Ornette's request, I called Ahmet Ertegun, the president of Atlantic, and cautioned him that he had not acquired the rights for this release. Subsequently, they paid him a substantial advance and issued the album. He never paid me for my services. In fairness to Ornette, I should mention that I never billed him. This was typical of my conduct, effectual for my clients but not self-protective. To support Ornette, I saw John Hammond at Columbia, Alfred Lion and Francis Wolff at Blue Note, and Bob Thiele at Impulse. I offered Bob Thiele a license for Ornette's self-produced concert at Town Hall for a three-year term. He liked the idea, but then he said, "You manage Ornette?" "Yes." He looked skeptical. That was intended as a hint, which I did not pick up. I went back to Ornette and said, "Hammond is interested in working with you, Lion and Wolff at Blue Note are interested, and I have a proposal to Bob Thiele at Impulse, and this is the deal." The following day, Ornette went to see Bob Thiele on his own. He also saw Lion and Wolff at Blue Note and made a deal with them for the Town Hall concert tapes. He then went to John Hammond, and *Skies of America* eventually followed from that. I had laid the groundwork. His morale improved, and his momentum was restored.

When we first met, Ornette had handed me the tape that he had produced of the Town Hall concert with David Izenzon, Charles Moffett, and a string ensemble. Izenzon couldn't hear himself, so he turned up his amplifier. His bass track was totally distorted, and they couldn't use the tape. I went to Dave Sarser, a remarkable engineer and a friend. At his studio, I met Ralph Ellison, author of *Invisible Man*, and Horace Parlan, the gifted pianist. David compressed the track; the distortion disappeared and the bass sounded normal. I brought the tape to Ornette. He paid for the engineering work and asked to borrow the tape. I gave it to him.

During that period, in August 1964, Bud Powell returned to America with Francis Paudras. Francis and I had corresponded regarding Bud. I invited Francis to dinner at the Carnegie Hall Tavern. As we ate, I urged him to return with Bud to Paris. "How can Bud survive the pushers here?" He replied that they were bound by contract to perform for two weeks at Birdland. "They flew us here and we must go through with the deal." I could see Birdland from our window seat, and I spotted a tall, portly man in a tan suit, running around the block, and recognized him. "Isn't that Bud?" Shamefacedly, he explained, "On our way over, I gave him the wrong pills."

About a month following Bud's arrival, I got a phone call from Nica Rothschild, the Baroness de Koenigswarter, whom I didn't know. "Bud has disappeared. Mary [Lou Williams] says that maybe you can help." I said I would try. The New York City Police Department, Missing Persons Bureau, staff member asked, "Are you a family member?" "No." "Well, I'm afraid we can't help you." "Please understand," I said. "We're talking about Bud Powell, an American treasure." There was a pause. "All right, we'll see what we can do." Then, at 3:00 a.m. the following morning, Nica called: "Mr. Stollman, the police have found Bud, seated on a doorstep in Greenwich Village. I've sent my chauffeur to get him. Would you like to come visit me in Weehawken?" Nica had a beautiful, modern flat-roofed house, on the cliffs above the Hudson River, whose panoramic picture windows provided a stunning view of the New York skyline. In its huge salon was a grand piano. On a large antique couch, in the center of the living room, dozens of cats were perched. Still more cats perched on couches that lined the picture windows. A small crowd had gathered: Francis Paudras, Ornette Coleman, and my youngest brother, Steve. As we waited for Bud, his teenaged daughter, Celia, and her mother, Mary Frances Barnes, arrived. Nica served us Château Lafite Rothschild.

Ornette cornered me. "Bernard, why aren't you helping me?" I said, "Why should I start again?" This was some months after I had done the other work for him. "We'll make an agreement, but"—this was just before anything had been released on ESP—"you must license the Town Hall tape to me; I'll produce the record of it myself." Ornette had left with me a two-track tape of a portion of the concert. I sat down and I typed out an agreement, and he signed it, as we waited for Bud Powell.

That same night, Francis Paudras played me a solo performance by Bud that he had recorded on his Nakamichi professional tape recorder, while Bud stayed in Francis's apartment in Paris. He had locked Bud in, turned on the machine, and gone out to do his work as a graphic designer. It was stunningly beautiful. When Bud arrived, he sat at the piano and played briefly. Then he pulled me aside and spoke to me in a soft voice: "Mr. Lawyer, can you help me? I don't want to go back; I want to stay." Mary Frances and their daughter Celia invited him to live with them in Brooklyn. Francis was dismayed, realizing that his idol would not accompany him back to Paris. Francis said to me, "I have to go back, but I need money." He had graphic images with him that he had made of Bud. I said, "All right, Francis, I'll give you the money you need, but I want to license this art." It was three hundred dollars. These images were used for the covers of his ESP album *Live at the Blue Note in Paris, 1961*, a tape that was brought to me in 1966 by Buttercup Powell and its producer, Alan Douglas. Francis wrote to me following his return to France. Phonogram wanted to put out a record by Bud, offering a thousand dollars. I had become Bud's manager. I wrote him back and refused, as it appeared to be too small an advance. In retrospect, I think Francis had personally assumed responsibility for the cost of Bud's hospitalization for tuberculosis and hoped to recoup part of it. I should have approved his request. Francis eventually licensed tapes from his collection of recordings by Bud to an Italian company. Over thirty years later, in a book he wrote describing his profoundly personal relationship with Bud, he characterized me as a scheming, unscrupulous, money-grubbing liar and recalled events that had never occurred. He blamed me for booking Bud into Carnegie Hall for the Charlie Parker Memorial Concert produced by Mercury Records. I had not been contacted by the producers and had known nothing about it prior to the evening of the performance. In 1997 Francis committed suicide. His book appeared the following year.

Shortly after the visit to Nica, I read in *Billboard* that Blue Note Records would release *Ornette Coleman at Town Hall*. I called the owners of Blue Note, and one of them came to see me, a dignified and genteel individual. They had paid Ornette to issue it, and he had then gone to Stockholm. There he recorded *At the Golden Circle*, including "Sadness," from the Town Hall concert. I proposed that Blue Note release the portion of the concert that Ornette had not licensed to me, and they accepted. We signed a mutual release, and ESP eventually issued *Town Hall 1962*. The remainder of the concert has never surfaced, and its whereabouts are unknown.

3 The Initial Years

When did you first imagine starting a record label?

In 1963 I volunteered to do legal work for Moe Asch at Folkways Records. I was fascinated by his dedication to documenting the folk music of America and of other cultures. I saw him as an unofficial extension of the Smithsonian. Pete Seeger was often in the office, providing support. I was struck by the fact that one could operate a record label with very modest means. The custom pressing plants made it possible to press five hundred LPs, place each one in a standard black jacket, paste a printed sheet of paper over it, and have a finished product. Moe Asch had launched his label in 1945 and devoted his life to this undertaking. When he died in 1983, his catalog contained over two thousand titles, all of which are available today from his successor, Smithsonian Folkways.

What was the purpose in producing your very first record, Ni Kantu en Esperanto, *in 1963?*

In 1960 I became interested in the international language and was briefly employed as a publicist for the Esperanto League of North America. The record was just an exercise, and I had no thoughts of doing anything beyond that. *Ni Kantu* demonstrated the sound of the language through poetry, a comedy monologue, and songs. It was marketed to members of the worldwide movement.

Late in 1963 somebody told you to go hear Albert Ayler play up in Harlem. What was that all about? Who was that person?

Granville Lee visited me. He had attended high school in Cleveland with another student who was enormously talented. They had formed a band and all through school they were performing professionally. He insisted that I hear his friend, who was going to play at the Baby Grand Cafe in Harlem on the following Sunday afternoon, between Christmas and New Year's. He said, "I won't be in town, but you can go; please, you must go hear him." He had said enough to intrigue me.

It was snowing when I trudged uptown from 90th Street to 125th Street. The Baby Grand was a popular piano bar. A few people were sitting there, wearing their coats, because the heat had not been turned on. The bartender busied himself polishing glasses. Elmo Hope was at the piano, with his trio, on an elevated stage. I sat and listened to them. Several minutes later, a small man in a gray leather suit, holding a large saxophone, brushed by me and jumped up on the stage. He had a black beard, with a little patch of white in it. He was not introduced and, ignoring the trio, he began to blow his horn. The other musicians stopped and looked at him. No words were exchanged. Elmo Hope quietly closed his piano, the bass player parked his bass, the drummer put his sticks down, and they all sat back to listen. He was playing solo, and he kept right on playing for twenty to thirty minutes, just a burst of music. It seemed like a second; it was no time at all! Then he stopped and jumped down from the platform, covered with sweat. I approached him and said, "Your music is beautiful. I'm starting a record label, and I'd like you to be my first artist." A small voice in the back of my head said, "Oh, you are, are you?" He reflected, and then he said, "I'd like that. But I have to do a session in March at Atlantic. After that, I'll be free and I will contact you." I was skeptical that I would ever hear from him again.

In June, however, the phone rang: "This is Albert Ayler. I'm ready to record." Moe Asch, the owner of Folkways, used a small and inexpensive studio near Times Square, so I directed Albert to the Variety Arts Studio. He arrived with his trio: Gary Peacock and his then-wife Annette and Sunny Murray. Gary was slender and austere, while Sunny was a big gregarious bear. There was no discussion. The engineer was lanky, blond, and low-key, one of the owners. They filed into the recording studio, and the session began. The engineer left the door of the control room open, while Annette and I sat outside listening. As the music played, I was enthralled, exhilarated, jubilant. I exchanged glances with Annette and said, "What an auspicious beginning for a record label!" She nodded her head in agreement. Then I found out that it had been recorded monaurally. I was horrified! We had assumed it would be in stereo. In forty-plus years, no one has ever cared. The engineer had done a superb job of miking. *The Penguin Guide to Jazz* says *Spiritual Unity* [recorded July 10, 1964] is one of the hundred top jazz records of all time.

Once you started thinking of a label, did you have a sense of what the potential could be?

Not at all. It wasn't a thoughtful decision, just something I was drawn toward doing.

After the Ayler session, you knew you had one record. What did you do?

I was thrilled with that record, so I was very much charged up with the idea of going forward. I wanted to explore this new music. A few months later, the October Revolution in Jazz gave me an opportunity to meet the community. The festival took place in a tiny café at West End Avenue, a block from where I lived at 90th and Riverside. The Cellar Café was out of business, and there was no electricity. Bill Dixon and Carla Bley had formed the Jazz Composers Guild, which sponsored the festival. Just inside the entrance, Paul Bley was seated at an upright piano, and standing next to him was Giuseppi Logan with a wired-together clarinet. I positioned myself next to them, as it was the only way I could be certain to hear them. The only lighting was from candles on the crowded tables. I met Marion Brown, Burton Greene, Sun Ra, the entire community of free improvisation composers.

Archie Shepp stood on the steps outside, puffing his pipe: I invited him to record for the new label, but he was under contract to Impulse. I invited all of the artists I found. Sun Ra was slated to perform with his Arkestra in a Newark loft. He gave me the address, and I went. I was greatly impressed by his music, and the playing of bassist Ronnie Boykins prompted me to invite him to record. He said he would like to record when he felt ready, and would let me know. We remained acquainted, as he was repeatedly featured on other ESP albums. Ten years later, he informed me that he was ready. It would be the last album made by ESP before it suspended operations for many years [Ronnie Boykins, *The Will Come, Is Now*, February 1974].

Were you still working as a lawyer at that time?

Yes, I was continually working, struggling, as a lawyer. I had a private practice. I had sought employment with other lawyers, but these were depressing experiences because I knew within myself I wasn't going to be a conventional lawyer. I wasn't interested in the kinds of work that lawyers typically performed.

When you started ESP, how did you imagine the enterprise as a business venture? Did you have any particular business models, beyond Folkways? Were you thinking at all as a business?

I just plowed blindly ahead, without giving a great amount of thought to how it would be sustained. I had no model to go with other than Moe Asch and Folkways. He was focused on documenting our culture, and it was clearly a not-for-profit enterprise. It became my calling. It took over from my law practice very quickly, because it was closer to my heart. I wasn't judicious in my approach to a livelihood or a career.

As the label was coming into being, how did you figure out financing?

I went to my mother, just after I recorded Albert. There was no way I could have gone forward without her help. She came up with the equivalent of a young executive's salary for two years. ESP was possible because of her; I had no other source of financing. My law practice was skeletal.

Why did you go to your mother about this and not your father?

She was the business head of the family, a brilliant woman, pragmatic, and a Taurus. My father was an artist, and all he wanted to do was sing. He sang for anyone who would listen. If he were in a room with a group of people, he would have to sing. He needed to be the center of attention, and he sang well. One didn't discuss anything to do with money or business with him.

You asked her for your inheritance at the time. How did you know there was an inheritance?

My parents were prosperous. They had worked hard all their lives. I felt that they would probably be able to provide funding. I wasn't sure how much I would need or how much they could afford, and I didn't ask for a specific sum.

With the Ayler session, you had the studio and the engineer. How did you go about putting together the packaging, the design? How did you find people to work with?

My first art director, Jordan Matthews, had been a producer for ABC. He brought in Howard Bernstein, who did many of our covers. I found Richard L.

Alderson in the course of my efforts to manage Bud Powell. When Bud returned to New York in 1964, after years in Paris, he was in terrible physical shape. He had been hospitalized in Paris for tuberculosis, he had liver problems, and he was an alcoholic. When I shook his hand, it was the strangest experience, like grasping a soft pillow. I tried to record him. I put him in the studio with two young musicians, and the tape eventually ended up with Mainstream Records in England, with a picture of me on the back [released as *Ups 'n Downs*, 1973]. But the session was a failure, and it should never have been issued. I have no idea how this tape got to Mainstream. Then in March 1965 two young men, producers at Mercury Records—this was before Mercury was sold to Universal—decided to stage a concert at Carnegie Hall, the Charlie Parker Memorial Concert. They invited several prominent artists, and it was going to be a recording session. I hadn't been contacted and knew nothing about it, but I found out they had booked Bud. I went to Carnegie Hall for the concert and met Celia, his daughter, and her mother, Mary Frances Barnes, at the entrance. Bud was with them, and I noticed that his hands were bleeding. "He fell down," Mary Frances told me. I excused myself and went backstage. An audio engineer was seated at a recording console, and two men stood behind him, the producers, listening to the concert over the speakers. I heard Bud announced. It was clear that he was unable to form chords. It was pathetic. When he finished, I said to the engineer, "I'm Bud Powell's manager and his lawyer. I must take that tape. It can't surface anywhere." He turned to look at the two young men for instructions, and they said, "Give him the tape." I destroyed it. The engineer was Richard Alderson, who would become ESP's engineer! Most of our albums were recorded by him, and he was the producer of ESP albums by the Fugs and Tom Rapp [Pearls Before Swine]. He had a small studio that Harry Belafonte had financed, where Lincoln Center now stands.

But how did you manage to get people to do the cover art, for example, when presumably you couldn't pay them very much?

I picked people who were unknown. They became famous, as their covers for ESP brought them recognition and commissions for major labels and other clients. In keeping with our outlook, they enjoyed complete creative freedom. The large LP format helped. Some covers featured photographs, often without words, a style that was quickly adopted by Elektra and other labels. Howard Bernstein and Dennis Pohl were inundated by offers.

The covers and liners for *Spiritual Unity*, [Ayler's] *Bells*, and *Pharoah Sanders Quintet* were Jordan Matthews's concepts. I decided that silk-screening them would have a primal quality, suitable for ESP. I personally silk-screened the first *Bells* LPs.

Howard and I found each other again recently after thirty-five years. Howard did the graphics for Ayler's *Spiritual Unity*, the Byron Allen Trio, for the Giuseppi Logan albums [*The Giuseppi Logan Quartet*; *More*], the Holy Modal Rounders [*Indian War Whoop*], very phantasmagorical. He did the Fugs color cover that we used for the first album, *The Village Fugs*. He did the Cromagnon record. He did the original cover for *Music from the Orthodox Liturgy*, but it was rejected by the producer as inappropriate.

Were there ever any recordings that you decided later you didn't like?

Not one. Many recordings were by artists I had not heard before I commissioned them. In the arts, there are circles inside of circles. If someone plays with another artist, whose work you admire, you know they're at a certain level of creativity. By granting them carte blanche to do whatever they choose, they assume full responsibility. As a premise, it works.

And that was the same with the cover art?

I never dictated cover art. They came up with whatever they chose to do, and it reflected the vibes of the time. I didn't want an institutional look, such as those of Blue Note and Impulse. By getting away from that, we were able to remain unpredictable.

When you were starting the label, how did you see your role with respect to the music?

I saw my role as a very limited one, as that of a curator and editor, who nurtured an emerging community of composers.

Where did your affinity for that type of music come from?

One influence was my father, who loved to improvise and harmonize. I grew up with that. During the Second World War, my parents often drove the sixty miles from Plattsburgh to Montreal in their 1941 Buick Special sedan, with their older children crowded in the back seat. My father would sing as he drove, and my mother would harmonize with him. I approached music with the tacit question, Is this art? Entertainment is something else. Bernard Berenson, the art critic, and Sol Hurok, the impresario, were among my models. I was footloose, and I had no wife or children, and my legacy after a lifetime of commitment would be this body of work that highlighted and spurred on the careers of a certain community of composers.

What did your parents say when they later heard and saw what you were doing? Did they ever meet any of the musicians?

They came to performances and met many of the musicians. Tom Rapp and his group, Pearls Before Swine, slept on their living room floor in sleeping bags. My father enjoyed talking with them.

The first time my mother heard Albert's *Spiritual Unity* album, I was watching her. She was a woman of very few words, and she just smiled in pleasure. Their sensibilities were sufficiently developed that they picked up on what was going on. She never offered any kind of critical comment, but took it in stride, appreciatively, proud of my work.

Following the October Revolution concerts, why was it the musicians responded to you? What did they have to go by? Was it because you'd already recorded Albert Ayler?

The word had gotten around that there was a new label, and the artists were desperate. No major label would record them. And there weren't any other small independents like this one. They were mature, in their twenties and thirties— they were ready to be heard. I had made a good faith serious bid, and they didn't have a better idea. I think it was that simple. What risk were they taking? The artists I met at the Cellar Café, who accepted my invitation to record them, became the nucleus of the label. I surmise that they had probably heard of my recording Albert.

So, in those days, you didn't encounter much distrust as an independent record producer?

There wasn't a lot of money involved. They knew they were highly unlikely to sell thousands of LPs. No one imagined that it would be commercially viable.

They didn't look at it that way, of course, because their art was very important to them. I knew from the inception that it might be a generation before this music would be accepted. I couldn't give them the promotion that a major label could. I didn't have the staffing, the resources, or the expertise to do a proper job. I knew I could issue and distribute their records. What happened beyond that was out of my control. I think that they assumed they would derive income from their record. Most of them had not recorded before. So, they were naive, and I was as well. What I could not do—and never claimed I could do, but they nonetheless imagined or expected I would be able to do—didn't happen. The vast majority of the records sold five hundred or a thousand units, while a few of the more celebrated recordings were repeatedly pressed.

However, they gained something priceless. They had an album, and it was prestigious; they could seek engagements. It was a galvanic thing that launched them. If I were the grandson of an immigrant whose father had become wealthy, it would have been an appropriate occupation for me, but I had skipped a generation. I was subjected to harsh criticism over the years and deep suspicion, and praised as well. Some of my detractors came to understand the significance of my work on their lives and careers, and I am not greatly distressed by the criticism. You do what you feel you want to do and can do, and let the chips fall where they may.

In September 1965 the label released its first dozen titles all at the same time. These included dates by Paul Bley and Sun Ra; first records by Pharaoh Sanders, the New York Art Quartet, Giuseppi Logan, Bob James, and Ran Blake; as well as Albert Ayler's first American record and Ornette Coleman's Town Hall concert. What was your purpose in launching the label that way?

It was a matter of critical mass. Putting out one album, then a second, and a third would have lessened the impact of our emergence. One afternoon, months earlier, when I was strolling on East 57th Street, I observed a large crowd on the sidewalk outside the Sidney Janis Gallery, for the opening of a new show. Inside, I found works by Andy Warhol, George Segal, and the Chilean sculptor Marisol, among others. The gallery described them as the Pop Art movement. The message was clear: launch your enterprise with a splash and a unifying theme. Put a frame around it and give it an identity as a movement.

The tactic worked. We called it simply the new music. The critics praised our releases. We were unable to find a market in the United States, but Europeans and Japanese responded. The quantities were not substantial, but it was encouraging.

How did ESP go about promoting its releases in those first years?

We attracted college student reps at several schools. We gave them LPs, and they helped us to get publicity on college radio. There was little else that we could do, because commercial radio would not play us, and this remains true today. We were a well-kept secret, except to a few jazz publications and some exposure in the *Village Voice* and underground newspapers like the *East Village Other*.

4   While It Worked

After that initial flood of releases from ESP, the dozen titles that came out in September 1965, the label released forty-five more titles over the next eighteen months. As you continued after the first dozen, how did you figure out what to do, whom to record?

Karl Berger sent Gato Barbieri to me. I was lying on the office couch, and suddenly Gato Barbieri was there with his wife, Michele. They looked down at me and said, "Karl sent us." And I said, "When do you want to record?" I had no idea what he sounded like, but he was very impressive in his bearing and demeanor, and I trusted Karl's judgment. He had just recorded for ESP. It was often like that. ESP didn't have a systematic approach that might include submission of a demo, or an audition. It was circles inside of circles.

So you hadn't heard of Gato Barbieri, his work with Don Cherry?

No.

In the spring of 1966, a number of ESP artists embarked on a concert tour of colleges in upstate New York, which resulted in several albums [Sun Ra, Nothing Is . . . ; *Patty Waters,* College Tour; *Burton Greene Trio,* On Tour]. *How did that adventure come about?*

The owner of the printing plant that was printing our album covers was a friend of Omar Lerman, a prominent music writer and a director of the New York State Council on the Arts. He introduced us, and Omar was very knowledgeable and kind. The council gave us seventy-five hundred dollars during the early months of the label, to do a one-week tour of five colleges with music departments. I hired David Jones, a highly regarded classical engineer, gave him a checkbook, and instructed him to manage the tour as well as record it. ESP sent Sun Ra and his Arkestra, Ran Blake, Patty Waters, Giuseppi Logan, and Burton

Greene. When the tour was over, David returned with the tapes, and I turned the tapes over to the artists, asking them to listen to their own work and to select enough material for an album. It worked. David told me that it had been an ordeal for him, coping with the personal needs of all the musicians, and vowed he would never do it again. When ESP artists went into the studio to record, they never did second or third takes of their pieces. The sessions were brief, typically forty-five minutes, and that was it.

Did the label engage in sponsoring other concerts or tours?

Infrequently. The Fugs had an underground hit on Folkways before they joined ESP. We paid for musical instruments, posters, and a publicist, and paid the rent for the Astor Place Playhouse, where they performed for a few months. In 1968 we staged a free concert on Pier 17, which would later become the South Street Seaport, at the foot of Manhattan. Sun Ra and his Arkestra performed without charge. Jim McCarthy of the Godz gave a solo performance, and so did John Hall, who is now a member of Congress. A huge white yacht was moored along the pier on one side, and on the other side was a Portuguese full-masted training ship, with two hundred cadets in white uniforms. A macrobiotic restaurant, the Paradox, was closing on that day, and I paid them for all their remaining food. They delivered it to the pier, and ESP was able to feed Sun Ra and all of the other performers. A huge crowd formed, and the Sun Ra Arkestra played a long set. The captain of the ship allowed the cadets to join the crowd on the pier, and they danced with the local girls. The captain saw our concert as a salute to Portugal, an observation shared by Portuguese journalists who were present, and ESP has since enjoyed a highly favorable reputation in that country. A recording engineer acquaintance warned me not to try to record the event in a conventional manner, explaining that the long electric lines needed to reach the end of the pier would act as antennae, picking up radio signals and ruining the undertaking. The engineers who had been hired for the job were neophytes and unaware of the problem. I foolishly disregarded his warning, and the tapes were useless. He had bicycled down to the scene with his portable tape deck on the handlebars and recorded thirty minutes of the concert. The sound was flawless.

How did you see what you were doing at ESP with regard to the usual industry practices?

I saw the industry as an enemy to the creative process, and I drafted a new standard for the treatment of artists. Each production would be a collaborative undertaking, in which the artists would have full control over the repertoire and the recording process. Our slogan became "The artists alone decide what you will hear on their ESP-Disk."

The typical recording industry contract has thirty-six to forty-five pages. We use a two-page agreement, and it is for a single album. The industry agreement grants ownership of the album to the record label. ESP co-owns the album with the artists in perpetuity. By jointly owning the master and administering their publishing rights through our Global Copyright Administration, LLC affiliate, we are partners.

As the label grew, you soon branched out into other types of recordings. How did you make the transition from the free jazz that was the core of the label to other projects like the Fugs, Pearls Before Swine, even the nonmusical albums?

I didn't want ESP to be a niche label. Art is anarchistic, and when it becomes categorized, it loses impact. I wanted people who were innovative and inspirational. *The Coach with the Six Insides*, the Jean Erdman theater piece based on James Joyce's *Finnegans Wake*, and other productions were selected using this criterion.

Were you concerned with avoiding a particular public perception of the label?

The label was not to become identified as representing only one particular sector of music. Art is ephemeral, and change is always under way. Any art form can become clichéd and derivative. I thought the label should be a documentary device to capture audio art. The format didn't matter; it could be Tim Leary talking about LSD [*Turn On, Tune In, Drop Out*]. It was important to confound people.

Did that help enlarge the audience for the free jazz people?

I was hoping that this approach would reach a larger audience than the very small community who were interested in free improvisation. I was always surprised to find people who embraced all of our repertoire.

The label had a certain success with the Fugs. How did that affect your ongoing approach?

It meant that we were doing more business, and I could pay my staff. Our U.S. distributors stocked our free improvisation titles on consignment to obtain the rapidly selling Fugs and Pearls Before Swine, folk-rock artists. In 1968 we were forced out of business.

The success of the Fugs didn't change what you wanted to do with the label?

No, I didn't go out to the pop music community and recruit artists. That wasn't our focus, and I was not interested in commercial music designed to be entertainment. A few folk-rock singer-songwriters—including Randy Burns, Jerry and Don Moore, Mij, Les Visible, Cromagnon, Octopus, and Louis Killen—came to ESP and were recorded. The Fugs were Beat poets and anarchists. They were against the war in Vietnam. I had numerous reasons for wanting to work with them. But pop music groups as such? Any commercial group would have had lawyers, managers, and demands for promotion budgets. They would have needed a small army of people to support their enterprise.

How did you see the label's role in the culture of that time?

Our role was to document the work of the community of newly emerging composer-performers of the generation who were identified as free improvisational, who had followed bebop and its immediate successors, such as Coltrane. ESP filled that need.

As you moved from the free jazz to a wider perspective with the label, you also started recording European musicians.

ESP put out one record by Gunter Hampel [*Music from Europe*, 1967]. By the time it came out, he had his own label, Birth Records. Other European musicians who joined ESP were the Free Music Quintet of Pierre Courbois, the group of Nedley Elstak, and Czech artist Karel Velebny. If I had been able to continue, ESP would have recorded more European artists. They too were in desperate need of wider recognition and stigmatized because they were Europeans.

How did you find out about Karel Velebny?

I'd gone to the MIDEM [the annual international music industry convention in Cannes, France] in January 1968. The Czechs were enjoying their "false spring," a brief period of freedom from the Russians. They were intoxicated by it, and they staged the gala that year. Marta Kubisová, the most popular singer in Czechoslovakia, sang to celebrate freedom! It was thrilling. At their reception following the concert, a young member of their delegation approached me and said quietly, "You will come to Prague." On a hunch, I flew to Prague! It was late January, and Prague was dark, cold, and damp, and they burned soft coal, so a soft rain of soot fell. I visited their official record label, Supraphon, where they played me Karel Gott and other artists. Their sounds were all commercial, so nothing came of it. The sun came out, and I hired a cab driver as a guide. We spent hours visiting exhibitions of historical art, the great old churches and monuments in Prague. When evening came, I visited the jazz club and asked for the name of their most celebrated jazz artist. I was told it was Karel Velebny. At my request, they found him for me, and he appeared within twenty minutes. He suggested that we step outside, to avoid prying eyes and ears. We walked out in the darkness, and I said, "I hear you're the most prominent jazz artist in Czechoslovakia. I have an American label, and I'd like to record you." "What do you want?" "I want you to take it as far out as you can go." He looked at me, stupefied. Then he paused and said, "We are going on tour; we will be in Germany in a few weeks." I said, "When you get to Germany, find a studio and ask them to call me in New York. I will pay for the session." He agreed. About a month later, the phone call came from the studio in Germany. I said, "Record him. Send me the bill." I paid the bill, and they sent me the tape. Then a few weeks later, I received photographs from him. He'd been in a terrible car accident. I thought, What a perfect metaphor for the state of his country. The Russians had suppressed the freedom movement. I put a photograph of him lying in a hospital bed, all bandaged up, on the front cover—and a nude shot of him standing and playing the flute on the back cover. The album [SHQ] did not sell, as we were on our way out of business then, so it did not receive promotion.

I went to the MIDEM in January 2008 and met a friend who was a Czech publisher. He wants to release the album in his country, where Karel Velebny is revered. We shall license it to him [Velebny, who died in 1989, also founded the Summer Jazz Workshop in Frýdlant, Bohemia, in 1984, which has since been named after him].

Even from the start, did you see the free jazz records at all from a political perspective?

Yes. Art is profoundly subversive. If you're living under a system whose government is disseminating lies, art is a refuge. It's difficult for the government to control, if it's not verbal. Art is inextricable from the free expression of ideas. It subliminally conveys a spirit of freedom. In the late '60s, we had a system that was drafting American youth for the Vietnam nightmare, and we have a recurrence of preemptive war now, and the official lies that go with it.

What was your relation with the East Village Other, *the underground newspaper? They were receptive to the records you were producing, and you even did a record with them.*

The Fugs were part of that Lower East Side community of artists, poets, and writers. They trusted me. The newspaper's editors asked me to do a record that would help finance the paper. They brought the artists to the session.

When did you first become aware of errors or faults in your handling of the label as a business?

I knew from the start that I was woefully incompetent and not suited to deal with both the creative side and the business administration side. I never saw it as a business. It is rare that one can wear two heads. Some artists have phenomenal business acumen, but most have one orientation or the other. And my orientation was to hear what was going on. I never asked, "But will it sell?" That is no way to run a business, if you look at it as a business. If you look at it as something different—as a commitment, a calling, an obsession—no, I didn't make mistakes. To regard it as a business would have been preposterous. ESP planted seeds that might yield a harvest in a year, ten years, or thirty years. How does one derive a livelihood in this manner? I wasn't married; I didn't have the normal concerns about getting married and having children and assuming the responsibility to support a family. I met women from time to time who were extraordinary, who would have made superb wives. I wasn't about to settle down.

Because of the money from your parents, weren't you able to keep the label going until that ran out?

Yes. And it ran out because I had been put out of business in '68, when we were doing phenomenally well. The government closed my business because of our opposition to the war.

With respect to business practices, how did you determine your royalty rates and why did some believe it was too low?

I think our original price when we started the label was $4.98. Over the span of a few years, it became $6.98. A $5.00 retail was $2.50 wholesale, and 25¢ would have been 10 percent of $2.50, domestic. And foreign export would have been 12.5¢. The rate was 10 percent of wholesale. That was not wildly off the mark. The records themselves were not ever—for any of the artists—deemed to be a significant source of earnings. The artists would make more from a tour or a series of concerts in a few weeks than they'd make in a year from a record. The records were a vehicle for promotion. And this had been true of the industry throughout its history. The record labels and their producers, recognizing the vulnerability of the artists, would make sure the studio costs were huge. You had to use a Columbia Records studio if you were recording for Columbia, and you would incur astronomical studio costs, promotion costs, and breakage allowances.

Did your royalty rate change in those few years?

Not only did it not change, but we paid royalties to few artists. During those three years, we kept records of what the sales were. We saved those files and are busy issuing statements that go back to the beginnings of the label. When ESP resumed operation six years ago, we changed our royalty rate to 10 percent of wholesale for all recordings, unilaterally—including those that had been re-corded during the early stage of the label—to reflect current prices.

But most of the time you were paying advances?

Three hundred dollars to a leader, fifty to a hundred dollars for a side person, and they all shared ownership of the album.

How did you determine these sorts of arrangements?

Artists who got together to record for ESP produced their own albums and often exchanged roles. A sideman on an album might become the leader on another album. They were all improvising. We decided that the leader should have a share of the royalties as the composer (he was generally the composer), as a performer, and as the leader. That's three shares to one share for each of the sidemen. That is the ESP formula. All the performers share in the benefits of the sales of the record.

Whether downloads or record sales, we have become efficient in our ac-counting practices. We did not pay substantial royalties during the first years or during the years we were out of business. We didn't pay royalties on the licens-ing either, because licenses were general advances, and then we'd receive ab-surd, fictitious royalty statements that were useless for this purpose.

So what did you do wrong, and how did musicians understand what was wrong, or right? Are there any particular things that you can point to as your failures in that era?

I have no regrets over any decision that I made during that time. My commit-ment to document the music was total. So, although I received criticism, it was more from people who didn't get recorded than from those who did. And of those who did, some were verbal in the first few years, but as time went on, they became far more tolerant, recognizing how important their first record was to their career. Few records ever recouped their production costs in the early years.

Was there a point where this bad reputation was beginning to surface?

Writers have written critically about ESP regarding its royalty accounting prac-tices. Our artists, as they have mellowed, are far more sympathetic to the label, and they now often cite its importance in launching their careers.

And certainly a number of the musicians kept coming back to you, complaints or not.

Yes. There is no ESP musician today with whom I can't communicate amicably, or who would decline to work with ESP regarding a retrospective or current project involving his or her work.

5 Decline and Fall

In 1968 the label fell over the edge. What were the circumstances? How did that come about?

I had a team of four, including the shipping clerk and his assistants, who were the Godz. We had three albums on the charts by the Fugs and Pearls Before Swine. One was at position 30 on the pop charts. We were hot. Then, I received a call from an industry figure associated with Warner Brothers—that Warner wanted to buy our label. And I said no. One morning, weeks later, the phones stopped ringing and the orders stopped coming in. Obviously, something was going on. The records were available in the stores, but they weren't coming from us. I went to the pressing plant in Philadelphia, and I toured the facilities. I couldn't find any Pearls album sleeves, or any of the Fugs. We had shipped them thousands in advance in anticipation of orders. The sleeves had disappeared. The plant had gone into business on its own with our products, bootlegging them. We were out of business.

And this was the plant that you always dealt with?

Yes.

Was there nothing you could do?

We could have sued them in federal court. We would have had to prove what they were doing, which probably wouldn't have been that difficult to do, but no federal laws against bootlegging existed at that time. The Johnson regime had found a way to silence our criticism of the war in Vietnam. Strict federal laws were enacted in 1974 to deal with bootlegging, but it was too late for ESP.

How did you come to that conclusion? Did you have anything concrete?

There were hints that we were being wiretapped. Why did the Philadelphia plant suddenly decide to go into business on our product, unless they had gotten a government okay? That was my theory. Why would they deliberately destroy an account, unless they had been authorized or directed to do so? That's a reasonable assumption.

You saw traces that the records still existed?

They were widely available in the stores! Tom Rapp [of Pearls Before Swine] told the public he had sold two hundred thousand records. I believe this was the correct figure. We had sold twenty thousand to thirty thousand—the rest were bootlegs. The Fugs too, their sales estimates were about the same.

Where did the Fugs and the Pearls go from there?

Tom Rapp and Ed Sanders were approached by a CIA man, who signed a personal management agreement with them and took them to Warner Brothers Records. He pocketed Tom Rapp's seventy-thousand-dollar advance and disappeared. Both groups no longer wrote or recorded songs that challenged the war, so they had been effectively silenced.

Did the bootlegs affect the jazz titles as well?

They weren't selling. The U.S. distributors tolerated our jazz; they put it on their shelves on consignment, and they could return it any time. They weren't legally obligated to pay for it until they sold it. Once the popular groups were no longer supplied by ESP, they no longer had any reason to handle the jazz, and they returned their stock to us.

As far as that purgatory of the label for the next few years, what did you do for pressing the new releases? It seems that as many as several dozen records were produced between '68 and '74.

I have a vague recollection of using another plant, whose product was of poor quality. In 1974 our remaining stock was sold to an Italian company, as I faced reality and closed the company.

Regarding the COINTELPRO surveillance, did you have any signs that you were being spied on?

I moved from 156 Fifth Avenue, where our offices had been, to an apartment house at 300 West 55th Street, on the top floor, in 1969. I engaged in a telephone conversation with someone, and I used an obscure phrase. Then I got a call from a prominent music industry lawyer, asking me whether I wanted to take on a client. As we chatted, he used the identical phrase. The likelihood of a coincidence was very remote. I concluded that the government was monitoring my phone calls. And he was in on it.

Do you see all that springing from your having two pop bands who were political, particularly the Fugs?

Lyndon Johnson's daughter got married, and the *East Village Other* album recorded the broadcast on August 6, 1966, intercutting the announcer gushing about the ceremony with ghastly audio images from the war. That was the first blow. The second was "Uncle John," a song by Tom Rapp of Pearls Before Swine, which labeled Johnson a war profiteer. The third was "Kill for Peace," a song by the Fugs. Johnson would have been enraged.

What was your reason at the time for not selling to Warner Brothers?

I had just started the label. Why would I cash out? It would show me as an opportunist—which was not how I saw myself. And I sensed that this was a ploy sponsored by the government to shut us down. Our government has two ways to deal with opponents: one is dirty, and the other is to throw money at them.

Did these troubles dog you beyond that period?

It was a very dark period, during which I lived in obscurity as a state government lawyer until I retired at sixty-two. I reopened ESP in 2003, at the age of seventy-four.

In the mid-1970s, you did continue to work in music a little. Didn't Columbia Records even hire you for a while?

They actually signed a producer agreement with me to find new talent for Columbia, and I brought them a roster of candidates who were artists that I would have issued on ESP. I signed a deal with them for the Charlie Parker broadcasts, recordings that I had bought from Boris Rose. I acted as the middleman. They wouldn't deal with Boris Rose, an underground individual, but they would deal with me. I went to Washington with my wife as volunteers on Jimmy Carter's transition team following his election, and I lost that connection by being out of touch.

I had assisted my lawyer brother Norman to obtain employment with a major music lawyer, and he eventually became vice president for International Legal Affairs for Columbia Records, based in London.

But how did Columbia think of you, at that point in time?

In 1965 I had contacted Columbia custom pressing. They sent me a salesman, Bruce Lundvall. Eight years later, he was the president of Columbia Records. He and I negotiated the licensing agreement for the Charlie Parker material, and he hired me to scout for new talent for Columbia.

With regard to the legendary Boris Rose, and the many radio broadcasts that he taped, what was the legal status of such material, some of which ESP released over the years?

He did this night after night for almost forty years, fifty-thousand hours of live music. The vast bulk of it is in the public domain. The courts have not dealt with whether radio and television organizations can assert any legal interest in their broadcasts apart from the rights of producers of shows. No copyright existed in sound recordings until 1974. No right of publicity exists in the estates of deceased artists if they were residents of New York. The courts have never adjudicated whether broadcasts are in public domain, and the broadcast organizations prefer that it remain a gray area to minimize exploitation of these materials. The rights of living artists to protection against unauthorized use of their names, likenesses, and performances are now protected by copyright laws and laws regarding the right of privacy, unauthorized exploitation, and unfair competition. ESP contracted with the estates of Charlie Parker and Billie Holiday.

How did ESP manage to continue in that period of 1968–74? Where were the resources?

My mother had lent me a certain amount of money. Much of it remained, as we had been largely self-financing. My rent was low and my expenses were as well.

We did some sales, but from 1968 to 1974 there was no longer distribution. We limped along. In November 1974, I got married and we moved to my country place, Acorn Hill House in the Catskills. I had no employment, and my wife wasn't working. In 1979 I took the federal and state civil service exams, at the age of fifty, and obtained employment as a staff lawyer with the New York State Department of Transportation, at seventeen thousand dollars a year, which was not enough to cover our living costs.

In that period between '68 and '74, did the label's difficulties affect your choices as a producer?

Putting out a record for commercial reasons was never contemplated. It would have been very detrimental to our credibility.

Did these difficulties provide an occasion for new alliances in some way?

Bruce Lundvall at Columbia Records provided us with needed funding from the independent producer agreement and the Charlie Parker licensing. Phonogram in Europe licensed some titles, but the agreement was cut short after two years, presumably under pressure from the U.S. government. Then Japan Phonogram surfaced and licensed titles from us in 1970.

Did the decline that began in 1968 affect your past relationships with musicians?

Not really. I don't think they were aware of our troubles. Major labels were signing them. Some were getting teaching positions in colleges and universities.

Their ESP albums had given them passports to careers. They weren't preoccupied about sales of their first album.

According to the ESP catalog, even though the company shut down in 1974, you did continue to produce some records afterwards. What was that all about?

While I had no funding, I kept producing records. It was irrational, as these productions had no apparent future. I believed ESP would return to operation.

After eleven years in government service, I retired in July 1991, with a small pension and social security. In December of that year came a proposal from the German dance label ZYX to release every ESP title for the first time on CD. I sent them all of our masters, including several that had never been issued, creating the graphics for those that had never been packaged for release. The catalog became 125 albums. They released all of them, with a forty-two-page color brochure, and sold them worldwide, providing ESP with renewed interest from the music industry and the music-buying public.

How did you end up buying the farm near Woodstock?

I had purchased tickets to the original Woodstock Festival in 1969, but access was blocked by the state police. Instead, I visited a real estate broker in Ellenville, New York, and looked for a secluded property bordering state land for a country home. I found an idyllic parcel of seventy-five acres, with meadows and woods and a stunning view of a mountain peak. Acorn Hill House was my weekend home until 1974, when we moved there. Onno Scholtze, our audio engineer from Philips Phonogram in Holland, had brought his family to live there for a while at the beginning. He found employment with a manufacturer of audio tape, and he opened a recording studio in our old red barn. Onno recorded two young Native American rock musicians from Florida in the meadows of the farm: Sun Country [in 1969; the band later reformed as Tiger Tiger]. The Tiger brothers were sons of Buffalo Tiger, chief of the Miccosukee tribe, a branch of the Seminoles. They had met my father in Florida, where my parents had retired, and he sent them to me. Members of the tribe wrestled alligators for tourists; in later years, they opened a casino in Miami and became wealthy.

What was the perception of the label in this period of decline, among musicians?

We didn't talk about it with anyone.

Did you take on any outside legal work through this time, in or out of music? How much did others know about your predicament?

I never sent out distress signals and did little legal work, except for Dizzy Gillespie.

6 On Individual Artists

Bernard Stollman was asked to speak more at length about a number of the artists who recorded for ESP.

Albert Ayler

Albert produced four records for ESP: *Spiritual Unity*, *Spirits Rejoice*, *Bells*, and *New York Eye and Ear Control*. *Spirits Rejoice* was done in Judson Hall [September 23, 1965], which we rented solely for recording purposes. W. Eugene Smith, the famous photographer, came by and took pictures of the session. So did Guy Kopelowicz, the Associated Press photographer from Paris, a good friend of the label. ESP recently acquired tapes of Albert's last performances in 1970, at the Fondation Maeght in the south of France. Several years ago, Revenant Records acquired the tape of his performance with Cecil Taylor in Copenhagen, as well as recordings from Cleveland and elsewhere, and issued the *Holy Ghost* box set. All rights to these performances now belong to ESP.

As Albert was recording his session at Judson Hall, I asked him whether he would be willing to do a short work. He smiled resignedly and nodded in agreement. One of the songs on *Spirits Rejoice*, "Holy Family," is the result. It is less than three minutes in length. I realized, to my chagrin, that I had violated our commitment to recognize the artist as the sole authority to determine the content of his work, and I vowed to myself that it would never happen again.

ESP staged a concert at Town Hall on May Day, 1965, which yielded the *Bells* album as well as Giuseppi Logan's *More*. While Albert was waiting to perform, he asked me to the basement for a private talk. His musicians would not play until they were paid, he told me with some embarrassment. It was early in their careers, and they were apprehensive as to whether they would be paid. I had the necessary funds, so I paid them.

In 1966 he asked me to visit him at his aunt's apartment in Harlem. He told me he had been invited to sign with Impulse. They were offering him a $2,500 advance and he asked for my advice. I said, I thought it might help his career, to have the support a major label could provide. We lost touch with each other after that, as he recorded several albums for Impulse, produced by Bob Thiele.

He came to visit me in November 1970 and told me with much satisfaction that he had a quarter-million dollar deal to tour Japan for the first time, in December. He played me a tape he had made of spirituals, taking them way out. They were magnificent, but my hands were tied. Two weeks later, he was found dead in the East River, under circumstances that are still unknown.

We represent Albert's estate now. His wife, Arlene; his daughter, Desiree; and a son all live in Cleveland. Desiree has a son at Ohio State on a football scholarship and a daughter who is entering a nursing career. Albert's father is in his nineties, and his brother Don died a few years ago.

Sunny Murray

I recently retrieved two masters for him: *Sonny's Time Now* from the Japanese licensee and *Big Chief* from BYG. They are being reissued under his direction.

I saw him in Paris a few years ago. At the apartment of a mutual friend, we had dinner together. Over the years, from time to time, we've always reconnected.

Pharoah Sanders

We met at his original recording session for ESP, which was his debut as a leader [*Pharoah Sanders Quintet*, September 20, 1964]. He was extremely shy. Unless you knew him well, he was not garrulous. The session was in the loft of the late Jerry Newman, a highly regarded audio engineer. Pharoah didn't greet me; he just approached the engineer regarding the placement of the microphones. When it was over, I paid the group.

I met him again three years ago, backstage at the Iridium. A beautiful set— he was singing through his horn—it was quite arresting. In his dressing room I sat next to him, identified myself, and complimented him on his performance. He seemed pleased, but I can't be certain, because he didn't say anything.

Paul Bley

Following the October Revolution festival, I visited Paul at his downtown apartment and met Carla. She looked at me quizzically. Paul and I discussed the pending album, *Barrage* [October 20, 1964]. It was recorded at a midtown studio, with Alfy Wade as engineer. As usual, I provided no input. He was satisfied, I believed, because he quickly decided he wanted to do a trio album [*Closer*, December 12, 1965]. I didn't attend that session. I visited him again a few years ago at the Blue Note, performing with a trio. I hadn't seen him in over thirty years.

Giuseppi Logan

When Giuseppi made his first album for ESP, I stood with Richard L. Alderson, the engineer, in the control room. I thought the piece they were playing was stunningly beautiful. It sounded totally spontaneous, as if they were engaging in an engrossing conversation. Suddenly, I heard a "thwuuunk," and I realized that the tape had run out. The engineer and I were so absorbed, we hadn't been paying attention. I thought, "Oh God, this remarkable thing is lost. It was interrupted in the middle, and it's gone." Richard got on the intercom and said, "Giuseppi, the tape ran out." Without a pause, Giuseppi said, "Take it back to before where it stopped and we'll take it from there." So, Richard wound it back and played some bars of it and hit the record button, and they resumed exactly what they were doing—there was no way of telling where the break had occurred. It was unreal. [Stollman's note to the 2008 reissue of *The Giuseppi Logan Quartet*, 1964]

I hadn't seen him in ten years; he had vanished. Then, one early spring day in 1979, I made a rare visit to the Manufacturers Hanover bank at the corner of 57th Street and Ninth Avenue, where the ESP master tapes were stored. As I approached the corner, I saw a street musician playing a battered clarinet held together by wires and recognized him as Giuseppi Logan. Of all the places to play on the streets of Manhattan, he had picked a spot directly above the vault in which the tapes of his recorded performances were stored, about which he could not have known. When I stopped to speak with him, he gave no sign of recognition but leaned over and whispered in my ear: "Nixon has exploded a bomb off Amchitka." Some years earlier [in 1971], Nixon had authorized an atom bomb test under the waters of Alaska. I gave him a small sum, and he brightened and said, "Now I can go home and practice." Efforts were made, over the years, to put him in contact with people with whom he could play and record his music, but his mental faculties were impaired and he was unable to perform. He had last been seen in Seattle some years ago, and I looked for him there during a visit in the late 1990s, but no one in the music scene recalled seeing him.

In the summer of 2008, he showed up at the Vision Festival in lower Manhattan. He has since acquired an alto sax, a bass clarinet, and a flute. He's been practicing, trying to get his strength back together. ESP has provided some support, and he has expressed a fierce desire to perform his new works.

Marzette Watts had recorded the Judson Hall concert in 1966 that ESP produced, of Giuseppi [playing thirteen instruments] with a small chamber ensemble. It was exquisite, but Marzette told me afterwards that the recording had failed. I was devastated! When I reached him on the phone in 1997, he confessed that he had lied to me and claimed he had done this to protect Giuseppi. We agreed that he would turn the tape over to me, and I volunteered to pay him for his services. He died before we could conclude the transaction. Giuseppi is presently being cared for by the Jazz Foundation of America and has returned to recording.

Roswell Rudd

Roswell Rudd had a large loft on Chambers Street in Manhattan and several young children. I remember visiting him there, and this was probably the origin of our agreement to record the *New York Art Quartet* [November 1964]. Roswell and I maintained contact over the years. I saw him in Woodstock in the '80s and recently at the Rubin Museum in 2006, where I caught him during the reunion of his Dixieland band at Yale, Eli's Chosen Six. It was spectacular!

Sun Ra

He had made over seventy-five records for his El Saturn label in the '50s and '60s. When he signed with ESP, he had never had general distribution—El Saturn was sold only at their gigs. His first two studio albums with ESP, *Heliocentric Worlds*, volumes 1 and 2, in 1965, brought him wider public recognition. During that same period, ESP sent him and his Arkestra on the college tour [*Nothing Is . . .* , 1966]. He was generous in response to ESP requests for his time and his music. Later, ESP produced the Town Hall concert [*Concert for the Comet Kohoutek*, 1973], and he was given a large advance to bring back recordings from his pending Mexican tour, but the Town Hall appearance was our last project together.

Following Sun Ra's first visit to Egypt in 1971, he and his Arkestra were stranded at Kennedy airport, broke, on their return. He called me at 11:00 p.m., and I drove to the airport in my old station wagon, paid for cabs, and he came with me back to Manhattan. My parents had an apartment at 5 Riverside Drive. They were in Florida, and I was staying there. Ra stopped by for tea—by then it was one in the morning, and he wanted to talk.

He told me how he was stopped at the Egyptian border by a guard, who examined his passport and was affronted—Sun Ra, in the Ptolemaic religion, is the term for a deity! He wasn't going to admit Ra and his musicians into the country. Sun Ra asked the guard to call the director of the Egyptian museum, who rushed out to the airport and engaged Sun Ra in conversation. They talked Egyptology, including hieroglyphics. Ra had studied the Rosicrucians; he was knowledgeable about Egyptian lore. The director said to the guard, "He is who he says he is. Let him in." He invited Ra to appear on Egyptian television. The group also went out to the pyramids. While they were there, a German documentary film crew was filming and saw Ra and his musicians, so they filmed them. When they finished, Ra sent someone over to confiscate the film.

The day after the Kohoutek concert, Ra came to my apartment. I had moved to West End Avenue. The label had been shut down—what was I doing staging a concert at Town Hall? He came by with a small group of his followers to show me a film, *Space Is the Place*. It was shot partly in the Rosicrucian Garden in California, and it showed Ra stepping out of his spaceship. There were shots of young women in scanty attire, introduced gratuitously. I said, "The film is fine, but take that material out. There's no point to it." Then they left. The master tapes of the Kohoutek concert were stored openly in the office, and they vanished during his visit. I never saw him again. The engineer had done a monaural reference tape for the concert, and this was used by ESP many years later for the record.

Frank Wright

John Coltrane was playing with his quartet at the Village Gate during the Christmas holiday. I was greatly impressed by the playing of a guest artist, a saxophonist. When the set ended, I approached and complimented him on his playing. I asked who he was. He said, "I'm Frank Wright, from Cleveland." "Do you have a record label?" "Oh no, I'm not on any record label." I said, "Well, you are now." He'd been pressing pants in a dry cleaning shop in Cleveland before he came to New York. Shortly afterwards, he formed a group and went into the studio [to record *Frank Wright Trio*, November 1965]. And he did a second album for ESP [*Your Prayer*, March 1967]. Then he came to me, and he said, "Bernard, I'm desperate. I can't get any work in this country." I said, "You have no problem, Frank. You're going to Europe." He said, "I am?" "Of course, you are."

And he did. A year and a half later, Frank returned. He was ebullient and dressed beautifully. "Bernard, I've made twelve albums! I'm touring everywhere. It's wonderful." I said, "I'm very happy for you, Frank." That was the last exchange I had with him. Frank married a French woman and had a child and lived the rest of his life in France.

Burton Greene

He made two records of his own with ESP [*Burton Greene Quartet*, December 18, 1965; *On Tour*, April–May 1966]. And he was on both Patty Waters records. Marion [Brown] performed with him on his first album, and his second album was from the college tour. Burton was one of the most outspokenly critical individuals regarding ESP for many years. He recently acknowledged, when I chided him, that while he had made numerous recordings over the years, none of them had made money. He acknowledged that his impressions were incorrect.

Patty Waters

One afternoon Albert Ayler phoned and asked me to visit him in a handsome group of buildings that predate the Revolutionary War, on Astor Place, across from the Public Theater. It was a beautiful afternoon, and he opened the door of a lovely, sun-filled apartment. He smiled at me and stepped aside. Patty Waters was standing behind him. That's how I met her.

I had never heard of her, but I knew that Albert would not mislead me. A resourceful woman, she was working as a ticket taker in a movie house, barely surviving. She invited me to her apartment, a tiny room with an upright piano. I said, "Play for me." She sat at the piano and played some songs. I said, "What would you like to do as a record?" "I want to do the great standards, like Ella." I replied, "That's fine. But not on ESP. You have to do your own material." Patty found Burton Greene, who had just recorded his first album for ESP.

She and Burton worked it out between them. She sings and accompanies herself on piano through the first side of her album, *Patty Waters Sings* [December 19, 1965]. Then she does "Black is the Color of My True Love's Hair," and Burton starts to tear apart the piano at that moment, so that half of the album is Burton and his trio backing her. They were all her originals, except one that she'd written with another woman. I think it's one of the finest albums I've ever had anything to do with. But it's topped by Patty's *College Tour* [April 1966], which had different mixes of musicians with her, song by song. Her work has been praised by Yoko Ono, Patti Smith, Diamanda Galas, and by critics.

She didn't stay active as a musician in the years that followed, and we lost contact. She lived in Santa Cruz, and part of the time in Hawaii, raising her son. When she came to the Vision Festival in 2003, Burton and bassist Mark Dresser played with her. ESP may release it.

Perry Robinson

Henry Grimes's trio record [*The Call*, December 28, 1965] was as much Perry's as it was his. He's a very fine clarinetist. I've run into him in the past occasionally. It's partly my fault; I could have taken some initiative with him. I had no rationale or justification for not giving him the same attention I've given to others. He projects modesty, humility, diffidence. He's highly regarded by his fellow artists.

Marzette Watts

I knew him as an independent engineer with his own recording studio. When I visited his apartment on Cooper Square, he had a few small paintings on the wall. I didn't know at the time that he had studied at the Sorbonne. He said, "Bernard, I'm going to do an album." "Yourself? Are you a musician?" "Yes," he said, "I taught myself." He had such aplomb, that when he said something it wasn't halfway. I said, "All right, Marzette, you will do an album." He brought together Sonny Sharrock, Karl Berger; a lot of people played on that album [*Marzette Watts and Company*, December 1966].

The Fugs

Jordan Matthews came to me one day, and I was depressed. Our initial releases weren't selling. "My company's not happening," I told him. "The American public is not interested in this music." He said, "You've got no problems. You've got the Fugs." "What do you mean?" "I've talked with them. They want to be on the label."

They went to Richard Alderson's studio and made their album [*The Fugs*, 1966]. It was a lot more polished than their first record, and Ed Sanders's songs were more prominent in it. When they did the suite "Virgin Forest," which was the culmination of the album (and which I later learned had been composed by Richard Alderson), I performed with them as one of the rude chorus. "Kill for Peace" is on the album, and that song was certainly very antiwar and antiestablishment. I took no part in counseling them. That record was really their unfettered moment.

The material put out by Folkways [*The Village Fugs*, 1965] was charming. Sexually, it was raw; it wasn't political. And then, from the unreleased Folkways material, came "CIA Man," which appeared on *Virgin Fugs*. That had been part of their original material, but they were angry with me when I released it, a violation of the label's principles. ESP was sued by the Fugs, but they lost the case.

After *The Fugs* started selling, I bought their first album from Folkways. Moe Asch couldn't care less how much they sold, as he didn't want anything to do with them. I released that album on ESP as well. *Virgin Fugs* came out later: when I bought the master from Moe, the tapes included additional songs. It meant we had another album of material. By then, relations were strained with Sanders. They were feeling their oats; they had a manager. They had been on the Tonight Show. They had all kinds of major breaks—some of which ESP had engineered, because it hired a publicist for them. Their drum set, their instruments, their microphones, all kinds of stuff, silk-screened T-shirts, posters, advertising—ESP underwrote it all, providing first-rate professional support.

We'd never had a pop group, with underground buzz, and we played it to the hilt. We booked the Astor Place Playhouse for them. I signed the lease and advanced the down payment for the rent. They performed there continuously for a few months [January to May 1966, appearing weekly, according to Sanders in his history of the Fugs on the group's website; during this period other ESP artists also performed there, including Albert Ayler and Sun Ra]. And the night they opened, the fashion editors and the major media came down as their guests, and ESP put out a spread for them of macrobiotic food, which they ignored. But they went back uptown and wrote very supportively. It was a major breakthrough.

They did a free concert in Tompkins Square Park on the Lower East Side for a crowd of several hundred fans. As they were performing on the stage, a police captain came by with a detail of four officers and made his way through the crowd. He mounted the stage and said, "I have a report of a bomb threat. You'll have to clear the area." Nobody moved. He climbed down off the stage and disappeared. The Fugs resumed their performance.

Peter Edmiston became their manager. He was in partnership with Charlie Rothschild, a well-known manager who represented Judy Collins and Allen Ginsberg. Edmiston took the Fugs and the Pearls to Warner Brothers and stole Tom Rapp's advance. After that, he vanished and hasn't been seen since.

Godz

They were all sales clerks at Sam Goody's, the record store. One of them became ESP's art director [Jay Dillon], another became our sales manager [Larry Kessler], and two were just helping the shipping clerk [Paul Thornton and Jim McCarthy], because we were shipping a lot of records. At one point, Larry Kessler came up to me and said, "Well, we're going to record tomorrow night." "We?" "Yes," he said, "we call ourselves the Godz." I had no idea until that moment that they had any such aspirations. I said, "Where are you going to record?" He said, "Herb Abramson's," which was a studio we used. I said, "Do you want me to hear you?" "Oh, yes. We're rehearsing in Natasha's apartment tonight to prepare for the session." Natasha was my executive assistant.

On a hot August night, I visited her apartment. It was humid. We turned off the lights, so we wouldn't have heat from the bulbs. As we sat on the floor in the dark, the guys started to do a song. They imitated the sounds of a passel of cats on the back fence during mating time, doing this like a choir. I decided we would call it "White Cat Heat." I allowed the session to go forward, and it was clear that I was going to subsidize it, no big deal. At seven o'clock the following evening, the session began. I decided that my presence might intimidate them, so I waited about forty-five minutes. At a quarter to eight, I entered the studio. It was on West 56th Street, and it had been the original studio of Atlantic Records. Herb Abramson had been a founder of the label with the Ertegun brothers. I found them sitting around. Paul Thornton, realizing that I was a little taken aback, greeted me. "Would you like to hear it? We just finished it. We're editing it now." I said, "You finished it in forty-five minutes?" He said, "Yeah, we just ran with it." So I listened, and I was delighted. I said,

"We'll call it *Contact High with the Godz*." I was obviously inspired. It was followed by a second album [*Godz 2*, 1967]. For the third one [*The Third Testament*, 1968], they invited a large number of friends, who contributed crowd noises and choral effects. It has kind of a rowdy party quality to it, which works.

Promoting them was an impossible challenge. They would try to perform, but they would get in fights; it was total chaos. I rented them a concert hall in the Times Square area and sent out flyers—they showed up but no one else did. Larry Kessler and Jim McCarthy were at each other's throats. "I'm the leader!" "No, I'm the leader!" That kind of thing. Those were the only records they ever made in their lives. We sent review copies of their records to the press, and one famous critic loved them, Lester Bangs—which was a tremendous plus, of course—but nobody else did. I think we re-pressed the first one, because I know the artwork changed. So, we pressed at least a thousand altogether of that one, maybe more.

I didn't bother to stop to figure out whether it worked or not. The investment was minimal and I liked their work, so I just kept documenting it. Now that ESP is back, we're going to do a Godz box set. Their records were pressed in Italy, by Abraxas, in the '90s. That gave them a new lease on life—and they sold reasonably well, five hundred pieces a year.

Pearls Before Swine

One day in 1966, two tiny reels of tape arrived in the mail at the ESP office on the twelfth floor of 156 Fifth Avenue. They were postmarked Eau Gallie, Florida. At the end of the day, I sat alone in my darkened office to audition them, and as I listened, I was moved to tears. I called Tom and asked him to visit a local studio in Florida with his group to make a professional demo. Two weeks later, a seven-inch square box arrived, wrapped in kraft paper. On the cover were handwritten notations: "garbage," "trash," "disgusting." Inside was a reel of tape. The Christian fundamentalists who owned the studio apparently could not refrain from expressing their opinions of his lyrics.

I brought the group to New York and they stayed in my parents' living room in sleeping bags. The first record was recorded in Richard Alderson's studio [*One Nation Underground*, May 1967]. I was the gofer; I went out at two or three in the morning to the delis so that Tom and Richard could work without interruption. Tom was pleased and gratified at the reception the first album had received, and he saw that he had complete latitude to do whatever he wanted. The second record [*Balaklava*] was done a year later. Then Edmiston signed him to a producer agreement and brought him to Warner Brothers.

The Pearls records got extensive airplay on college radio. Rumor was that there had been vast sales of the Pearls albums. They didn't come out from us; they came from the pressing plant. We didn't get rich on it.

Yma Sumac

In 1946 she came to New York with the Inca Taqui Trio, a group of dancers and singers, performers, playing instruments, flutes. She and her cousin, who also sang, wore exotic Inca costumes. I saw them perform on my family's new black-and-white twelve-inch TV set and was spellbound. Four years later, Capitol Records selected her for their first ten-inch LP, and she was their first Latin artist. One side of the album was produced by Les Baxter, while the other side was produced by her husband, Moisés Vivanco. Vivanco's side is spectacular! The other side is schmaltzy, not very interesting. I bought the record and became an early aficionado. Her series of LPs for Capitol had huge sales. Then, she and her husband were accused of being communist sympathizers, and they fled the U.S. They were invited to tour in the Soviet Union for two weeks, and it was extended to six months.

She and her husband divorced, married again, and divorced again. In 1965 she was living in Beverly Hills, where I visited her. She was a tiny woman, with huge lung power from having grown up in the Andes. I'll never forget the comment she made. Apparently referring to her treatment by our government, her eyes flashed as she said, "The one thing I cannot stand is injustice." It could have been her anger about her divorce. She agreed to record for my new label.

I had to find a musical director for her. She was divorced from Vivanco, and I could not imagine who would be suitable. A year later, she called me. "Bernard, I want to end my contract," she said. "I have the opportunity to do a rock album." What was I to do? I gave her a release.

Back then, when ESP was producing mostly free jazz, I didn't worry whether or not she fit the label. ESP was going to be whatever I decided. I wasn't at all put off by the idea that I had an artist who had had world popularity, who had sold many millions of records, who was now in decline; nobody was talking about her any longer. I thought, If I can capture some of her work, why not do it? My own appetites, that's all it was.

In 2006 ESP licensed a recording of her concert in Bucharest in 1961 [*Recital*] from a Romanian label that had originally issued it on LP. It was out of print and had never appeared on a CD. But ESP has a new album featuring her U.S. concert debut at the Hollywood Bowl [August 12, 1950], which is gorgeous, plus the soundtrack of the Jack Carter Show on television [aired March 3, 1951] and a mambo that is joyous, funny, and high-spirited.

7 About Some Records

So many records in the ESP catalog are distinct and unusual. Bernard Stollman was asked to elaborate on the people and circumstances behind some of them.

Jean Erdman, *The Coach with the Six Insides*

Jean Erdman, who is ninety-two and retired in Hawaii, was a very creative choreographer who had produced a theatrical performance piece based on *Finnegans Wake*. Her husband, Joseph Campbell, was a famous scholar and an authority on James Joyce. She had brought together a number of talented performers, and the music was composed by Teiji Ito, who was married to the documentary filmmaker Maya Deren. His brother was also a musician. Somewhere along the line, I met one of them and became aware of Jean Erdman and her work.

Recently, I found a black-and-white video of the production. Jean Erdman herself danced in it. ESP will reissue the album with the DVD, which enhances the experience immeasurably.

William Burroughs, *Call Me Burroughs*

My youngest brother, Steve, knew Gaït Frogé, who had the English Bookshop in Paris, a cultural landmark. She had acquired the rights to do the record, from Burroughs. She wasn't able to do anything with it—she was basically a bookstore owner. We just got the record from her—complete with the graphics, the whole thing. [This was Burroughs's first record. It was recorded in the bookshop's basement by Ian Sommerville and released in Paris in the summer of 1965. ESP released the U.S. edition in late 1966.]

Movement Soul

[The first volume, subtitled *Live Recordings of Songs and Sayings from the Freedom Movement in the Deep South, 1963–1964*, was released on LP in 1966; *Movement Soul: Two* was first released on CD in 2007.] *Movement Soul: One* dealt with the plight of being black in America in the '60s, as distinguished from *Movement Soul: Two*, a much longer historical reference work. *Movement Soul: One* was just a brief documentary recorded by Alan Ribback [later known as Moses Moon], who was in his thirties. He had come back from Montgomery, where he had traveled with a portable tape deck. He had been at a church in Selma—a white, wooden-framed church—when it was surrounded by Klansmen who were screaming and threatening to burn it down. The parishioners inside, unprotected, were terrified. He had captured their voices trying to reassure each other; he was with them inside the church. It's hair-raising, because you pick up the voices, in panic and fear, and singing gospel. You sense what they are going through. The threat abated, but that moment was emblematic of the black experience of that time. A documentary on Martin Luther King used a portion of it on the soundtrack.

The CD *Movement Soul: Two*, which is not a reissue, is an anthology of different African American voices that span the century [including Mary McLeod Bethune, Ralph Ellison, Babs Gonzales, Thurgood Marshall, Bob Moses, and Fannie Lou Hamer]. It's a far more expansive collection. Michael D. Anderson assembled it from his own sources. It's fairly recent, since we relaunched the label. Mike wanted to do it, and I thought it was a very interesting idea, so we put it out. We haven't marketed it wisely, but I think we still may be able to do so.

Steve Lacy, *The Forest and the Zoo*

Steve Lacy visited our 156 Fifth Avenue office in 1966. He had just returned from Argentina. I had heard him in the Village years earlier, when his focus was on the work of Thelonious Monk. He said, "Bernard, I need money. I'll sell you a master." It was of a concert in Buenos Aires. I bought it for ESP without having heard it. It featured a front cover painting by his friend Bob Thompson. I learned only in 1991, when the tape was to be duplicated for the ZYX licensing agreement, that it was out of phase. The Sony engineer who spotted and corrected the problem, Ken Robertson, was a direct descendant of Karl Marx.

I saw Steve in Paris some years later and visited him and his wife at their loft. He and I went to a café, in a small gathering, and Joseph Jarman was in the group. He had a nice disposition, very philosophical.

Slavonic Cappella Ensemble, *Music from the Orthodox Liturgy*

Alexis P. Fekula was a Wall Streeter of Ukrainian descent. David Hancock had recorded his ensemble of fifty opera singers in the cathedral in Garden City and sent Alexis to ESP. I thought it was beautiful. Howard Bernstein created an imaginative cover, but they were horrified by it. They said it was not in keeping with Ukrainian church art. So, we quickly replaced it with a more prosaic cover of burning candles.

Charles Manson, *Sings*

The music was recorded [in 1967] several years before the crime spree. Manson had formed a friendship with Dennis Wilson, and it was recorded in his studio. The Beach Boys took one of the songs ["Cease to Exist"], made it their own, and recorded it with a different title ["Never Learn Not to Love," on their album *20/20*], which did not endear them to him. I heard about the Manson album; in fact, I saw the cover and tracked down its producer, Phil Kaufman, in Los Angeles. The year was 1970 [the original record was called *Lie*, with a cover photo of Manson on the front of a renamed *Life* magazine; the CD reissue on ESP contained additional material]. I said, "This record seems like an interesting idea. I'd like to make a deal with you concerning it." He said, "I've got a couple hundred copies left." I said, "Come to New York, bring the tape, and we'll make a deal." "The reason I'm coming," he said, "is because a group of his followers surrounded my little house, with knives, and they were screaming at me, talking about killing me, and they wanted money to help Charles. I want no part of that. I went outside my house and fired a pistol at them. I don't need that. I'll bring it to New York." I faced the possibility of a visit from them myself.

We made an agreement. A lawyer who represented the estate of Wojciech Frykowski, one of Manson's victims, had sued Manson successfully following the conviction. So, royalties go to Frykowski's family.

But why did I put out the record? Because I thought the songs had a peculiar kind of individuality to them. Manson was, of course, a total maverick—in the sense that he was an enemy of society, and he'd been in and out of prison since childhood. He was a victim and also a perpetrator. I thought his story was fascinating, and I also felt at the time, and I still feel, that the government used that trial to try to discredit the hippie movement. They used him as a poster boy for hippies, and these youths were the ones who were challenging the system with regard to the horrible war in Vietnam. I saw him, in a sense, as a political victim as well as a psychopath. I had no sympathy for his conduct, and my hunch was that he and the Family were probably doing a brisk business in coke. These murders, other than just being a wildly lunatic thing, were characteristic of cocaine deals gone bad. Coke dealers do atrocities. They don't just kill. How was he making a living? How were they surviving? I concluded that they were probably dealing coke. The reason that never came out in the trial was because too many famous names were involved.

In choosing to take on the album by this pariah, I was influenced by Alfred Knopf, a Jewish publisher who published *Mein Kampf* in English. One of his songs, "Garbage Dump," is extraordinary, and there are a few others, including "Big Iron Door." Some things stick in your mind. I never had a second thought about doing it, but realistically I was already out of business. I bought Kaufman's two hundred records from him, and I shipped them to our distributors. I pressed five hundred myself. There wasn't a second pressing. ESP's former distributors took them—then they all contacted me, claiming that the stores refused to handle them. But none were returned, as they all sold.

8   A Word or Two on
Recording Engineers

Aside from Spiritual Unity, *which was recorded by an engineer known only by his first name, Joe, the first few ESP dates were recorded by Art Crist. How did you find your way to him?*

Art Crist was on staff at Bell Sound Studios. Whatever we did at Bell Sound, he engineered. I knew that Art was a jazz pianist, and very accomplished, but his role with us was strictly as an engineer. He was sympathetic, and musicians seemed to like him.

What about Richard Alderson?

He did the bulk of our recording. Richard was an accomplished composer, arranger, and producer. He was very involved creatively in the music, and he brought in studio musicians to work with Jerry Moore and Bruce Mackay. He would make suggestions to the Fugs and to Tom Rapp of Pearls Before Swine. Some arrangements were by him but uncredited. "Virgin Forest," the elaborate suite on *The Fugs*, was his work.

Richard seemed to be able to cope with everything we put out. He engineered the first Patty Waters record—with Burton Greene plucking the strings inside the piano, and Patty screaming. Richard took it in stride. I trusted his judgment. The engineer's vibe is critical; musicians pick up on it. He looms large in the history of ESP.

What was your experience of David Hancock as an engineer?

He did the Sunny Murray record and Albert Ayler at Judson Hall [*Spirits Rejoice*]. He also went to Millbrook, New York, to record Timothy Leary [*Turn On, Tune In, Drop Out*]. It was a session where Leary engaged in a monologue. When David returned from this assignment, he played the results for me.

Leary had spoken at length, with long pauses between each phrase. It would have been impossible to release in that form. David agreed to edit it to remove the pauses. When I visited him again a few days later, the floor of his work space was littered with pieces of tape. He had made thousands of splices to remove the long intervals between words, and Leary now appeared to speak briskly. David was a pianist and Satie's most celebrated interpreter. He toured the world as a performer, but he was also a classical recording engineer, who recorded with two mikes. He was highly regarded by the major labels for recording large orchestras. He carried a portable Sony deck, at thirty IPS [inches per second], twice the speed of conventional tapes. It results in a superior recording. David recorded Ayler at Judson Hall at thirty IPS.

Was there any particular reason why you kept working with different engineers?

There was no hard and fast rule as to who was going to do what. Herb Abramson's studio, A-1 Sound, was the site of a number of recordings, where he lent it out for our use with another engineer, Onno Scholtze. All of the Godz albums were done by Herb Abramson in his studio. He was very comfortable with the group. He was aware enough to appreciate what they were doing.

You originally knew Onno Scholtze from your connection with Philips?

He was their engineer, and we became friends. He knew I had a house in the Catskills, and he moved his wife and his two daughters there, where they lived for about a year. He worked for a tape company for a while, and he did some audio engineering at my farm, using our old barn. Then he returned with his family to Holland. He had moved here to see what he thought of America. He found it too hard. And his relationship with Philips was very solid.

Onno recorded Mij, Erica Pomerance, Cromagnon, and Octopus in Herb Abramson's studio. He loved to experiment, and he was in charge of research for Philips in new technology such as amplifiers, speakers, earphones, and microphones. Once he sent me a set of quad phones and a disk. ESP briefly issued LPs that carried instructions to create quad sound by employing a set of rear speakers wired out of phase.

9 Close Encounters in the Music Business

Over the course of his years in the music business, Bernard Stollman crossed paths with many notable figures beyond the sphere of ESP's activities. Here he recounts episodes involving the more well-known artists.

Barbra Streisand

Mike Wallace had an interview show on television [*PM East/PM West*] in 1961, and one of his guests was a tall, slender young woman, whose movements and gestures were beguiling. She was funny, wisecracking, and I thought she was attractive. I found her phone number in the directory and called her. The time was about midnight. She took the call, and I told her who I was. She responded by engaging in a long melancholy reflection on life. When she finished, I said, "Well, let's have dinner." She agreed.

At the appointed hour, I showed up at her apartment, a studio walk-up in Chelsea. She came to the door, looked at me, and said, "Yes?" I said, "How do you do? I'm Bernard Stollman." She did a double take. "This isn't some kind of a joke, is it?" "A joke? No." "What did you say your name was?" I said, "Bernard Stollman." She said, "Oh. Okay, I'll get ready." She went back to freshen up, leaving the door open. I didn't enter the apartment; I stood at the door. I could see a poster of Anthony Quinn on the wall. We walked from 23rd Street up to 44th Street to her favorite Greek restaurant, the Pantheon. Spyros Skouras, the Hollywood producer, was there at a back table with his family. As we sat down and ordered, and all through the meal, women buzzed around and pleaded for her autograph. I found that she was appearing in a Broadway musical, *I Can Get It for You Wholesale*. We never really got into a conversation. When we finished the meal, I walked her part way toward the theater. I suggested we get together again. She said, "Okay. September." It was June. She was embarrassed. "I have a boyfriend in the show. He's terribly jealous." The boyfriend was Elliot Gould, whom she later married. We parted company. I thought that was the end of the story. It wasn't.

About two weeks later, I get a call from my bank, informing me that my account was overdrawn. I said that this was not possible, as I had just checked my account and there was money in it. "I know, we put it in your account by mistake. It belonged to another person with the same name." I said, "Would you mind giving me his phone number and address?" "We don't do that; it's a policy of the bank. I think I'll make an exception in this case." So, I called him and asked, "Are you Bernard Stollman?" "Yes." "Well, *I'm* Bernard Stollman!" He said, "I know about you. I've gotten your mail and calls for you." I said, "I've never heard of you. Maybe we should meet." He agreed to come to my office. He was very dapper, with wavy blond hair and blue eyes. I saw no family resemblance. He was an architectural engineer. I asked, "Do you have a girlfriend?" He said, "Yes." "Let me see if I can guess her name. Would her first name be Barbra?" "How do you know that? Oh, you're guessing." "You're right, I'm guessing. Let me try her last name: Streisand." He said, "How did you know?" "Because I took her out by mistake. She thought I was you." He said, "I'll have to call her and tell her that it was not a practical joke." And he called her at the theater.

Jimi Hendrix

It was August 1966, a beautiful sunny afternoon. I was strolling along MacDougal Street in the Village and heard the sounds of an electric guitar wafting up from a basement. I was never particularly enthused about electric guitars, but I liked what I heard. So, I descended the stairs to the Café Wha? The door was unlocked, and the club was empty. At the very rear, a musician was standing and playing his guitar, a small amplifier by his side. When he stopped, I approached him and said, "Your playing is beautiful! I have a record label. I'd love to record you. Are you free?" I told him the name. He said, "I like that idea. But I've just gotten a plane ticket to go to London. When I come back, I'd certainly like to discuss it with you." He was very open. And he remembered our encounter.

In January 1968 I visited London en route to the MIDEM, the international music convention in Cannes. While shopping in a department store, I heard music and approached the sales clerk. "What is that playing on your phonograph?" "Why, that's Jimi Hendrix, don't you know?"

I didn't see him again until after the Woodstock festival in '69, in the midtown Manhattan office of his manager, Mike Jeffery, with whom I had made an appointment. Jimi was waiting for me when I arrived in the outer office. He approached me and said, "Bernard, I just want to tell you how much I appreciate what you are doing with ESP-Disk." I thanked him, and then I excused myself and entered his manager's room. Jeffery sat hunched over a big desk. He didn't look up at me or greet me. I told him I had asked for the appointment because I thought that Jimi would benefit from meeting and associating with the artists of ESP. "I have some people I work closely with who are cutting-edge musicians, and I believe he would benefit from knowing them." Of course, I should have talked to Jimi, but I was following protocol. Jeffery replied curtly, still didn't look at me, "Not interested." Jimi had vanished. I don't know if he overheard the conversation.

I didn't know it at the time, but Jimi had recorded in my living room. He was staying in Shokan, just a mile from Acorn Hill House, the farm I had bought near Woodstock. The farm had a rooming house, and Juma Sultan was renting a room from me. He was Jimi's percussionist at the Woodstock festival. Jimi would visit Juma at the farm, and they made a trio recording with Mike Ephron, the British pianist [who had played on Alan Silva's ESP record the previous year].

Yoko Ono and John Lennon

I met her in 1965 at the Paradox, a macrobiotic restaurant I frequented in the East Village. She stood in its window holding a large black burlap bag and a tiny tape recorder that kept repeating a brief message. It was one of her Fluxus happenings. She invited people to climb into the burlap bag and experience the sensation of returning to the womb. We discussed whether this experience could be packaged with a record but found no solution. A few weeks later, Tony Cox, her husband, visited the ESP office. He brought the manuscript of a book by Yoko, *Grapefruit*. It contained a series of Zen exercises. He told me that Yoko wanted to know whether we would publish it. I explained to him that we had not considered publishing, as we were caught up in the fledgling record label. I didn't see Yoko again until I ran into her in London with Lennon, in January 1967.

Lennon had met Ono at the preview to her show at the Indica Gallery in November 1966. I was returning from the MIDEM and stopped in London on the way back. Barry Miles ran the Indica Bookstore and Gallery, and I dropped in on him hoping to obtain distribution rights for an LP he had assembled featuring two maverick Soviet poets, Yevgeny Yevtushenko and Andrei Voznesensky, declaiming their works in Russian. A small sign at the entrance to the gallery announced an exhibition by John Lennon and Yoko Ono. I wandered through the gallery, examining the work, and as I emerged, I saw them at the top of the stairs behind me. I turned and greeted Yoko, and she introduced me to John as the founder of ESP-Disk'. His only comment was "Oh, yes. Paul has the Sun Ras." When I impulsively asked him to distribute ESP on Apple Records, he assumed an attitude of mock disdain. "What? *Us* distribute *you*?" He then dropped the pose and explained earnestly that Apple was having terrible problems with EMI and that there was no way they could contemplate taking on anything new.

The following year, on a sunny summer morning after attending a late-night jam session at Sam Rivers's Studio Rivbea, I was still asleep when the phone rang at 9:00 a.m. in my sublet pied-à-terre on West 10th Street near Fifth Avenue. The call was from my bookkeeper, Rose Schmidt: "The president of Capitol Records is here to see you."

"Does he have an appointment?" I quipped. "I'll be right there." The ESP-Disk' office at 156 Fifth Avenue was just ten short blocks away.

Stanley Gortikov, the label head, was stiffly erect, with a crew cut. He could have been mistaken for a Marine combat officer. Tucked under his arm was an LP wrapped in brown paper. "John and Yoko asked me to give this to you. They would like to know whether you wish to distribute it."

Titled *Two Virgins*, the album's front cover featured a full-length black-and-white frontal nude photo of the pair.

I told him I would listen to it and get back to him. We shook hands and he left. Moments later, the office phone rang. It was Ron Kass, the American business manager of Apple Records. "Well, what do you think of it?" he asked. "I haven't heard it yet, but I have great respect for Yoko as an artist." There was a brief moment of silence. "Well, John's a pretty good musician too, you know." I acknowledged that this was true.

It was Friday. I told Kass that I would be visiting Europe the following week, and we agreed that I should go see him at their Abbey Road office in London on Monday morning to explore a possible distribution deal. I didn't tell him that the trip would be for this sole purpose.

On Sunday I flew to London. The following morning, when I arrived at Abbey Road, no staff member was there. Tony Casetta, an acquaintance of mine and the owner of Dischi Bluebell, an Italian record label, was babysitting two young children. Peter Asher was the only other adult present. He invited me to join him in the legendary Beatles recording studio to listen to a tape of a new artist he was producing. With sinking spirits, as I sensed that my trip to London had been a fool's errand, I followed him into the control room. The recording had been grossly overproduced, but I liked the singer and the song, and I was candid about it. Undaunted, Peter then played a simple version, which hit the mark. The artist was James Taylor and the song was "Fire and Rain." I hung out for a few hours at Krank's, a large, attractive vegetarian cafeteria in the neighborhood, repeatedly trying to reach Kass by phone. At the end of the day, I returned to New York.

Months later, the front cover of the New York *Daily News* featured a headline regarding a massive raid on the Columbia Records pressing plant in Pitman, New Jersey, by Hoover's FBI as well as state and local police. Several thousand copies of the *Two Virgins* LP were seized as obscene. On the weekend that I had traveled to London, Bill Cosby and his business partner Roy Silver, president of Warner Brothers Music, were also crossing the Atlantic to London, and they were negotiating with Ron Kass on behalf of their Tetragrammaton label while I was left unattended at Abbey Road. According to the news article, Cosby and Silver made a distribution deal with Kass for the LP, which included their commitment of $250,000 to build a new recording studio. If ESP had become embroiled in the running feud between J. Edgar Hoover and John Lennon, it would have meant disaster for the label.

Janis Joplin

I met Janis Joplin, alone in the empty Village Theater on lower Second Avenue. I knew who she was, but she didn't know me, and I didn't introduce myself. She was in a foul mood because her group, Big Brother and the Holding Company, was late in arriving for a sound check. They were to perform in a benefit, in which Tom Rapp was also scheduled to perform. I didn't know then that she had written to her sister, "I'm going to New York to record for ESP-Disk." She never reached us and was signed for management by Al Grossman, who brought her to Columbia Records.

Emmylou Harris

It was a Tuesday night hootenanny at Gerde's Folk City in midwinter, 1968. Among the performers were John Hammond Jr. and Emmylou Harris. She played twelve-string guitar and had a bell-like voice, and she was singing songs that were very affecting, including a mournful tribute to the cane cutters of the Caribbean islands, who worked like slaves to harvest sugarcane. When the evening was over, I informed her that I had a record label and loved her work, and walked her to the subway. It was 2:00 a.m., and we stood chatting for a while. Snow was softly falling. There was no wind; it was totally quiet. We were alone in the darkness. I said to her, "Those songs are beautiful. Did you write them?" "Oh no," she said, "they're traditional songs. I don't write songs." "Do you write poetry?" "Every girl writes poetry." I said, "Well, if you write poetry, you can write songs." She hesitated for a moment to reflect on this and said, "Well, I don't know. I could try. But I think they'll be terrible." I said, "Yes, your first song will be terrible. The second song will be fair, and the third one will be good." "Do you really think so?" I said, "I'm absolutely certain." "I'll think about it." Then she went off to the subway. Six months later, I was having a late breakfast at a diner in the West Village. Suddenly, a young woman burst through the door, ran back to my table, and kissed me. It was Emmy. "I've written a song, and it's good!"

Forty years elapsed. No contact. One day I picked up the *New York Times* and read a review: "Emmylou Harris came to the Beacon Theatre, and aside from her usual magnificent performance, she introduced two new spectacular songs she's written." Some months later, I called her road manager, Phil Kaufman, who had brought me the Charles Manson album. "I understand Emmy's coming to New York to play at Joe's Pub." He said, "Come as our guest." So, there was Emmy, gorgeous as ever, white-haired, playing her twelve-string guitar, solo. One of her songs could have been the reflections of a classical Greek philosopher on the meaning of life. I have never heard or read anything more profound. When the set was over, I waited a respectful interval, then went back to her dressing room. She sat there, resting. She didn't look at me or greet me. Her only comment was "It's so hard to write a song." It concluded a conversation that had begun forty years earlier.

10 A Short History of Licensing

How did the licensing arrangements start?

Phonogram wanted a European distribution deal. There was a buzz about ESP, and they liked that. The director of the company came to New York, and we struck a deal for our folk-rock albums. They released Jerry Moore, Pearls Before Swine, and the Fugs.

What was the difference for them between pressing it there and importing copies from the U.S.?

They made more profit by paying us a royalty and not having to import. And they had their own pressing plant. Generally speaking, licensing is a bad idea, because there's no accountability. That was in 1968. Then, over a year later, they asked me to visit them, and I went to Holland. They told me that they wished to terminate the agreement at the end of the second year of the three-year contract. There is no doubt in my mind today that the American government pressured them to do this because of our opposition to the war in Vietnam.

With that first licensing deal you received a fee up front, but did they ever pay any royalties?

No. Typically, there would be a general catalog advance. Then, presumably, statements would follow, listing sales of each album.

Since that is a general advance, what do you do with that?

It goes into the company, then we wait for the statements of sales and pay the artists their share. On foreign licensing and sales, the royalty was 12.5 cents per LP, half of the domestic rate. So, they would have gotten royalties. I don't recall whether we got any statements. Three years later, we were just about out of business when Nippon Phonogram licensed our records in Japan for a three-year term. We had already licensed in Japan to JVC in 1967, but that agreement had expired. JVC had released albums by Charlie Parker and Billie Holiday.

After Nippon Phonogram, next there was Base, in Italy in 1980. What was your arrangement with them?

It was just a two-year contract for three or four titles, Fugs and Pearls. They continued to make and sell those records for ten years. We received no statements—because they knew they could escape responsibility. We would have had to sue them in the Italian courts, which are notorious for long delays. Italy was then experiencing a huge amount of bootlegging.

How did they find you in the first place?

They tracked us down. When ESP was going out of business, these same people bought our remaining stock. I opened an envelope from them two weeks later, and it contained seven thousand dollars in cash! And they came back to us six years later to make this small licensing deal. They offered us a nominal amount of money. We were struggling. I had just come down to New York with my wife; we had bought a co-op in midtown. I had started working for the attorney general's office. ESP, at that point, was inactive. So, I didn't think very much about it.

Again, what happens with the advance they gave you? Where does that money go?

It goes into our survival.

Did ESP still exist as a legal entity?

The corporation never closed. Every year we filed a return.

ZYX was the next licensing arrangement, in Germany. How long did that last?

From '92 to '98. ZYX was a dance label, and it had global distribution. They licensed the entire catalog, all 125 albums, with a substantial general advance. They released all our records on CD for the first time. They had been urged to take this course by music historian Tom Klatt, who had become an ESP enthusiast in the '60s, when he marched in Germany to protest the war in Vietnam and was beaten by police. Tom wrote liner notes for the ZYX releases and shared the task with Urban Gwerder, founder and editor of the Swiss underground publication *Hotcha*, who had been tending his cows in the Alps but came down from the mountains to Zurich for this purpose. Also drafted was Hans Schreiber, a noted writer who lived near Tom in Dortmund, Germany. ZYX published a forty-two-page color catalog of all these releases and marketed ESP to their customers throughout the world. They revived interest in our recordings. We spent much of the advance getting everything remastered and packaged. Then we waited for the royalties to come in. Their statements were false, claiming there had been almost no sales. Apparently this was typical in international licensing, this disdain for accountability. During the last year of their agreement, they licensed vinyl rights to Abraxas in Italy, which was unlawful, and the LPs were being manufactured and distributed by Abraxas/Get Back. We were not aware of it and received no statements. Then I visited a record store in Brooklyn and saw our LPs.

Ben Gieskes, the Dutch fellow who ran Calibre, came to us in 2000 and made an agreement to license our product. He must have known about the ZYX/Abraxas agreement. Calibre reissued some of our titles, then they brought in Abraxas and the contract was assigned to Abraxas. Gieskes kept going broke, so Abraxas eventually made a formal agreement with ESP for both vinyl and CDs.

Wasn't there an initiative with the Smithsonian around 1997? What happened to that?

There was a series of trips to Washington with my ex-wife, just at the time we were in the process of getting divorced. We went to the Smithsonian, sat with the executives there, and explored a deal. My wife said, "Look, it's your legacy. Let the Smithsonian have it." I said, "Yes, but I'm not ready to do that." It would have been twenty thousand dollars a year for ten or fifteen years, for each of us—seven hundred thousand dollars in installments. I didn't want that. Would they also pay artist royalties on top of that? In theory, yes. But in practice? It was a possibility that never happened. They would have paid us off over a period of years, and then it would have been over with. She may have been right; I can't say. But I kept going, and it's been growing. I can't speak to what would have happened, but it would have been just available. They wouldn't have been pressing anything new.

11 In the Wilderness

What did you do after you closed down ESP in 1974 and moved with your wife to Woodstock?

The area, like much of upstate New York, was economically depressed, and local lawyers were not responsive to my overtures to join them. We struggled for five years to make ends meet, until my wife suggested I take the state and federal civil service exams. My grades were acceptable, so I visited various state agencies in Albany. In 1979 I was hired to an entry-level position as a staff lawyer at the New York State Department of Transportation for seventeen thousand dollars per year. It required a daily round-trip commute of three hours, and I was fifty years old. After a year, we rented an apartment in the Albany area. In the course of my work, I would speak from time to time with members of the staff of the attorney general in New York City, and I eventually decided to visit New York and look for a position in the Law Department. I found one in the Mental Hygiene Bureau, which served the needs of the psychiatric hospitals and facilities for the developmentally disabled. My impressive sounding job title was Assistant Attorney General. Our offices were on the forty-sixth floor of 2 World Trade Center. We remained there for seven years, until the New York State Department of Law moved to 120 Broadway, a stately old building nearby. During my eleven years in state government, I avoided contact with friends and ESP artists, as I felt responsible for the failure of the label. On my sixty-second birthday in July 1991, I retired from government service with a small state pension and Social Security. My wife and I left New York City and returned to Acorn Hill House. In December of that year, we entered into the licensing agreement with ZYX to reissue the entire ESP catalog on CD. A year later, my wife and I separated. The Catskill farm we both loved was sold. I withdrew to a mountain cabin near Woodstock, living alone for a year and a half with a black Persian cat and pondering my next direction.

What happened after that, in the decade before relaunching ESP in 2005?

Lost years. I returned to Manhattan. I floundered—I guess that's the word for it. I hadn't seen my parents for several years. So, I felt I was free to go down to Florida and spend some time with them; it was nice. During that period my father had been placed in an assisted-living facility, which angered him, but my mother had no choice, as he was now a hundred years old and susceptible to falling when he wandered about at night in the apartment.

When did your parents pass away?

Within that period, my father died, my mother died, my brother Norman died [December 1996], and his son. Four deaths within one year. I have a sister living in Hollywood [Florida], so I stayed with her. After my brother's son died, his family wanted me to help a little bit. I got his affairs together, some paperwork, and I took over his little room back in New York at the Hotel New Yorker. I lived there about a year. On that floor of the hotel there was a record label, some artists living there; it was like a bohemian place. Tesla the scientist had lived on the same floor for ten years. So I stayed there, and time went by.

Where did you go from there?

After that, I stayed for a couple of years in my brother Steve's building on Houston Street, which he sold recently. I have no clear recollection of what exactly I was doing. In the back of Steve's building—he didn't live there—he had a mezzanine, and that's where I was staying. Then he had a party, and a friend of his, a brilliant woman who was in the computer software business, had an apartment in Stuyvesant Town that she wasn't using. She rented her one-bedroom apartment to me for nine hundred dollars a month. I was there for seven years. It was very comfortable; the area was nice.

What animated you to start thinking about the label again?

I never wanted to close it in the '60s. Here were the masters and we're licensing them, and they're robbing us. I thought, What would I do ideally if I had the resources? I would run the label again. I never really lost my interest in it. So this was the moment. If I was ever going to do it, it would be now.

What happened was I had a small inheritance from my parents. I was foot-loose; I had no ties. I thought, Why not bring the company back, if it's possible? For whatever reason, fate has brought me to this point. Why not see what I can do with the company that foundered earlier? Raise the ship again; see if it'll float. And so I went back. It wasn't that difficult. The masters had survived somehow. The quality of the tapes was excellent; they hadn't deteriorated at all in the bank safe-deposit boxes in Manufacturers Hanover at 57th Street and Ninth Avenue.

It's very curious how things played out. Anything could have happened, any number of disasters. I had my health; I still do. I had built up a small nest egg, enough to get the thing launched. I thought, Why not carry this forward? I'm still around, and the music still has not been widely heard. So, bring it back and give it another shot. And that's exactly what I've been doing.

12 Revival

How did you go about reviving the ESP label? What facilities did you use? Who was your staff?

When plans for relaunching ESP began to take shape in 2003, I hired Michael D. Anderson, Douglas McGregor, and Rob Lake. Mike was a music historian, radio personality, and musician who had toured with Sun Ra as a member of the Arkestra. Doug had just graduated from Syracuse University with a degree in accounting and skills in audio engineering. Rob had just graduated from Wesleyan University with a degree in music. We worked from my apartment in Stuyvesant Town. When it came time to start pressing records, ESP rented a room in the office suite of Harvestworks, at 596 Broadway near Houston Street. Harvestworks is a nonprofit organization that helps artists use computer-based technology. After two years, in March 2007, we relocated to a ground-floor space at 990 Bedford Avenue, in the Bedford-Stuyvesant section of Brooklyn.

Was there any sort of master plan for the label when it relaunched in 2005?

We wanted to go backwards and forwards at the same time. We would reissue the archival materials, and in some cases issue them for the first time. Meanwhile, we would record cutting-edge new artists. The Billie Holiday set [*Rare Live Recordings 1934–1959*, a five-disc box] was one of Mike Anderson's contributions.

We've cut back somewhat from the pace of our initial releases, but we're still putting a lot out. We have frequent new releases, including vinyl. We keep signing new artists and reissuing titles from the original catalog. Our course has been fairly consistent, back and ahead simultaneously. I think the underlying premise is still the same, except that the CD business has somewhat gone down and vinyl's come up. We seem to be doing all right with vinyl, and the margins are nicer.

Tom Abbs subsequently joined us as ESP's general manager and A&R man.

Tom plays upright bass and tuba and has been a musician for twenty years. He brought in many of the new artists. And Adam Downey has been engaged in production and promotion.

By 2010 ESP had produced some eighty releases in the new era, including half a dozen reissues on vinyl. Has business more or less matched your expectations?

Our business has expanded considerably. We have added distributors internationally [besides Western Europe, these include Scandinavia, Poland, the Czech Republic, Argentina, Croatia, Singapore, Indonesia, Greece, South Africa, and India], and we are cultivating specialist stores that have survived. Our distributors are upbeat and optimistic. Our new releases have been well received by critics, and we are getting airplay.

As a corollary to your renewed involvement with the label, you have also been developing related interests. What have you been up to in the realm of music publishing?

Our publishing arms, Syndicore [BMI] and ESP-Disk' Music [ASCAP], publish all works that are released on ESP. Publishers elsewhere in the world collect royalties for us within their territories from records that are sold and other uses of our works. ESP has an affiliate, Global Copyright Administration, LLC, which represents composers who publish their own music. GCA establishes subpublishing relationships for them throughout the world. GCA acts as their agent for collecting royalties for live and broadcast performances, mechanical copyright royalties for the use of their songs by record companies, and synchronization royalties for film and television soundtracks. It has created a database to administer this program that is highly efficient. GCA represents Sam Rivers, Cecil Taylor, D. D. Jackson, Nellie McKay, and the publishing catalogs of ESP artists, as well as the estates of Eric Dolphy, Bud Powell, Sun Ra, Art Tatum, Albert Ayler, Jaki Byard, Horace Tapscott, Blind Willie McTell, and many others. Its website is gcaworld.org.

For GCA, I have had someone running it: an accountant who is also a DJ, Robert Keefe. In addition, he's the one who has been putting together Royalty Share for ESP, the online database that we are compiling. Every artist will eventually be able to access every transaction, every sale, anything that happens to any of their records.

How did these efforts first come about?

We found that many composers and performers with their own publishing companies have neglected to compile their catalogs and are not knowledgeable about their global rights. It began early in my professional career with research for Mary Lou Williams, Bud Powell, and Dizzy Gillespie. In later years we did extensive work for the Art Blakey and Chet Baker estates. We screened all their bootlegs and legitimate records and determined which works had been recorded and published or neglected. We found titles that had never been published but were on records. We saw a need, and GCA is addressing it.

ESP ad, *Billboard*, July 16, 1966.

David Stollman, father of Bernard, in front of ESP office. New York, 1966. Photo by Daniel Berger

Bernard Stollman. New York, 1966.
Photo by Daniel Berger

Albert Ayler. New York, 1966.
Photo by Daniel Berger

Left to right: John Gilmore, Ronnie Boykins, and Sun Ra. New York, 1966.
Photo by Daniel Berger

Left to right: Perry Robinson,
unknown man, and Sunny Murray.
New York, 1966. Photo by Daniel Berger

Henry Grimes and Cecil Taylor. New York, 1966. Photo by Daniel Berger

Milford Graves. New York, 1966. Photo by Daniel Berger

Roswell Rudd. New York,
1966. Photo by Daniel Berger

John Tchicai. New
York, 1966.
Photo by Daniel Berger

Marion Brown. New York, 1966.
Photo by Daniel Berger

Alan Silva, Judith Dunn, and
Bill Dixon. New York, 1966.
Photo by Daniel Berger

Gary Peacock. New York, 1966. Photo by Sandra Stollman

Godz. Clockwise, from upper left: Paul Thornton,
Larry Kessler, Jay Dillon, and Jim McCarthy. New York,
1966. Photos by Sandra Stollman

Giuseppi Logan. New York, 2009. Photo by Margo Ducharme

a.   b.

c.

d.

a. ESP 1002 Albert Ayler Trio, *Spiritual Unity*. Cover by Howard Bernstein   b. ESP 1004 *New York Art Quartet*. Cover drawing by Saul Stollman   c. ESP 1007 *The Giuseppi Logan Quartet*. Cover by Howard Bernstein   d. ESP 1016 *New York Eye and Ear Control*. Cover by Michael Snow.

II

ESP-Disk' as Lived and Witnessed

Naturally, every person has his or her own point of entry in ESP's history. In seeking out these many witnesses to the label's role in recent—and current—cultural practice, I wanted to reflect the wide perspective that is its legacy. So, most of the people who speak here are musicians, and the majority of those played free jazz, or still do. But there are also idiosyncratic folkies, and rockers, and theater people, as well as a few writers and a recording engineer too. Nearly all of them were involved with one or more records in ESP's original catalog; two appeared only on the revived label in recent years, and another, as archivist and researcher, brought forth historic new releases. The few musicians in these pages (and one adventurous producer) who did not work with ESP offer a sense of how the label was heard and received beyond its immediate sphere of action.

Given the distance in time from ESP's early burst of productions—four to four-and-a-half decades in most cases—I remained keenly aware of just how much I was asking of people to cast their memory that far back, to dredge up as many details as they could muster. Most respondents managed to do so marvelously well, though for some their powers of recall were inevitably frayed by the wear and tear of all those years on body and mind. Inherent to such an exercise is the curious play of emotion over time, and for any musician who had a relationship with the ESP label there were expectations and disappointments, pride and rancor, yet seldom indifference. Surely these reactions were a familiar palette of sentiments toward many record companies, yet somehow their vibrancy held special sway in regard to ESP. On the one hand, Stollman was known as a musician's advocate; on the other, most of these musicians would not have recorded what and when they did if not for him, so they were in a vulnerable position. Perceived slights, largely about money, were quickly compounded by suspicion, hearsay, sloppy business habits, and a sinking reputation so that what he did wrong may well have paled in comparison to all he was thought to have done wrong. Still, if time does not entirely heal all wounds, it allows for nuance, understanding, or at the very least a recognition of the complexity of human interactions. Some musicians who speak here, therefore, offer a more generous outlook than they might have in earlier years.

There are, of course, those who got away. Some simply refused my request, for no express reason—Pharoah Sanders, through his manager; Henry Grimes, through his wife. Others I almost sought out but did not get that far—Randy Burns, Perry Robinson, Mij—wishing to impose some degree of moderation on my project. The multiplicity of voices that follows already provides ample perspective on the label's claim, "you never heard such sounds in your life," and how that was lived through the course of these many paths. Still, there were others who would not yield, no matter how much I tried to elicit their cooperation in the interests of history, art, and science. Knowing my chances were slim, due to longstanding disputes, I persisted for a while in pursuit of the Fugs as well as Patty Waters. One of the Fugs, the late Tuli Kupferberg, had been in declining health, so he never replied to my letters and phone messages. The other, Ed Sanders, did send me one brief email message (March 7, 2009), laid out like a four-line poem: "I will be dealing with these / issues in the future, / and I am not at this time / giving interviews on this subject." Patty Waters also replied by email (December 10, 2008) to say, "I am not anxious to be interviewed. I'm just one of many who felt disappointed that he didn't pay royalties as he'd promised. My albums were enthusiastically received and sold quite well, I'm told." A year later (November 15, 2009), declining my final effort, she added, "Bernard in 1966 had me sign giving him publishing rights to all my music. He has cleverly robbed me." The conditions that gave rise to some of her claims are addressed in other parts of this book. Stollman points out, however, that at ESP "the publishing was shared, in contrast to the prevailing practice then, which was for the label to acquire the entire publishing rights." As for royalties, in 2008 ESP settled all its back royalties that were due her and has continued to send her statements and checks for current sales. I leave these charges here, though, because they represent the suppositions held by a number of artists over the years, both those who recorded for the label and those who never did.

All the same, Patty Waters has spoken about ESP in past interviews, so it is worth quoting her from a less fraught moment. As she told Robert L. Campbell, "I really think ESP has a fantastic place in history, and it put me in a position where I was making history. . . . I'm very, very grateful to Bernard" (*Cadence* 21, no 3 [March 1995]: 23, 107). Concerning the Fugs, Ed Sanders has written at length about their relationship to ESP in 1965–66. On the band's website (www.thefugs.com/history2.html), he presents many details in not too different a manner from what Stollman recounts in this book, while expounding on the Fugs' success and colorful activities at that time—as well as their investigation by the FBI in the wake of their ESP album that landed on the charts. He does not dwell much on the specifics of their problem with the label, beyond what he says was too low a royalty percentage and dissatisfaction with the contract overall. We do know, however, that ESP's release of *Virgin Fugs*, previously unissued from the original Folkways tapes that ESP bought, was a rare instance where the artists in fact did not decide.

But the purpose of these interviews is not so much to air the arcana of an improbable company's trace in the world, though that does have some importance historically. Rather, it is the people themselves who count most here, in all their wild variety: how they found their way to ESP-Disk', what that relationship might have meant, how it played out. In my interviews with these artists, their experience with the label was inevitably part of a continuum, so that whenever possible we also discussed where they were coming from, the context and community in which they worked, and where they went from there. After all, ESP was—and is—still just a record company.

The interviews that follow were conducted in person, by phone, and in a few cases by e-mail, between October 2008 and August 2009, with the majority dating from winter and spring; the last two were done in January 2010. For the most part, they are presented chronologically, in the order of when they were completed. (Several interviews were placed more intuitively; these were also edited differently, pared to the essentials of a few responses without the questions.) No other method of arrangement seemed a natural fit, given the variety of subjects. The reader will find, however, that the experience is much like following the ESP catalog as the records appeared. You never knew what you would land on next, expectations were always confounded, and yet sometimes intriguing connections emerged. In the end, any order will entail a process of discovery, between known and unknown names as well as unforeseen perspectives, anecdotes, and ideas from throughout the ESP horizon past and present.

Ishmael Reed

Novelist, poet, and essayist Ishmael Reed was still working on his first novel, *The Free-Lance Pallbearers* (1967), when he was invited to read a passage from it for the *East Village Other* album recorded by ESP on August 6, 1966. He had helped found the *East Village Other*, one of the first underground newspapers in the United States, with Walter Bowart and others in late 1965. The paper survived, through a series of changes, until early 1972.

How did the East Village Other *record come about? How did you get involved with the paper in the first place?*

It was Walter Bowart who organized the project. He was a painter and bartending at Stanley's on Avenue B [at East 12th Street]. We all used to hang out at Stanley's, get into fights, and drink. Painters, writers, Amiri Baraka, Hubert Selby Jr., all came in there. This Polish guy ran it, Stanley Tolkin. He was a patron of the arts. We were all down and out. We didn't have any money; we'd borrow money from him, then pay him back. So, somebody had hired me as a reporter at a community newspaper in Newark; then they wanted me to be the editor, to put it together, and I asked Walter Bowart to design the dummy of the paper. He did these surrealist collages, and I said, "You know, I don't think I can use that." So he said, "Why don't we start a newspaper down here?" I named it the *Other*, because we were all reading crazy stuff like science fiction and Carl Jung's introduction to *Paradise Lost*, where he talked about the Other being in the world, Satan. So I said, "Let's name it the *East Village Other*." I didn't have time to work on it. I quit the paper; I was working on my novel in Chelsea, up on 23rd Street. And Allan Katzman was a friend of mine; he used to come to my house every day. I said, "Go over there and help this guy start this paper." He became managing editor; he was a poet. So, I'm writing my novel, and they're giving me a lot of publicity, the *East Village Other*. My photo was in the paper, and excerpts from the novel. Walter Bowart comes to me and says, "We've got all these people—Andy Warhol, the Velvet Underground, Allen Ginsberg—and we're going to make this record." The label was there, ESP. We went over to the studio, and I read some of my novel—and in the background was the Johnson daughter's wedding.

That made the record a rather controversial release for the label, politically.

They were afraid that there were going to be a lot of problems because we had taken Charles Kuralt, I think it was—one of these guys who was narrating the wedding, he had the bells and all that—and Luci Baines Johnson, and I was reading my novel, which was like a metaphor for what was going on in the administration and politics. Harry Sam was sort of like a Lyndon Johnson figure. We were doing a lot of collages and ridiculing Johnson in the newspaper; the war was going on in all this. So, all that was mixed in together—I'm reading and you hear, in the background, the wedding bells and Charles Kuralt.

Did everybody come in to work on the record at the same time?

Yeah, we were all there in the studio. I think the Velvet Underground was there when I was recording, coming in and out. I think even Ed Sanders was in there. That was one of the ideas, the Electric Circus; that was Bowart. He was a genius.

Had you seen or listened to any of the ESP records by then? Albert Ayler?

Well, Albert Ayler was a guest in my home, and his brother. Carla, my wife, we had a place on Second Avenue. I knew all those people, Marion Brown. The reason I left New York was I had too many distractions. I'd go out in the morning and get the paper; I'd come back at four o'clock in the morning. It was too interesting. I said, If I had remained in New York, I would have died from an overdose of affection. I wanted to go to the most barbaric place in the country where nobody cares about culture, so I went to Los Angeles and I began my second novel. I had to get out of here, man; it was a party every night.

Gunter Hampel

On vibraphone, bass clarinet, and flute, German musician Gunter Hampel was among the first to pioneer a distinctively European free jazz sound; he was the second European artist to record as a leader for ESP (*Music from Europe*, December 21, 1966—preceded only by Karl Berger's *From Now On* two weeks earlier). In 1969 he founded Birth Records, which has continued to release numerous recordings of his music. Around that time, he also established a base in New York so that his musical activities, along with his various collaborators, embodied a truly transatlantic perspective.

In the winter of 2009 he performed twice in ESP's monthly concert series at the Bowery Poetry Club in Manhattan: in February, doing a solo set that was followed by Giuseppi Logan's first club gig in many years; and in March, joined by the Haitian drum ensemble La Troupe Makandal.

When did you become aware of the ESP-Disk' label? Were there certain records you heard?

Around the time I made my *Heartplants* album [1965], which has gone down in history as the first European record of our *own thing*, we heard Giuseppi Logan on ESP; the Ornette Coleman concert at Town Hall; and, I guess, Pharoah's record; and the Fugs.

How did you happen to record Music from Europe *for ESP?*

It goes back to Benny Goodman. He stormed on stage with his NBC-TV cameraman while I was performing with my group at the Comblain-la-Tour jazz festival in Belgium—we were playing a section where we both used bass clarinets, like on my ESP recording [with Willem Breuker]—and he asked me, "Can I tape your band?"

Benny really featured my band in his nationwide *Benny Goodman Show*—I never saw it—stating that he heard in us the most advanced music he had ever heard in his life. It was probably our bass clarinet playing. Decades later I learned that Benny had already played the bass clarinet on one of Red Norvo's recordings, as early as 1933. Bernard Stollman must have seen the show because he sent me a telegram: "Go and record this great band; send me the tapes and the bill." He published the recording but never paid the bill. . . . Well, I am starting to settle this with ESP now.

At that time I also met Jeanne Lee, who later became my wife and mother of my two great children, Ruomi and Cavana. One week after the recording, she started to sing with my band, from January 1967 until 1997—thirty years, just like with Marion Brown.

Were you living in Holland, where it was recorded, at that time?

Yes, in Amsterdam and in Düsseldorf, Germany.

Were you aware of people who had heard the record?

When I hooked up with Marion Brown in Europe [1967–68], who was also on ESP, he had heard it. That was in Antwerp, Belgium. I had moved away from Germany—I knew I was on my way to the U.S. I wanted to get to New York, but I had to get out of the German culture. So, I experienced Belgium, Holland, and France, and then I went with Jeanne to the Bronx in New York, in 1969.

Is there any way to describe the special bond you forged with Marion Brown in the course of three decades playing together?

Many years ago, when our sons were eight and twelve, Marion and I took them with us on tour around Europe in my Citroën station wagon, as part of their education. As Marion put it, we wanted to let them know firsthand how adventurous and troublesome our profession as a jazz musician is and how heavy it is for us to make our money. So, Djinji and Ruomi were very relaxed about it, as if nothing was of any interest to them. They had their earphones on listening to hip-hop, they helped us set up the vibraphone and organize food and sell our recordings, and they found it pretty boring to accompany their dads into the jazz clubs with all the old people listening. Until one night, there were almost only young people in this club; I believe it was Saarbrücken, close to the French border. When they saw that these kids were digging our music, they woke up and started to appreciate the pretty stressing monotony: play, sleep, ride, play, sleep, ride.

But another thing happened. They took their earphones off, and we started to have real conversations. I guess that was the beginning of our father-son relationships in both families. Because all the time Marion and I, both Virgos, had the most deep and thorough conversations, no one can imagine. When we played, we just continued to have these conversations in our music: one man from Atlanta, Georgia, the other from Göttingen, Germany.

How did Music from Europe *fit into your own discography?*

The ESP record was the first with all my own compositions. In a way, it was like a first outing, which was followed by my real worldwide breakthrough, *The 8th of July 1969*—my compositions, arrangements, instant composing, instant conducting, with three European and three Afro-American greats: Anthony Braxton and Steve McCall from Chicago and vocalist Jeanne Lee from New York.

The other day, my neighbor in New York yelled, "Gunter, they're playing your new record on the radio!" It sounded so fresh, as if it was just recorded and not forty years old. But that is why I trusted to invest all the money I had into my own record company. I am making music they call *timeless*. In 1964 my music had reached that quality that separates music from music. Once you have worked your stuff out, then you have the responsibility to make sure the music survives the ups and downs of the business in order to keep growing.

Did the experience of making the ESP record influence the creation of your own label a few years later?

Well, since Bernard never paid me, I decided to set up my own label, Birth Records, and keep the music under my control. Bernard didn't restrict me as to what music I should play. That was unique, because every other producer up until then had commercial requirements about playing hits or standards. His statement that "the artist alone decides" about the music woke me up. It showed me that I, as a jazz musician, have that choice. I could take charge of my own freedom and my own fate.

How do you see the change in audiences, over the past forty years, for the music that you as well as the ESP label started to produce back in the 1960s?

In the '60s and '70s we had thousands of listeners at jazz festivals and big concerts, but now people listen more at home on their sound systems. People today have lost their guts to trust in anything; they've lost the awareness of their own feelings, except the kids.

I mostly work with young talents now. I'm happy to meet them and give them my music to learn from. I gave the reissue of my ESP album *Music from Europe* to at least twenty young musicians in Berlin, Hamburg, and Cologne—they love it. In my children's workshops, I teach five- to thirteen-year-olds how to improvise and how to communicate with each other and have fun *playing* music. When I play my recordings for them, they understand it because they learn how to improvise themselves. This music, old or new, is like nourishment for them, to use our ideas to learn from and do it their way.

The current generations really are under the spell of commercialism. They have been separated from good music and consume the garbage of a merciless industry that preys on their mind and spirit. Our society is a mockery of the life we should and could have, if we were an enlightened society.

The jazz music we are all playing, from the beginning up to my generation, is such a vital fountainhead of body and soul manifestations. It's nourishment for the abused human soul—we need not just to preserve the old music but to learn the contents of this music, to learn from it and help children use human communication as a platform to rebuild our society. You should see what my children's workshops are making out of these children, once I have shown them how improvisations, real improvisations, are achieved and what it does to the human mind besides awakening.

It's time we learn from our own achievements in jazz and share this with the rest of the people we are living with.

Michael Anderson once said on WBGO, "Jazz music is the bible of the new age."

Let's read it.

John Tchicai

Born and raised in Copenhagen, of a Congolese father and a Danish mother, saxophonist John Tchicai came to New York in 1962 to take part in the new music. Over the next several years there, he worked on eleven albums. In 1964 he made two records released by ESP: New York Eye and Ear Control (a leaderless sextet that included Albert Ayler, Don Cherry, Roswell Rudd, Gary Peacock, and Sunny Murray, recorded July 17, 1964) and New York Art Quartet, the group he cofounded with Rudd (recorded November 26, 1964, and featuring the poet Amiri Baraka on his own "Black Dada Nihilismus"). The following year, he was a member of John Coltrane's large ensemble on the landmark session Ascension. In 1966 he returned to Denmark and has mostly lived in Europe ever since (except for the 1990s, when he taught in Davis, California), recording and touring widely. The New York Art Quartet reunited briefly in 1999 and made a record. In recent years, he has been living in southwestern France near Perpignan, even working with traditional Catalan cobla ensembles on one project.

How did you first become aware of the ESP label?

I think it was when we had the Jazz Composers Guild; the label started about the same time. We met Bernard when he came to one of our concerts. Then Sunny Murray and others told us about it, and we got involved.

Albert Ayler was the first one that he recorded; when he started to do Albert, then it became known. I knew Albert from Scandinavia, so it was probably through him. He used to live in Copenhagen at a certain time; that's how the connection came to Stollman.

Of the two albums you made for ESP, New York Eye and Ear Control *was recorded just a week after the first Ayler date. Was that actually made for the label?*

No, it was not for that intention, as far as I know. The idea was just to make a soundtrack that Michael Snow would work with for his film, then later it became a record.

Did you ever see the film?

It's a very interesting document. I saw it recently in Torino. I was playing with Sunny Murray and an Italian bassist. They showed the movie as the first part of the concert; we played the second part. I was so surprised to see the movie again, because I didn't remember a lot of that footage. All of a sudden, I see myself standing in front of a small Volkswagen beetle, getting into it with my alto saxophone case. There are some very nice shots of everybody—Albert, he's naked, must have been summer; it was very nice to see him, with his white spot in the beard. A nice shot of Don Cherry also. There were also some nice shots, I'd totally forgotten, of me and my wife at that time, a Danish girl, where we sort of caress each other—I don't know who got that idea, it might have been mine. You see us kissing and sort of fondling each other [*laughs*].

Do you remember how the New York Art Quartet *record came about for the label?*

Roswell and I went to Stollman and talked to him about it. I just remember we were up at his office on Riverside Drive, sitting there with the contract papers and stuff.

Was the New York Art Quartet *record helpful to you in any way?*

I think it did quite a lot, not so much in America, but in Europe people became aware of it. The record opened up many possibilities for me, in order to be able to play in Europe—that and the records I did with the New York Contemporary Five [with Archie Shepp and Don Cherry].

The New York Art Quartet had a fairly brief existence as a group, from about the middle of 1964 until the beginning of 1966. In the fall of 1965, you returned to Copenhagen for a visit and lined up several concerts for the quartet: at the radio house and also at the Montmartre in Copenhagen; in Gothenburg, Sweden; and in Hilversum, Holland, as well as in Amsterdam, where you opened for Ornette Coleman's trio. Since only Roswell was available, you called on Danish bass player Finn Von Eyben and South African drummer Louis Moholo. How would you characterize the difference between the two versions of the quartet?

That was more like two bandleaders who tell the other guys how it's supposed to be. We also didn't have much time to rehearse together, so we just had to get the repertoire in shape. It wasn't like in the regular New York Art Quartet, where we were more on an equal basis in terms of improvising. But there too it was only Roswell and me who supplied the written themes.

Following your return to New York, the quartet did not manage to perform much after that. Didn't you and Roswell do a gig near Carnegie Hall?

We played with Charlotte Moorman, the cello player, in a gallery on 57th Street. It was just a trio; Milford was not there. I think it was improvisation we were doing. What I remember most is that she was also playing the typewriter, and then she was breaking some glass in a bucket, very impressive.

Do you consider the ESP albums important in your own development as a musician?

Yes, with that quartet it presented the music that we wanted to create at that time. Without that record, people wouldn't know our ideas about how to make music. I think also the critics were aware of the differences between our way of collective improvising compared to the way that other people played. They noted the specific point that we had which was special for us, the polyphonic way of playing compared to the others, and more of a classical European influence in our way of structuring the music, in the Art Quartet.

Without that company, a great part of the so-called avant-garde musicians wouldn't have been known. Because none of the other companies did anything with those people. After that, several of the musicians that were involved with ESP could go to Europe and stay in Paris and get recording contracts.

Paul Thornton

A founding member of the experimental rock quartet the Godz, Paul Thornton had been making music since receiving his first guitar and Hank Williams albums as a child. With their playful anarchy, the Godz produced four records for ESP: *Contact High with the Godz* (1966); *Godz 2* (1967); *The Third Testament* (1968), as a trio; and *Godzundheit* (1973), a cobbled-together affair after they had been championed by rock critic Lester Bangs. The group disbanded by the 1970s, but they gained many fans in later years. In 1996 a tribute album was produced in London, their songs interpreted by Stereolab, Royal Trux, and others. Sonic Youth was another band influenced by them. In 2008 a new tribute album was produced in Eureka, California, mostly with groups from Humboldt County.

How did the Godz come together as a band? How old were you?

I was twenty-three, the oldest in the band by a couple of years. There was a club back then, Folk City; for about six months I used to play there just by myself. But I'd always go visit Larry—he lived on 11th Street between Second and Third; Jimmy lived on Avenue D and 7th Street—and then walk over to Folk City. We'd always get our guitars out and play, so they came with me. That was the first time we ever played anywhere as the Godz, the four of us, tiny little stage.

How did you first meet? Weren't all of you working at ESP?

I'm an old Tin Pan Alley man. I grew up around Hell's Kitchen. As a kid when I'd walk over to Broadway I had two choices: left was Central Park, right was Broadway. The Brill Building was down the street from the only Sam Goody's store at the time, on 49th Street. Jimmy McCarthy was already working there; he grew up working in record stores. I'm walking down the street and Sam Goody walks out. Because I've got long hair, he says, "Look, there's a guy back there with long hair; we're starting a new department. You know anything about music?" I say, "Yeah, I hang out at the Brill Building. I make 45s, record my songs." He says, "Well, come in here; I want you to meet Jimmy McCarthy. Would you like to be a salesman?" About a week later, Larry Kessler comes in from Baltimore, and he gets a job there. Somebody at Sam Goody's says to Larry, "We heard of this label, ESP. They're looking for somebody to work there." So he goes out and gets the job.

Within about a month's time, he came in as a sales manager and becomes vice president—still getting the same salary! Once I started working for Bernard, I was the traffic manager, shipping clerk. Jay Dillon was already at ESP. He was the graphic designer, so that's how we met Jay. The whole music industry was trying to remanufacture the Beatles, because that was the biggest thing. So Bernard says, "Like the Beatles came along and really took over. I'm looking to start a group like that." That night, we're over at Larry's place, and he says, "The guy's looking to start a group. Why shouldn't it be us? We sit around and play every night." Somebody thought of the name, the Godz. Bernard got pissed off. He told Larry, "You're the vice president. I ask you this, you say, 'Yeah, I'll do it.'"

So, how did you manage to convince Bernard to go along?

Larry said, "Look, we have the same right as everybody else. You're not going to sign anybody until you hear us audition." A woman at ESP had an apartment down on 3rd Street at Second Avenue, so he says, "You go there, and I'll listen to you." So, we went there—I had some claves; Jimmy McCarthy had a guitar worth about five cents—and we sat on the floor and did a song called "White Cat Heat." It's a song where it doesn't make any difference what we play; all we do is meow. We start at a normal meow and get more intense, then it levels off. I think Jay played the psaltery. We ended as soft as we started out, and we meowed. I said to myself, Well, I had nothing else to do tonight anyway. We ain't going to get anything out of this. And Bernard says, "That's fantastic. I want to sign you to the label."

At that point, were any of you thinking in terms of songwriting for the group?

I don't think we even know how those records came out sounding like that. Larry Kessler and Jay Dillon had no idea how to play music, I think; they just picked up an instrument and played it. Jimmy had made an album; he used to have a band. I knew what we were doing was new and nobody did it before, but I didn't think about that.

What was the response to your records? Was there any effort to promote them?

Bernard set up a concert at Duke University, in the Civic Center. We were there for three days; that was the first big thing. We also played at the New York Coliseum. It was a ski show; there were go-go girls. We were supposed to do two sets. When we went up and played, they said, "We can't dance to this," so they didn't dance. When he heard our set, the guy who was running the ski show told us, "You don't have to do the second set." Larry looked at us. "You want to do the second set?" "Yeah, I'll do the second set." So we went back and did it regardless.

Did the approach of the band change much from one record to the next?

On the first album, we played with a shit acoustic guitar, a psaltery. After that, people were sponsoring us. We got a Gibson electric guitar, a Shure PA system, amps; Jay Dillon got an electric organ. So, it was even weirder, and by then there were more tracks to record with.

Was there a sense of developing an aesthetic for what you were after with each record?

[*Laughs.*] I think that was a key to our success, not knowing what we were doing.

Did you do many concerts?

We didn't do that many. That was always my complaint, because I like to play. I'm still playing. We just did another album. We completed it the end of this summer [2008], but they don't want to put it on ESP. I would. They want to try something else.

Don't the other members of the band have an ongoing dispute with Bernard?

I'm not involved with the dispute, and Bernard knows it. One of the guys got a big law firm. They asked me to come up when it first started, two years ago. I brought my wife with me and we decided—after we were there maybe twice— we're not interested. It's the principle. Maybe it's true Bernard didn't make a lot of money, and if it's true, how do you expect to be paid a lot of money? We're known all over the world; nobody would have ever heard of us if it wasn't for Bernard. That's the way I look at it. I'm satisfied. How many musicians have got all these albums out and you can go in every country and buy them? To me, it's also important doing what I'm doing. I don't care what happened forty years ago. I enjoyed it!

The music that the Godz made has been described variously as psychedelic rock, protopunk, garage band. How did the band describe its own music?

When the first album came out, Bernard referred to it as "organic tribal body rock." We didn't like him saying that, so we said, Let's all go home tonight and name our music. That night, about three o'clock in the morning, I'm watching the Late Late Show, a Jimmy Cagney movie, *13 Rue Madeleine*. Sam Jaffe was head of the French underground, and I'm thinking, Wow, underground, underground music. That sounds better than the tribal body rock he called it.

James Zitro

Several months after appearing on Sonny Simmons's second ESP date, *Music from the Spheres*, drummer James Zitro made his first album as a leader, *Zitro*, recorded on April 13, 1967. With its distinctive photo montage on the cover portraying him in silhouette against a burst of clouds, the record featured a sizzling sextet on compositions by the leader as well as by tenor saxophonist Bert Wilson and pianist Michael Cohen, all of whom played in the sextet on the Simmons session. These two dates represent Zitro's entire recorded output from his few years in New York, but he has continued to work as a musician on the West Coast in the decades since.

Who were the other musicians on your album Zitro? *Where did they go from there?*

The alto player, Allan Praskin, graduated from high school just in time to make the *Zitro* record. He later left the country and has been over in Eastern Europe, I think, for years and years. Bruce Cale, the bassist, was from Australia; he and I went and played with Zoot Sims for a while, shortly after that album. I've lost track of him. Warren Gale, the trumpeter, was born in L.A. but resided with the rest of us in New York for a time, before settling in San Francisco and joining Joe Henderson's band. Michael Cohen, the piano player, was also originally from Los Angeles and later went to Berkeley; he became a lawyer in San Francisco. Actually, I met him for the first time in Copenhagen in '64.

That was a good time to be there.

Absolutely. Then I moved to Paris and lived there for a year and played with all kinds of heavies that were coming through but didn't have an American drummer. So, I got a lot of opportunities given to me real early. When I came back to the States and did the *Zitro* album, it was right after I had played with John Coltrane in San Francisco. That was the turning point in my life, because the last thing John said to me was "I'll see you in New York." It didn't take me long to put together my band and take off and go back there. Bert Wilson was already friends with Sonny.

When you played with Coltrane in San Francisco, did you just sit in with him at some club?

That's basically it. The Jazz Workshop was happening, and everybody in town who could play was in there. So, it opened up a lot of gigs for me in that area.

Did you meet Bert Wilson in New York?

No, I took Bert with me. We hooked up in L.A. Bert has been in a wheelchair since the age of four—he had polio, and they told his mother he'd be dead by eight, but no, Bert still lives; he's almost seventy now. But the reason I mention that is it was quite a caravan to New York. I had Bert in the back of a station wagon and his wheelchair strapped to the roof. And my wife and my one-year-old baby, and my drums, and all our possessions were packed into this station wagon. We drove clear to New York City.

How was it arriving in town like that?

When we got to New York City, we went straight to the Lower East Side, which was a real dump in those days. Bert didn't even get out of the car because we ran into Barbara Donald standing in front of her pad. So, as if we didn't just drive three thousand miles, she says, "Oh, don't even bother to get out of the car. We got a gig in Baltimore." And I say, "A gig? For when?" She says, "Tonight!" So, we turn and drive to Baltimore, playing music in this club called Peyton's Place. It was classic, man. At this point, I don't even know Sonny—I mean, I waved at him out the window once, but that was about it. So now we're on the bandstand together. It's a totally black neighborhood, a totally black club, and the riots erupted the weekend after we left. Anyway, here we are; I'm setting up my drums on the bandstand, and word comes to me that the doorman says, "If that white boy plays one note in here, I'm going to stab him." So, I've got this message now, and I'm getting some funny looks from people in there. I think I was the first white guy to be in that place. So I tell that to Sonny, and Sonny says, "Oh, yeah? I'll take care of it." He goes over to the guy and he says, "Look here, brother, if he don't swing, we'll both stab him." I overheard that one, and now

I'm really inspired! "Okay, here I am." So, Sonny kicks it off; the shit goes flying. Man, it's instant harmony. He turns around and looks at me and says, "Where the fuck did you come from?" I said, "I'm right behind you, boss. What do you got?" So, he calls off this little phrase thing, and then he just starts playing. It was pretty much total improvisation. Now, Bert Wilson was on the stage too with me, and so was Barbara Donald.

Right, so you weren't the only white person.

Yeah, the other white people. The bass player might've been Juney Booth, I think. Anyway, the music is ass kicking, at the end of which the doorman comes over to me and says, "Welcome, brother, the shit is happening."

After the gig in Baltimore with Sonny Simmons, did you play together much in New York?

Daily. We all went back to New York and found places on the Lower East Side. I moved the family into some cockroach nest in Alphabet City. We were playing at St. Mark's Church. It was Sonny and Bert and Barbara and me. We were playing just about every day, with several different bass players. We had nothing else going on in New York. Nobody worked; everybody was just biting the bullet for a minute and trying to make it happen. So, we got pretty tight. And then, in a very short amount of time, Sonny had this record date—he had done one album for ESP [in August 1966], he and Barbara. Then, the record date is due [December 1966], and we're supposed to show up at the studio. So we go there, and we're on the elevator going up. The door opens, and Sonny's giant presence is in the elevator, saying in his low voice, "Let's hit it." That was it, man. We set up the instruments, the music started, and it was first takes.

After that, I went back and pestered Bernard to give me a date, because I'm a composer. I write music for my band. I showed him a sample of what we had in the can, and he said yeah. So, I brought the guys out, those who weren't already living in New York.

What was the response to your record?

Well, it received a four-star review in *Down Beat*. The people who like that kind of music have responded very positively. Over the years, people would keep telling me about my album, and I was always shocked, because I hadn't heard that it sold one copy.

So, when did you leave New York? What have you been up to since then?

After that date, I took off to Europe for a little while for a vacation with my family, awaiting the release of the record. I had high hopes for its promotion, possibly a gig set up to create exposure other than as "a bunch of white cats from California." However, I see now that I was rather naive about that, given their lack of knowledge and money. Then we moved out to Berkeley in 1968. I rented a house at just the right time and managed to get a deal, so I moved the whole band into duplexes in a one-block area with the same landlord. We had music going twenty-four hours a day, on Curtis Street in Berkeley, Curtis and Delaware. We made a bunch of recordings in-house, Sonny and Bert and me. There's one album called "Christmas with Uncle Sonny." We never tried to release any of them. It's absolutely outrageous. The shit is so tight, because we spent day after day playing music.

Then, in 1970 I got a call from Charles Lloyd, and Charles had my whole rhythm section—Jack DeJohnette had just gone off with Miles—so it was Kenny Jenkins on bass, and Michael Cohen, and for about five years we worked with Charles.

After that, I left L.A. and moved to Big Sur and put out an album in 1978 called *New Moon in Zytron* with Dave Liebman, for Michael Nesmith's company [Pacific Arts]. Then in the '80s, I moved up to Marin County, and Dave Liebman and I hooked up. He's a monster. We had a wonderful time playing together. We were both superinfluenced by Trane, and we immediately went there. After Dave went back east, I brought the band back together with Bert, and we started recording. We've released a couple of albums under "Bert Wilson featuring James Zitro."

In the '90s, I went back to school because I moved to Santa Cruz, and there was no way I could support myself in music unless I was going to teach. I got credentials as a therapist and a counselor, with mental health and substance abuse. So, then I got hired by the county of Santa Cruz to be the Proposition 36 guy, which was intended to get people out of jail and go to treatment. That's what I've been doing and then flying up to—Bert is in Olympia, Washington. There's a sextet that we formed up there, and we've done some recordings. And I still play a couple of nights a week here in Santa Cruz, with Don McCaslin who plays piano and vibes. We have a couple of low-energy gigs; that keeps my hand in.

Where did you grow up? What was your formation that launched you into all this playing?

I was born in Paterson, New Jersey, and then my parents moved to Buffalo when I was quite young, and when I was a teenager they moved out to California, to Santa Barbara. My mother was an opera singer, my father was a pianist, and they concentrated on the classics. When I was born, I kind of fell out of bed into music. My mom was accepted by the Met in New York. She was a heavy hitter, but then she tossed it in and became a housewife, much to all of our chagrin. When I was four years old, I was taking piano lessons. And when I was two years old, I was playing with wooden spoons on my grandmother's pots and pans. So, it was clear to me that I'd been a drummer before. It came so easily that I was shocked that everybody else couldn't do it. So, it was a source of power as a kid in school. If I wanted to get recognized, I'd just grab a pair of bongos or something and blow everybody's mind. And I stayed with it religiously all my life—I went through all the school bands; later in college I was playing gigs every night to pay for school. I never had a day gig until I got to be fifty. And, lo and behold, I've worked my way up to where now I'm ready to retire. So, I'm going to retire probably in this next year and go back to chasing moonbeams with the music.

Sonny Simmons

Born in Louisiana, raised in Oakland, California, alto saxophonist and English horn player Sonny Simmons first became known as coleader, with Prince Lasha, of the 1962 date for Contemporary Records, *The Cry!* Following that session, during his first stay in New York, he and Lasha recorded with Eric Dolphy (notably their composition "Music Matador") and the Elvin Jones/Jimmy Garrison sextet (*Illumination!*). A few years later, during his second stay in New York, he recorded his first two dates as leader of his own group, which included his wife, trumpeter Barbara Donald: *Staying on the Watch* (recorded August 30, 1966) and *Music from the Spheres* (recorded December 1966), both for ESP.

Before moving back to the West Coast, he worked briefly with Bill Dixon's University of the Streets Orchestra in 1968, alongside Jacques Coursil, Marzette Watts, and Sam Rivers. Due to personal difficulties, from the late 1970s to the early '90s he ended up homeless and often played music on the streets of San Francisco. Gradually he returned to actively performing and recording (especially in Europe), and lived in France for a while before settling in New York, where he lives in the Hell's Kitchen district with pianist Janet Janke, who has been an important factor in his continued survival. Late in 2009 he was a featured performer in ESP's marathon benefit at the Bowery Poetry Club for the Jazz Foundation of America and subsequently played in ESP's monthly series there.

How did you first connect with the ESP label?

I came to New York, me and my ex-wife, the trumpet lady Barbara Donald, in 1966. We drove all the way from Los Angeles to New York City. Psychedelics, revolution, all kinds of shit was happening. I was in the mix. So, the word went out among musicians like myself that were playing something different and new, inspired by a lot of other forerunners of this great music. Byron Allen, another alto player, told me this in his home: "Sonny, they'll make an album of you right away. They're looking for you." At that time, I had a wife and a little baby boy, and I'm trying to take care of them.

I went and talked to Bernard Stollman. He had a hard deal for musicians; he didn't want to pay you nothing. So, I fell victim to that out of desperation, trying to survive in New York City. Because they weren't giving no jobs for that kind of music. My wife and I talked about it, and she said, "Let's do it." I said, "Okay, because we're a rare hookup together, and it might not happen again. So let's do it now, while we're alive and well and young and pretty." We done it, but the money wasn't shit. I had to almost kill the guy. And he never got over that shock: I was going to throw him out of the fifth-floor window in his office, because it was open and I was pissed enough to do it. He didn't want to pay me no money. His mother saved his ass; she ran out of the inner office and said, "No, no, Sonny, don't hurt him." She was going to write a check. It was just enough to keep me quiet for a minute. So, since I had raised so much hell with Bernard about how he was treating me, I didn't go back any more, because she was afraid of me after that, the whole family was.

But then you even did a second record for ESP a few months later.

Yeah, well, he came up with some money, and my wife—she's new on the scene—this was good for her. So, I did the second one for a lot of different reasons. Those records are historical. I can't believe people are still buying them.

Those sessions sound as alive today as they must have forty years ago.

That's the way the spirit was. I had the right cats—the pianist, John Hicks, was a young cat. His dad brought him all the way from Philadelphia to New York City for this date, because he was sort of protecting his son in the wicked city.

How did you know of him to get him on your date?

J. C. Moses, the great drummer, told me about him. And a few other people were talking about John Hicks, the new young pianist from Philly, sounds like McCoy. I said, That's cool, at least he's hip to the modern harmonics. So I grabbed him and took him on this date—first date he'd ever done was with me—then I made him become noticeable in the music world. It was a great date. But the second date, it was so jive dealing with Bernard. I wanted to do it with the same group, but it wound up the time passed, and I'm stuck with some other players.

Well, that record sounds good too.

It does, but I really had to work hard. I put up with a lot of stress to deal with that last one, because I wanted to get some of the black jazz musicians who were here that were into the music. But he didn't want to pay nobody. So, I had to negotiate with these cats. After that, we left New York City, my wife and I, we went back to California in '69. I didn't bother with him anymore. We were working in places like Baltimore, Maryland, and Washington, DC, in those days, but they couldn't use the interracial trip. It was like Jack Johnson with his white lady long ago—the great black boxer, champion of the world. I was in the same predicament. Because of that, I didn't get no work, no recognition, no press. And if there was any press, it was negative.

Were you consulted on the art production of those records?

I was involved with the photo shoot for *Staying on the Watch*. They were going to do some square shit that I didn't dig. Sandra Stollman was the photographer; she took a masterpiece. I coordinated that shoot. I said, "Let's go to Central Park." Standing on the watch, it was very appropriate, on a big high boulder in Central Park, with those buildings in the background.

Did the ESP records help you in any way after that?

Yeah, during that period back in the roaring '60s, among the hippies and people of intellectual ability about music who knew what was happening and knew the times they were living in, they were hip. But it was a small audience. I wasn't expecting anything.

Didn't the records sell more in Europe than they did in the U.S.?

That's true. I was over there, and they had them in the record stores. And the ESP record, *Staying on the Watch*, was number one. They put it right out front. I couldn't believe it. Everything else that I've done in the years since, they're in the back.

How was it working with Contemporary Records, which produced your first date with Prince Lasha in 1962?

Lester Koenig was great. I loved that guy. He treated me right as an artist, with decency. He had heart. When I did *Firebirds* [1967] with Prince Lasha for Contemporary, I was living in New York, and Lester Koenig sent for me. He paid my air flight, and money in my pocket, like I was supposed to be paid coming from that distance.

How did you first meet Barbara Donald?

I was working in San Diego at that time, the squarest place on the West Coast. It was because of this great boxer, Archie Moore. I came through there to play a gig at one of his hangouts, a big audio shop. Archie Moore came in one night— I used to see this brother, champion kick-ass on TV back in his day, in the '50s—and he said, "I want you to play at my place. I got a little party." He had property all over San Diego, so he gave me a beautiful apartment to stay in for free. He said, "All you have to do, Sonny, is play 'Jumpin' at the Savoy.'" I played it for days, that was my supper and rent, the whole trip, every time he hit the place. I met the trumpet lady there in San Diego, through Benny Harris, the great bebop trumpet player.

Why did you originally go to New York? Was that where you met Eric Dolphy?

I met Dolphy in L.A., Prince Lasha and I, back in 1960. We went to a nice hotel in West L.A. and the flautist Paul Horn was working the gig, and Dolphy would go over to him and play flute. That's where I met him, because I had heard his first recording, and it knocked me out. I said, This is my kind of playing. We getting away from bebop, and we're going into super rebop. I loved his dexterity on all three of those instruments. He was a master, and he played them all equal! When I got ready to go to New York after 1960, we were both reaching for a certain height of tones on the alto, which are referred to as the altissimo range, the high notes above top F, so I became very close to his music. I said, This cat is thinking the same way I'm thinking. So was Ornette Coleman when I heard him. And I'm doing this in Oakland, California. Nobody ever heard of me, but I was right in the mix with that.

Speaking of the late great Prince Lasha, when he and I were comrades in dealing with what we were dealing with in the music—and we were bold and courageous about traveling because we believed in this music so strongly—we would take felonious chances to keep this music going. So, when we arrived in New York City back in 1963, we became accepted right away. I couldn't believe the reception. We came together; we drove all the way from California.

When you left New York after your second stay, in 1969, was that for family reasons?

Yeah, my wife, her *papa* and *maman* were upper-middle-class white folks in California, and they still had racism surging in their hearts behind their young beautiful daughter, great talented trumpet player, hanging out with a black man. They couldn't live with that. I understood it because I was born and raised in the South. It didn't make me no never mind. I was just respectful and congenial to her people.

So you came back to California for her to be close to her family?

And I wanted to be with my family because my young son was just a baby. I didn't want to be in the class where cats run off and leave their babies with a white girl. I said, No, I'm not going to leave my son, so I stayed with him, and I caught hell for that, trying to still be a papa. I gave up a lot.

In light of the fact that ESP has reissued your records in the last few years, how has your music been received by younger generations of listeners and musicians?

The generations that have come up since, everywhere I play in Europe they gather around me like a guru. But they're all poor. They ain't no rich people who say, "Sonny, we're going to set you up right." The kids say, "I got this record, I got that record," and I know they're telling the truth. They're not slick talking trying to be hip on the jazz scene.

The kids are deep into it, with sincerity, and I appreciate that. But I wrote a beautiful romantic melody called "Too Late for Tears"—I'm still struggling, and even if something happened like a big windfall, I probably won't even be that moved. I'm going to take it. I'm going to accept it gladly, wholeheartedly, and be thanking the creator that I finally lived to get a little bit of this. But I didn't play music to become rich and have a lot of money. I played because I loved it, and it's in my soul, and I want to express it to the world.

I just don't play enough. And I've never performed here on a righteous level in New York City, not since the '90s. But I'm not a limelight guy. I stay in the shadows. I'm right here, and the whole new generation of musicians, they don't even hear me. I've grown to the point where I don't really give a damn anymore. I'm like Old Man River, I just keep rolling along.

Gary Peacock

Bassist Gary Peacock played on most of the Ayler sessions for ESP, as well as Lowell Davidson's sole recording for the label. In the late '60s, he left music for a while to study Zen Buddhism and subsequently biology, then taught music theory in Seattle. Since 1983 he has been a member of Keith Jarrett's trio with Jack DeJohnette.

The first time I played with Albert, I wasn't really familiar with his music. So he came over, and he just played; that's how we rehearsed. He was there one afternoon.

I was also doing work with Jimmy Giuffre then, and I had been out on the coast with Prince Lasha and Sonny Simmons [*The Cry!*, 1962]. Free playing has always been a major interest of mine throughout the years, and I've involved myself with several situations of free playing, even with Keith and Jack. But whether it's free or not, those are descriptions of form, and they really don't touch the essence.

Ornette was, I think, the first one who provided an opportunity for me to look really closely at my cherished ideas about what music was, about tonality, expression, creativity. My understanding of the essence expanded a great deal in the late '50s.

True art is a perennial affair. It transcends all the trappings. It transcends labels; it transcends periods of history.

Milford Graves

A native New Yorker, drummer Milford Graves was one of the prime percussion innovators in the new music of the 1960s. He recorded on ESP sessions with the New York Art Quartet, Giuseppi Logan, Paul Bley, and Lowell Davidson, as well as his own landmark date, *Percussion Ensemble*, a duo with drummer Sonny Morgan, recorded in July 1965. In those years he also worked with Montego Joe, Don Pullen, and Albert Ayler, among others, but by the end of the decade he went back to school to learn the skills of a lab technician, to better support his growing family.

In 1973 he was invited by Bill Dixon to become part of the new Black Music Department at Bennington College, where he has taught ever since, commuting from his home in Queens to Vermont two days a week, six months out of the year, spring and fall. Though his public appearances were less frequent after the 1960s, he still continued to perform intermittently, as in the duo with drummer Andrew Cyrille, *Dialogue of the Drums* (1974). In more recent years, he has released several records on John Zorn's Tzadik label, including two solo dates, a duo performance with Zorn, and a trio with Anthony Braxton and William Parker. A longtime student of martial arts, alternative medicine, and music therapy, he is also an accomplished acupuncturist and herbalist and has done significant research into the relationships between heart-rate variability, music, and healing.

How did you first come in contact with the ESP label?

Through the New York Art Quartet, it was through Roswell Rudd and John Tchicai. We had a recording date, in 1964, and that was with Leroi Jones, or Amiri Baraka. I had never seen Bernard Stollman; that was my first meeting of Amiri Baraka. I went to the studio. Lewis Worrell and myself, we had this partition, at Bell Studios. All I knew was that Roswell and John said, "There's a great poet." Bernard was smiling, and I was trying to read Amiri Baraka's lips, because I couldn't hear him through the partition. Then we went to the sound booth to hear the playback. I said, "Man, this is some deep stuff this guy's talking here! And controversial!" And that was my first meeting with ESP.

Who brought in Baraka?

I'm not too entirely sure. It could have been between those two guys, because they were on the scene downtown. And Baraka was on the scene. He was doing these concerts on Fourth Avenue in his loft; he had a series going on. So, he was familiar with all the musicians. Or it could have been Bernard who came up with that idea, because Bernard was a free jazz scout, to find out who was on the scene, who should he record.

Where were you coming from? You weren't so much a part of the scene until that moment?

No, I only came on the scene in 1964. I met John and Roswell through Giuseppi Logan. Because I had been in Boston, I was playing Latin jazz. I wasn't even on the scene with no so-called free jazz. I met him at a jam session—they used to have Sunday jam sessions at Connolly's. There was a house band with Sonny Stitt, and all these guys would go up and sit in. I'm a little lonely up there for the whole summer, so I go check it out. I'm in this place, and then Giuseppi goes up, and the guys were saying, "There's that weird musician." He goes up on the stage, and everybody goes off. He's the only guy up there; nobody wanted to play with him. So he's up there playing, and I just jumped up on the stage. When I went up there, I was an oddball, because they hadn't seen anybody play trap drums like me. I wasn't that conventional kind of trap drummer. I'm bringing in all this African, this Caribbean and Cuban stuff; I'm transposing this stuff on the set. I knew a little jazz licks because my uncle used to try to show me some jazz drumming, but I didn't want to deal with jazz drumming. I was too much into just the drums. I wanted to play all that backwoods stuff, the country stuff.

So, Giuseppi and myself we started talking. He told me where he lived and invited me over to his place, then I invited him over to my house. I had like a loft, and we started playing a lot. Then the summer was over, and I left Boston, and I told Giuseppi to come to New York. In September, Giuseppi packed his bags, got his wife and his son, and came down to New York. Giuseppi started roaming around, and he was on the scene. Because I wasn't really on the scene;

at that time I was still living in Queens. I was born in this area here, and then I moved to Brooklyn. Then I came back here again. But Giuseppi told me he had met these two guys, that was John and Roswell, and they were having this rehearsal. So I went to this rehearsal, and John and the band were there, with J. C. Moses on drums. They allowed Giuseppi to sit in, and then Giuseppi asked them, "Do you think that my friend can sit in?" So I sat in, and J. C. Moses got off of the drums, and J. C. Moses looking at me in the oddest way, man. After that, the rehearsal was over, and J. C. left, and I stayed around to listen to the tape. And I remember John and Roswell saying, "Wow, that's the type of drummer we want." They asked me, "Do you want to play in the band?" I said yeah, so J. C. lost his job. And J. C. was on my case after that—J. C. did not like me; I took his gig. That was it, and we had the record date.

You later introduced Giuseppi Logan to Bernard Stollman, is that right?

After the *New York Art Quartet* recording, Bernard approached me and asked me to do something. Fine, but then I thought about Giuseppi. I told Bernard, "I'm a young guy, and I have time. Let's give it to Giuseppi." I don't know if Giuseppi ever knew that. So I just recorded with Giuseppi as a sideman; that's how that took place.

Even before the New York Art Quartet *session, you recorded with Paul Bley's quintet for ESP,* Barrage *[in October 1964]. Had you been playing with Bley much?*

I did a few things with Bley, not that many.

On Giuseppi Logan's first record, Quartet, *Don Pullen and Eddie Gomez were in the group. You worked with Eddie Gomez on the Paul Bley date as well, and you also worked with Don Pullen for a while as a duo after that. Both of those musicians ended up going a more mainstream route, less open-ended. How would you characterize that distinction between the direction they started going and what you chose for yourself?*

It was a simple thing with Don. For Don, it was a matter of economics. At least that's the conversation we had, because I was trying to talk him out of it. When he went a more commercial type of way and took that job with Charlie Mingus,

I was trying to tell Don that he had the potential and the ability on the piano to take it a step higher than what was already being done out there by all the guys. I tried to convince him that it would be better for him to go as an independent and be a really great innovator, and not just another good piano player.

The great difference in the way I was thinking is that most of the people I played with were into a lot of written music. I was saying, Okay, written music and understanding how to chart it out on paper, that should be a prerequisite to learn how to play just very spontaneously and improvise. So, I used to listen a lot to the way people talked and the terminology they used, and it seemed like their words or their concept was different from how they practiced or what they were doing. I mean, the guys were great, everyone I played with. I would focus on that. I said, But how do we create right at that moment? We all have some structural things, but how do we really play off those structured things in a way that it's highly unpredictable?

From a scientific perspective, I used to say that's like the concept of Newtonian physics, where you can actually see that; it's very obvious. But when you get to the quantum guys, I always wanted to hang out more in the quantum community where stuff lasts for just a nanosecond. It would be all over the place—it's there, where is it, I don't know, it's over there now, we can't grab it! It's constantly going deep into the core of how nature functions. So, I was sticking to that principle. I didn't go for the ride. Let's put it like this: certain people were what we would call the core people, who stuck to what they did, regardless if you like them or not. I mean, Cecil Taylor is Cecil Taylor. He has his own personality, his own characteristics, but Cecil Taylor stayed with Cecil Taylor. He didn't go over and deal with pop and funk and rap. Cecil went and said, "This is what I do, man, and this is what I want to project." It's not about if it's good or bad. I'm saying, Do you have conviction? Are you sincere in what you do? So, that was my main difference. And everybody didn't do that. Or Steve Lacy— Steve stuck to his principles, regardless. And I'm thinking of Derek Bailey. I respect people like that.

They followed their own particular evolution that was dependent on themselves and what they needed to do.

That's right, and they didn't really have any control over that, because there's something bigger than all of us that pretty well tells us the path to take.

You also played on the Lowell Davidson date for ESP, Trio [recorded on July 27, 1965]. Do you remember anything particular about that session? Had you been playing with him?

Lowell Davidson introduced himself to me. What I really liked about Lowell Davidson was his smartness. Lowell was a smooth-talking guy. His volume was lower, but he had a certain way about him that I liked. Also, it's like the situation with President Obama. If you see somebody who is classified as African American and went to Harvard, this is special! Even in the black community. "Oh, he went to Harvard? He must be smart! This guy is really different!" So, when you're coming from a certain kind of environment, an area where there's lower academic standards, some people don't think they can achieve. And when they do see somebody that biologically looks like them achieve that level, they say, Wow! So, Lowell was like that. I said, "I met this black cat. This guy went to Harvard!" Look, I was a guy that was coming up too at that time. One of my other friends went to school with him, and they were among the few African Americans in the '60s that went to Harvard.

Lowell was working at a laboratory, and I would go up to Cambridge just to hang out with him. Because how many of my brothers do I know—I'm growing up in Bedford-Stuy, South Jamaica—that go to a place like Harvard and be in that kind of institution, with resources and the information they're getting? I'm saying, What are they teaching you, man? And he was telling me all this. I said, Man, this is some heavy-duty stuff!

And I remember one time he picked me up from Brooklyn to drive me up. I was going to spend a week up there in Boston with him, because I was doing a gig with him. I did something at Harvard with him and Gary Peacock; we did a trio. During that same year as the record. And so, we're in his little sports vehicle. We're speeding on the New England Turnpike, and all of a sudden we hear the siren, and the state trooper stopped us. Lowell says, "Oh, no problem, I can deal with this." I said, What is this guy talking about? Here's a six-foot, six-inch African American, and he's going to go out here with a white state trooper. What are you going to tell this guy, my man? This is in the '60s! They were talking; he smiles and pulls out some ID, and he got back in the car. The cop's smiling; he walked on. And I'm saying, Who are *you*, man? He says, "Well, you know, I work with a big laboratory up in Boston, with a big-time guy." He would take me over to the lab, where we had the use of an electronic microscope. I said, This guy's no joke.

How did you yourself get into the scientific end of music?

I always had the desire. I was a kid that had all the chemistry sets. I didn't have parents that were academically trained, in a sense—from the South, old-school. So I had to do a lot on my own, and growing up in this community that was always on the low academic level, I didn't have the best kind of environment to do that. I always wanted to be a scientist. So, when Lowell stepped into the picture, wow, that was it! And I got inspiration from the fact that he liked my drumming. He was a piano player, but he came with a tape one time, and I said, What are you trying to play like me for? And it was kind of an honor, because I respected this guy's brain and mind so much. I said, If this guy likes what I'm doing, I think I'm doing something.

Your own date for ESP was the first on the label offered to a drummer. What did it mean for you to be able to record that? How did you conceive of your approach to doing the record? How was it received?

I heard somebody say it was better than *Ionisation* by Varèse, because of the way it was done, for just two people, the way it was scoped out. That was supposed to be larger than a duo, so they kept it as the "Milford Graves Percussion Ensemble." It was supposed to be an ensemble, but people couldn't cut it. I had a few name guys in there, but they couldn't understand the concept.

Was it something you were working on already?

Well, if you talk to people around here in their sixties—I'm sixty-seven—they all know me as a drummer. In junior high school, I used to play for all the assembly programs. The teachers would ask me, "Could you bring all those bongo players?" Never congas, they'd always say "bongo players." And I'd bring all the drummers. I'd get all the guys in the neighborhood, because I was in it from the housing project and we used to be out on the bench playing at night. So, everybody knows me; I was the drum guy around here. I'd play the little local dances and put bands together. We were playing Latin jazz or backbeat or funk or Calypso. But the drum thing was always the power thing with me, because when I was born drums were in the house. My grandfather and my uncle were drummers. So, for some reason all the guys would come around me; they wanted to play those drums. Before they built all these houses, there'd be all these wooded areas on the side here, and I'd be in there beating on tin cans. I had guys like little messengers, "Come and go here, over there," like the talking drumming in the Congo they use, signal drumming.

So, I had always wanted to deal with that situation, and then in '65 I was fascinated by Indian music. I went and found Wasanta Singh, the guy who was Ahmed Abdul-Malik's teacher, and I studied tabla with him. As a matter of fact, he wanted to take me to India, because he said I had a great touch for tabla, but I was committed to doing free jazz. That led me to really studying Indian rhythmic systems, but then taking that with the West African, and taking that with the Afro-Cuban, the Haitian, the Brazilian stuff. I said, Man, this is it! So, I started contacting guys I knew who were percussionists in the African and Afro-Cuban thing, but they couldn't conceptually see the rhythmic structure I was dealing with at that time, like in seven beats, ten beats, thirteen beats. I had rehearsals, and guys couldn't play in that framework, in meters of ten, and seven, and nine.

These were rehearsals toward this record?

Right. I would get guys together. I would instruct them on what to do—I never told them like a pattern. I'd say, "Okay, I'm giving you nine beats [*counts them off*]." And they couldn't fit patterns in. I'd say, "You're overlapping; now you're going back into four-fourths." They couldn't hear it. And Sonny Morgan, he was just an unbelievable guy. He was the one who could cut it. So, we'd wind up with just a duo.

And what was the significance of the titles? "Nothing," with a series of numbers . . .

I was really involved with yoga—kundalini, nirvana. Bernard had said something about being nothing. I remember telling him, "I want it 'Nothing.'" I didn't make a commitment to Buddhism or anything, but I was reading all that stuff. Before that, I had started studying karate, and before that, I was doing martial arts. And I was studying Asian philosophy. So, by the time that record came, all of that was there. And then from the structural point, I was listening to certain things. I remember John [Tchicai] had a friend named Jan Tilton. I would go over to their houses and they'd be talking, mentioning Shostakovich. I said, Who's this guy Shostakovich? All these classical cats, so I started going to the library, and I had every classical side you could get. I was listening to a lot of Stravinsky at the time, and I said, Hmm, these guys are okay. If you're playing a lot of African music, everything would be right on there, it's a pulse. But these guys, it's not an exact pulse that you could put your hands on. It's like life; it's flowing. So I put all that in; I threw everything into the pie. And that's why if I play with classical people, it's no problem.

After all's said and done, four decades later, what is your assessment of the ESP label historically? How do you view its revival in recent years?

What I know is that with ESP, if you had a chance to record . . . I wasn't thinking about money. I asked a person, Who was going to record you during that period? If you recorded for somebody during that period, how much money were you going to make? If nobody was going to record you then, where would you be if it wasn't for ESP recording you and putting you out there? So, if Bernard Stollman or ESP recorded you, and you had a recording out, how were you going to publicize yourself? Are you going to be this kind of artist that's going to sit back and say, "I'm an artist and I'm not going to do nothing for myself," and you're going to depend on everybody else to do something? You can't depend on people doing anything for you.

You know, I come from a situation in this country with all the heavy-duty racism, and I have to go back to President Obama again, where there are African Americans saying, There's no excuse right now; there's no damn excuse. Don't blame it on white folks no more; there's no damn excuse. It's about you. Nobody can stop you but your damn self.

I look at the positives, because I can't deal with the negatives of Bernard Stollman. I just know one thing: nobody was recording us in the '60s other than ESP! And the pay that maybe you didn't get from Bernard, it neutralizes itself because if you had to hire a public relations person, you were going to have to pay him. So you're still going to come out to zero. It balances out, a plus and a minus. Now, ESP puts you out. What are you going to do after that? Albert Ayler became what, he started putting out—that's all through ESP. Myself, through ESP, I came out. And I remember sitting at a restaurant, in Brownie's one time. Bernard was sitting with another person, and I've got to admire Bernard about this too—we're sitting down eating, and Bernard made a comment about me; he says, "Oh yeah, this was a smart guy. I recorded him, then he started his own label." SRP with Don Pullen. Look, ESP publicized us all over the planet, so anybody complaining about Bernard, I have to ask people, You've got to check yourself out. That's over, man. Bernard was a businessman—he wasn't a charitable organization.

Everybody had their own kind of experience. I had a lot more communication with Bernard than a lot of people. I used to go up to his place. I met his mother. I met his father. They would come and sit with us sometimes, serve Giuseppi and myself something. You go talk to people. If Bernard would do something that I didn't like, you say something. And Bernard gave me some explanations, at certain times. So, to harp on things, Bernard was this and Bernard was that. I'm saying if Bernard approaches you now, you've got to sit down in a very mature adult way, and you have to say, "Look, Bernard, if we're going to do something, this is what it should be now. You can say either I will accept that . . ." And I see certain people recording for Bernard still, because this guy realized, "I need this publicity now, who else is going to do it?" So, sometimes you walk into something, you say, "You know what? I know I'm not going to get nothing out of it financially." Everybody looks at this little dollar all the time. It's not always about that exchange, at that immediate dollar level.

You've got to really look at something, take it apart. . . . For me, I would rather shake Bernard Stollman's hand and say, "You know what, buddy, after all this stuff, after all this beating each other . . ." and bringing out this stuff that just about was buried in the damn recording cemetery, this period of music. I said, "Man, if you've got the energy and if you've got the will to do this here, everybody needs to come back around again and work." With Bernard, you've got to say, "Hey, man, you started something. Look, you did what you did." Now how can we all get together and use our resources, instead of just burying this guy and knocking him. I mean, that's petty. I can't deal with that, if you've got any humanness in you.

Alan Sondheim

A self-taught musician drawing on several traditions, Alan Sondheim made two albums for ESP in the 1960s: *Ritual-All-7-70* (recorded in January 1967, in Providence, Rhode Island) and *T'Other Little Tune* (recorded in May 1968). In subsequent years, his musical practice was eclipsed by his work as a writer, artist, and theorist; he published books, had a career as a performance and new-media artist, and collaborated on numerous dance projects. More recently, he has resumed playing improvised music (on mostly non-Western instruments) and has released CDs on various independent labels. Currently based in Brooklyn, he has taught at a number of universities and works extensively in virtual worlds and with Internet art in general.

How did you initially make contact with the ESP label?

Around 1966 I was hanging out at Shakespeare and Company Books in Paris, where I met Joel Zabor [drummer and later novelist, as Rafi Zabor, *The Bear Comes Home*], who was on my ESP records. Steve Stollman was there, and he put us in touch with Bernard. I was playing saxophone then, unbearably badly—I was trying to play everything at the time. Then Joel went off to Copenhagen and I joined him, and we met up with Ted Joans and some bass player, and we got a gig in a club. Ted Joans was on trumpet; he was really all over the place. Eventually Joel and I played there a couple of nights, just the two of us. I was on Indian flutes.

Then you came back to Providence, where you were living. What brought about your first album, Ritual-All-7-70?

I think Bernard said, Do a record. So, we gave him a tape and that was it! The 7-70 was the name of the Ampex computer we were using. I think I was probably using what I use now to record, which is two mikes. As I remember, the pieces were done in one long twenty-five-hour session. The way I was thinking about it was that we would set up certain situations—for instance, on the second ESP record, John Emigh would be on sax at one end of the room, and I'd be on trombone, which I knew I couldn't play, at the other, and we would be playing over a distance of maybe a hundred feet, so there would be echoes. There was this conceptual bent to the music, which is more noticeable in the second album with the electronics on it, with the Moog synthesizer.

That second ESP album, T'Other Little Tune, *seems as much a continuation as a further development in what you were doing. How did that development play out?*

In that record, there's something that has held my interest all the time, which was to make pieces so complicated that a lot of what you were doing was sort of exploring the complexities. So, although that music sounds simple, we used—because Moog was plug-in cords—every single cord, and the modules were so complexly united that you would start to get strange feedbacks. I'm doing work now in Second Life, this virtual online world—the installation is unbelievably complex, both musically and visually. I'm fascinated by having to negotiate spaces that represent a kind of implosion of information, where information is everywhere. In '68, we ended up building our own synthesizer and used that a lot, live, until a few years ago. I knew what I wanted with it, but I couldn't do the electronics. Greg Johnson did the electronics, and we rebuilt them several times. We built it from scratch without any plans at all, after the second record.

But with the music, for the second record at one point, the piece called "Rock," we set the drummer up with his own mike, and we arranged it with the equipment so that the louder he played, the more the volume would drop; it produced this really weird kind of compression. So, we were trying even there to mess things up and to contradict what would be the normative way of playing and listening to these things.

How did you decide on that specific cluster of people for the records?

They were people I felt I could work with. One guy—Paul [Phillips], the trumpeter—complained that I worked him harder than he had ever been worked before, because I was really pushing on rehearsals, maybe because I felt I couldn't play anything.

But wasn't it all improvisation, with some conceptual elements?

Yeah, but it was tuned improvisation. It wasn't just a free-for-all, what people in the '60s were calling wipeout. I had listened enough to pseudo–John Coltrane *Ascension* kind of stuff, where everybody would get together who couldn't play instruments and think they were in heaven. You listen afterwards, it's like, This is the worst garbage I've ever heard in my life. We had rehearsed so much; I knew what to expect from the players, and I was able to work with them.

There is clearly a focus on different instruments, especially from you, who plays the most variety.

Yeah, too much. Far too much.

You were playing Hawaiian and country blues guitar, and also koto.

Well, see, on strings I'm comfortable. I'm just on strings now; I got rid of all the other instruments. On the session I just did for Porter Records [*Julu Twine*, duos with Myk Freedman, lap steel], I also use the Alpine zither, which is hard as hell to play.

When you pick up a string instrument that's new to you, are you looking into its traditions or are you adapting it to what you want to do?

I'm adapting it. Alpine zithers are used for edelweiss kind of music, German waltzes and so forth. They're played very slowly, and I'm playing them very jaggedly. I mean, they're amazing. You put a mike under them, and they sound orchestral; they're just astonishing. It's like establishing a sort of tonic field, like [Charles] Olson talks about in "Projective Verse," the poetic field. So, I'm thinking about music that way, but with a lot of practice and a lot of restraints.

Did you have much sense of what you were getting into, joining the ESP catalog at that time?

Yeah, and I think I always had an identity crisis over it. I do think I felt a little bit like a fraud. I don't want to put my music down too much, and I'm happier with what I'm doing now by a long shot—I was influenced by people like Bartok as well—but it sounded like jazz to a lot of people.

Because of the improvisational aspect?

But I was listening to taqsim also. And I was listening to ragas. I had done an interview with Ravi Shankar. I was listening to Indian music whenever I could—and that makes jazz seem simple. It doesn't make Charlie Parker seem simple. With ragas, the scales are different whether you're ascending or descending. It's a mess, for an outsider. So, that was influencing me. I felt close to the taqsim; I felt close to the Jewish Yemenite music. I had a lot of that kind of stuff. I was listening to all that probably more than I was listening to jazz, in the mid-'60s—and I was listening a lot to Albert Ayler, who just blew me away. On the label, I was listening to him, Giuseppi Logan, Sunny Murray. I still have the albums.

Was there much response to your ESP records at the time?

Not that I know of. Probably none at all. I wasn't on the scene, and I never have been. My whole career is made of moments—I have this "important" art book out that I edited, *Individuals: Post-Movement Art in America* [1977], but I was never part of the art scene. I'm not part of the poetry scene, but I have poetry books out, and I've actually run poetry series here in Brooklyn. So, I move in and out of scenes, but I don't have any stake in them. But it also means (a) I don't know the scenes that well, and (b) I don't get the playing gigs. It's all right.

On both of those early records—and especially on another release, The Songs, *a whole oratorio recorded a couple months after the first ESP album with the same musicians—you seem to have a special fondness for the use of voice. Where did that come in for you musically?*

I really like female voice. I don't like male voice, and maybe it's because I can't sing at all. The male voice developed in a direction that was almost more militaristic. I associate it with a kind of authority, whereas the female voice I associate with a kind of maternal discourse or open spaces, in a way. It's different; it sounds more melodic to me.

What was your musical formation? Did you study music while you were at Brown University?

I have a master's in English from Brown. But my first thesis, in the early '60s, was a bibliography of the blues, and it got out of hand. I was reading every book I could find, and the more I got into it—particularly books like Paul Oliver's *Blues Fell This Morning*—the more I began to feel that this wasn't my music. I was very much aware of being Jewish middle class. As a musician, I'm self-taught. The way I played guitar, I learned the chords in alphabetical order; that seemed as good a way as any. Then I was living for a while in Cambridge—in a house with Aram Saroyan and Clark Coolidge—and that's where I met Alan Wilson before he was in Canned Heat. We played together a lot. I didn't understand the Delta stuff until after I met him. And he had the best ear of any musician, better than any of the jazz people I played with. But I was playing weird when I was playing blues. I just couldn't stick with the blues form. I would get really bored. Al Wilson introduced me to John Fahey, and Fahey was going to bring out a record of me on Takoma Records, then he said my stuff was too repetitive.

After the ESP records you stopped playing music for a long time. What happened?

My music has developed in very quirky ways since those records. I wouldn't say at all now that it's related to jazz—I don't know what it's related to. I was interested in pursuing what I could do and not what I couldn't do, partly because of what I saw was an essence, which had to do with the race issue. Then I met Vito Acconci. We were very close friends in the early '70s. He was moving out of writing into performance, and I was doing performance; we were talking daily. I was doing a lot of filmmaking at that point, working with oscilloscopes and other kinds of electronic gear. And I didn't get back to music until the mid-'80s, when I was in Dallas for two years. I heard the SPK recordings and other "industrial music." I began to feel that I could do something in music that had some kind of meaning "otherwise" in the world, and so I had a group called Damaged Life; the phrase is from Adorno. Edie Brickell was part of the music scene there. I was teaching new media, and I brought all my professor friends down to see her. She was doing very amazing raw stuff.

Do you see any particular constants in your musical trajectory?

One of the things I was always interested in doing, even before the ESP records, was playing as fast as possible. I wanted speed. For me, when I can do something really fast I can actually zone out at the speed. And afterwards, if I do it well, I always have a sense of wonder that I did that. So, on keyboard I can be fast, and on stringed instruments I can be really fast. Then it becomes almost like moving shapes around rather than just playing; it's a different kind of a space for me.

And why does that attract you?

Because it pushes me to the limits of what I can do physically—which probably has to do with being Jewish. I felt very disassociated from my body; at the same time I was intellectual. I was also in revolt against that, so I wanted my hands on a stringed instrument to be able to take any shape I can think of immediately, which means really complicated chording. As a matter of fact, the dancer I work with now [Foofwa d'Imobilité], we do a piece called "Ennui"—sometimes Azure [Carter] sings independently—but he'll dance as fast as he can, and I'll play as fast as I can, until we can't do it anymore. It's usually about ten minutes, and we're just completely worn out.

What is your view of ESP's legacy and its revival in the last few years?

I think it's a really good idea that it's relaunching. What always worries me about these things is this idea of generations or resuscitation—which I understand totally, and I associate it with New Orleans jazz coming back. But, at the same time, I hope the music would be considered as current and relevant. If it's not, it's not that interesting to me. Among its new releases, for example, I like Yuganaut [*This Musicship*], because this holds its own *now*. As far as the ESP catalog, the music doesn't sound dated to me, by and large. What was odd was that music was almost like a crystal window that opened and then was shattered a few years later, because it was only a very short period that people were doing that. When I hear Giuseppi Logan, I still have the feeling, what on earth am I listening to?!

On a more theoretical level, I think that ESP was caught between ideological/social wars and cultural wars, and there was no way they could win, at that point. I didn't feel they were making much money—I didn't know how popular the music was, but I certainly knew it wasn't mainstream, and since then it's become clear that it was not enough to make a living on. So, Stollman stepped into a no-win situation. The good thing was that the music got out to people like me and to a lot of other people. My stuff, by the way, gets played on the air a lot—which is weird—and recently. So, I have this odd, very minor reputation, and that wouldn't have come about without ESP. I mean, ESP was a kind of legitimation that something had arrived.

It's interesting, because if you think of the Godz, and the Holy Modal Rounders, and the Fugs, and Pearls Before Swine, all of them are oddly community-oriented or communal, in a way. All of them are folk in a communal way that's got an edge to it, but a comfortable edge, a friendly edge. That makes you want to listen to them over and over again. And I think that was really important. It's another direction that ESP went in that's not talked about very much.

Tom Rapp

Just nineteen when he sent off a demo of his group, Pearls Before Swine, to ESP at the end of 1966, Tom Rapp saw a quick and unexpected rise to fame, if not fortune. Within six years, touring widely, he released eight albums of original songs, the first two (and most adventurous) produced by ESP. By 1975, disillusioned by the music business, he went back to school and studied economics, then law, eventually becoming a civil rights lawyer in the Philadelphia area; in more recent years, he moved to Florida, where he had lived as a teenager. In the 1990s writers and younger musicians began to seek him out again, and he performed publicly for the first time in twenty years at the Terrastock festival in 1997. Later that year, he appeared with others in New York to celebrate the release of the Pearls' tribute record, *For the Dead in Space*. He has performed occasionally in the years since and released CDs of archival material as well as previously unrecorded songs.

How did you first get the idea of sending your demo tape to ESP?

Somewhere I had read about the Fugs, and I thought, This is great. I went to the local record store and ordered a couple of Fugs records. They came, and they were funny, and they were on ESP. Friends and I would just sit together and play music occasionally, so we put together a tape, and we sent it to ESP. We said, You have the Fugs. We're not just like the Fugs, but you might be interested. And they immediately sent a letter or a telegram. Yeah, come sign up with us, do a record! It was easier in those days, apparently, to get on a record. We went up to New York, and we stayed at [Bernard Stollman's] parents' apartment at 90th and Riverside. The parents had an apartment that had maybe ten bedrooms, and a chandelier and a grand piano, overlooking the park, the whole deal. We'd hang out there, and we recorded at Impact Sound, which the Fugs and the Holy Modal Rounders were using. Richard Alderson was the engineer. It was a little place, just in back of where Lincoln Center is now, and it was one or two flights up—the whole block looked like a slum. So, we went up there, and the first album [*One Nation Underground*] we recorded in about four days, from beginning to end, including the mixing. It came out the same week as *Sgt. Pepper's*—it was a little bit overwhelmed—in May or so of '67.

Did you know about anything else that was put out by ESP when you first got clued in to the label?

In those days, the back of the albums had ads for everything else. So, I probably saw that they did Albert Ayler and jazz, which I really wasn't into. They didn't seem to have any other kind of pop or rock acts at that time, unless you count the Fugs and the Godz. And I think I knew that they put out albums of William Burroughs and Timothy Leary.

On the recording sessions for that first album, how did you come up with the arrangements and instrumentation that you used?

Essentially, we were four kids from Florida—I was still writing the songs on the airplane up to New York. At Impact Sound they recorded all kinds of things, so there were lots of different instruments at the studio—Middle Eastern groups and everything—so any kind of instrument in the world seemed to be right there, and we were allowed to use them. A lot of it was just impromptu: let's use that; that sounds really cool. If we had had to bring our own instruments, it would have been guitar and a bass. But ouds, and drones, and strange celestes, and all that kind of stuff, which I had probably never heard of—what is that, what does it do?—we had the advantage that the instruments were there in a huge buffet for everybody.

What do you recall about working with Richard Alderson and his contributions?

He was terrific. He had worked with Dylan. Richard was just incredibly cool, and he'd make really good suggestions. We all did the mixing with him, but to a great extent the goodness of the first couple albums is him. He knew a lot more options that were there, and we'd say, "What about this?" and he'd say, "Well yeah, but then there's . . ." And he brought in Warren Smith as the drummer. Warren's this wonderful jazz artist, and so all of the percussion ideas came out of Warren. If you subtracted Richard and Warren, it would be a far different album. But apparently for about a year or two, our first album was like the hippest thing in the world.

How quickly did it become apparent that your first record was a success?

Well, first, we'd hear it all over the radio, especially in the New York area. I knew songs from it were printed in *Sing Out!* and *Broadside*. And there was originally a full-color flyer of the Hell part of that Bosch picture [on the cover], and everywhere we'd go people would have it on their wall. And later, Fassbinder, the German director, used two of the songs from it in one of his movies—something I only heard about five years ago, frankly—in *Rio das Mortes* [1971]. You just become aware that people seem to know about it. Years later, when I was trying to track down what the hell went on, people in the music business told me that album probably sold like two hundred thousand copies maybe.

So, how did all this unfold? You make the record and then what—you all go back to Florida and this begins to happen?

Yeah, mostly everyone went back to Florida, and within a few months ESP said, "Well, let's do a second album." We weren't part of any promotion, and aside from hearing about it on the radio, we didn't know much what was going on. We didn't know how much airplay makes it extremely probable that you're doing very well. We knew we didn't have any number one hit on the AM radio, and we probably thought that's where success is, and anything other than that isn't much of a deal. So, we came back to Impact Sound over the next several months and put together everything for *Balaklava*. Again, that was with Richard, and there were instruments there, but we were just able to take a whole lot more time and think about things.

And you had certain conceptual approaches as well, like using those old recordings.

It was the middle of the Vietnam War, and I said we should put together an album that has this sort of theme, because the Charge of the Light Brigade was really the last time that war was glorious. I had records that I'd had for years, *Voices of History*, and they had Florence Nightingale and Robert Browning and this guy Trumpeter Landfrey, who did the Charge of the Light Brigade. So, I had two *Balaklava*-related items on that one record—Florence Nightingale and the trumpeter—and I thought that would be good to start and end with.

Though these records were getting attention, you didn't actually tour those first years, right?

Yeah. ESP never said, Let's tour. So, I was just interested in writing songs. I wasn't into any business end of it or anything like that. The one big problem was we never got any money from ESP. Never, not even like a hundred dollars or something.

Bernard has said that in 1968 they had a big bootleg problem that more or less shut them down.

Right, the Mafia and the CIA.

You've heard the story, obviously.

Yes, I have. My real sense is that he was abducted by aliens, and when he was probed it erased his memory of where all the money was. I think that probably makes as much sense as the Mafia and the CIA. But Bernard, to his credit— despite all the problems I had about never getting paid—he did get these products out there, especially the jazz and the experimental stuff. And then what happened to the people who did it, that's another story. But he did provide a conduit where a lot of good things got released out into the world.

You were twenty when you made the first record. The manner in which this happened relatively easily, and its success on the radio—was there an aspect in which it all seemed rather unreal?

Well, yeah, it's strange to be a kid who's just out of high school in Florida, to have stuff on the radio and records and all of that, especially at that time. That was the dream of every child that age: be in a rock band and have a record, and hear it on the radio, and meet all the girls. So, it was that dream, and it was very nice, but after the first album I spent more time probably in New York working on the second record and less time just being a kid in Florida anymore.

Did the fact of doing some politically charged songs create any problems for you directly?

No. Probably nobody in Florida knew they existed, first of all. Obviously now we know that things in the '60s were worse even than people were paranoid about at the time. But I never ran into anything like that. We weren't at that level like John Lennon.

After you signed with a big label, Reprise, did that affect your songwriting at all?

I really don't think so. Obviously, when you're writing songs, it's reflecting the environment you're in at the time. Having signed with Reprise, we were sent over to Holland. I was and my wife; she was from Holland. I got to write all the songs for *The Use of Ashes*. When we lived in Holland, it was the swans on the lake, and roses all over—not much like New York—but then, just across the fields, maybe fifty yards away, was a Nazi bunker, and the Dutch do not tear down these things, so it was an odd mix. I'm sure that affected the stuff. And the landing on the moon was then. In fact, I wrote "Rocket Man" on that day actually, when I was watching it on TV. It was only thirty years later I found out that Elton John really did get his inspiration for his "Rocket Man" from mine. That was cool, but I keep thinking, Why didn't I know this thirty years ago?

Apparently you never got much in the way of royalties during the Reprise years either. What happened there? As a big company with resources, did they do anything better for you?

They were fine. They were really wonderful. My manager, Peter Edmiston, who had signed the Fugs from ESP to Reprise, and us from ESP to Reprise, instead of my having a contract with Warner Brothers, I had one of those personal service contracts where he owned me and then he would sell stuff I did to the record company, so no money ever came directly from the record company. All I ever got the whole time was money he would give me to pay that month's rent or phone bill. So, I was on this really short leash—I suspect because, had I gotten some money in any kind of volume at all, I would have known what was going on.

At the end of that time—it was years, he had an office in New York, these records were out and I didn't have any money, I was living in Woodstock—I said, "Peter, I want to see the contracts that are between the record companies, because I have no copies." He said, "Come on down." I took the bus down. I went in and he said, "Oh, I've got to run, but here's all the contracts." There was one of those big padded envelopes covered with duct tape. He splits and I split. I get to Woodstock. I opened it up; it's full of newspapers, all folded up. Then I called him. His office is closed. He's not there anymore; nobody knows where he is. So, he was just gone with whatever—because I would hear, Warner Brothers would give you twenty-five thousand dollars up front, or fifty thousand dollars up front, and I never saw any of that. Peter said, "Well, that's not how they're doing it here, because of blah blah blah, and in fact you probably owe me a lot of money for all this money I'm putting out for rent." It was just insane.

Looking back, do you ever wonder about what you wrote and how you managed to do it?

Yes. In fact, just very recently I found out that a record company in England is going to be re-releasing *Stardancer* [1972] and *Sunforest* [1972], which were my Paramount/Blue Thumb Records. And I started thinking about it and reading the lyrics, getting stuff together to send to them, and I thought, Where did that come from? Where the hell did that come from?

It's just so strange, and I'm so far from it now. I've been doing shows occasionally, like at the Terrastock festivals, and I'm surprised how many people are out there that even heard of us. More than half of them are people who were not even born when I did those records! And they just love the stuff. . . . It's really a good dream: my sense was that I did whatever I was put here to do, so I'm okay now [*laughs*]. But there have been people who came up and said, "I was going to kill myself but then I listened to your song, and I didn't do it." It's just amazing.

So, in a way, I always think with Bernard, well, of course, I wouldn't have got to point B if I hadn't started on point Bernard. It's a lot of things: they were horrible at the time, but now I'm okay, so I guess they're all right, but it was awful at the time.

In 2005 the two ESP albums were remastered and reissued together. Joe Phillips, who did the remastering, said in the notes that the original tapes could no longer be found.

Well, sometime around 1976, Bernard tracked me down and came to my house outside Boston. He said, "Here, I have this for you," and he gave me these four boxes. He said, "These are the masters to the first two records," the four-track and then the two-track mixdown. I said, "Well, that's fine." I still have all of those. I actually have in my closet as we speak the original four-track master that Richard and all of us did in 1967.

Did you have any involvement with the ESP reissue?

I think I knew it was happening. I talked to Joe about it, because I knew him from years ago, and we discussed it. For some reason, the first album, *One Nation Underground*, after the initial vinyl pressing, all of the CDs and the later vinyl had different mixes. We had a song called "Morning Song," and Leonard Cohen said he loved that song, but in that song there's a verse and then there's a chorus with a swinehorn, a sound that was just tremendous when it popped up—it's not there anymore. It's just weird. I don't know where they got that different mix from. I'm talking about the ZYX and Get Back reissues, all of those. *Balaklava* seemed to be exactly the same as we had mixed it at the time, but *One Nation Underground* is as if someone got hold of some of the tapes and remixed them as best they could remember. It's been that way wrong for thirty years.

With ESP having relaunched in the last few years, do you think that reconfirms the value of many of the recordings from the '60s, rather than just seeing them as historical relics?

Yeah, I think actually they're all quite contemporary, because at the time they were so strange, people didn't know what the hell they were, and now there's a better context for them. I'm glad all those things are coming about, and I just wish that one day I'd get a check—for the two hundred thousand that sold, you know what I mean? That would be nice.

Are you writing songs anymore?

No, not really. The last song I wrote was called "Every Change Is a Release," a good recap of everything, I think. And I wrote one for my wedding when I married my wife, Lynne. And not much since, odds and ends here and there. Mostly what I do related to music is every year or so I'll go do a gig like these Terrastock festivals, or [*laughs*] I played at CBGB. I'm just extremely happy that they're going to be finally releasing *Stardancer* on CD over in England, because it was the last one that had never come out and it was really, after the first album, my favorite album of any that I did.

Warren Smith

The range of drummer and percussionist Warren Smith's experience in music, through more than sixty years, is truly phenomenal. He started working in family bands around Chicago at the age of fourteen, and by the end of the 1950s in New York, a decade later, he was playing with Kenny Burrell, Gil Evans, and new music composers. During the 1960s he worked extensively in the studios, on Broadway, and with numerous Motown artists, while remaining engaged in the jazz world and launching his own performance loft, Studio WIS, in 1967. For the next few decades, he was a music educator on the university level, but along the way he also played with Mingus, Miles, Muhal Richard Abrams, Sam Rivers, Max Roach and M'Boom, and Julius Hemphill. He worked on three studio dates for ESP, all in 1967: Pearls Before Swine's *One Nation Underground*, Jerry Moore's *Ballad of Birmingham*, and Bruce Mackay's *Midnight Minstrel*. He has played at a number of ESP-sponsored concerts in recent years, and his own record with the Composers Workshop Ensemble, *Old News Borrowed Blues* (2009), released by Engine Studios, is distributed by the label.

How did you come into contact with the ESP label and Bernard Stollman?

I was associated with a couple of studios as either a freelance percussionist or as a writer. Bernard's artists were flying through there, and there were all of these off-the-wall, iconoclastic groups, whether they were supposed to be jazz or pop or whatever, that I found myself associating with either as a writer or as a percussionist or sometimes drummer. So, that's what happened. I know they had an office on 20th or 21st Street and Fifth Avenue, and I had a studio on 21st Street between Sixth and Seventh, so sometimes I'd have to go over there to get my money.

You did get some?

Oh yeah. Because I put up a fuss, and I talked with his mother, whoever was handling it, and she'd come back in there and give me a check.

Were you connected with Richard Alderson's studio?

Yes. A lot of the projects came through Richard. Even outside of him—because Alan Douglas wasn't working through Richard Alderson's studio; that was some other thing. But the two of them as producers probably drew me into most of it.

Did you play with, or cross paths with, any of the free jazz players that were working with ESP?

Most of them. Because I was associated with the Jazz Composers Guild, and Bill Dixon and Marion Brown, all these people . . . I came here in 1957, and I had worked with Harry Partch, John Cage, and all the dance companies that were doing contemporary stuff, all these wild composers, but that's how I had associations with all these different musicians.

Recently, when Giuseppi Logan made his first concert appearance in over forty years [at the Bowery Poetry Club, on February 17, 2009, an ESP-sponsored event], you were the drummer. Had you ever played with him before?

In that same period of time we had crossed paths. There were a lot of those guys on the Lower East Side, where a lot of activity was happening, and I just knew Giuseppi by association. But I never actually played with him before last week.

Who called you in on that gig?

Matt Lavelle. There are these resurgences, you know. I remember seeing this in every evolution of jazz. I remember them bringing Bunk Johnson out, building him some teeth so he could play. So, hey, man, let's work with Giuseppi.

It was nice to see all of you on stage there with him, offering a certain nurturing, helping to carry him forward.

Well, see, also it's a respect for what you know is there. This is a human being who's fallen on bad times, there but for the grace of God, you know. And so we've always reacted to each other like that.

Do you recall much about working with Pearls Before Swine on their first record, over forty years ago?

Oh, yes I do! That was a fantastic project, that particular one. The songs that those guys had, and the lyrics—some of those lyrics haunted me all my life. Like the guy says [in "Another Time"], "did you cast an enchanting glance / through the eyes that all men use?" Which just reminds you of all the obstructions to progress and to helping people who are desperately in need that we've seen from that time to the present. And these things kind of live on.

Tom Rapp said that if it weren't for you and Richard Alderson, that record would have been completely different.

Richard and I got together and talked. I had done some of my projects there, so he knew all this percussion stuff that I had, and we just talked with Tom and he liked it. We used triangles and tambourines, and it just lit the thing up.

It's interesting that you continue to remember the effects of some of the lyrics from that record.

It shows you how some projects just explode and stay there. And the chorus in there was "Or have you come by again / To die again / Well, try again another time." And that's another thing that hits me here, because so many people almost want you to help them kill themselves.

I read only recently that he wrote that song after surviving a car accident that he essentially walked away from. And it was one of his first songs.

Wow! That's impressive. That touches me. I never thought it had that dimension.

Did you ever perform with Pearls Before Swine after that?

We had a reunion about ten or fifteen years ago.

How much did you work with the Fugs?

I did a lot of their stuff. Some of their albums, I had maybe five or six arrangements, like on "Coca-Cola Douche." And I was the musical director for a while. I conducted them at some shows at the Fillmore East, down on Second Avenue. I remember going through a whole conduction—oh man, that was great. I mean, they didn't need any conduction really; it was just kind of keeping everybody like, Hey, we're going to the next number.

How did you manage to avoid having the long-term money disputes that other musicians had with a producer like Bernard?

I was very fortunate—I taught school, because I had children. So, I was totally involved in music, but I made up my mind about two things that I would never argue about with another being: jealousy and money. If there was something about money, I always had enough wherewithal that I could walk away from it and let it resolve itself. A few times I had confrontations, but it never bothered me to the fact that, Oh, I'll never work with you again or I'll never speak to you again. I think probably the reason why Bernard and I have always been friends is because I never put that pressure on him. I didn't care whether he had the money or not—I was happy, and my family was cool. But that may be a rare condition when musicians depend entirely on their own creative efforts to survive.

Which is asking a lot.

It is! And it's rare even in this society—professional musicians, are you kidding me? I mean, shit, that's a blessing.

But how did you get to be so smart early on with all this? You're from a musical family . . .

Exactly. I grew up watching this business and being involved in it. My father and his brothers, and my mother's brother and sister, were involved in the post office as a subsidiary to the music, and just as serious about the music. So, I knew there had to be something. I started out studying architecture in school— it was as much a love for design and architecture as it was about money, but I almost flunked out of that so I transferred to music. And then I went into music education, purely about the economic factor. I mean, it's a fickle business, and I tell all my students that. Some of us make it, very fortunate that some of us do, but a lot of people . . .

Also, if you're depending solely on that, the compromises you have to make artistically are probably far greater than if you weren't desperate for that.

Yeah, and let me say this one other thing: I worked with the inception of the record company called Strata-East, and Strata-East—in fact, I think they even had an office in the same building as ESP—they broke up over petty disagreements about money and about, you know, "We finally got one artist that hit it big," Gil Scott Heron. A lot of people were saying, "Well, we should all be making more money." It literally disintegrated the company through petty accusations and jealousies. And through all that, I maintained my association with Charles Tolliver and Stanley Cowell, because we were all in this together. I wouldn't blame anybody for what happened. And when you look back on it, that was a great happening. The ESP catalog, the reason I was involved in it and so interested in it, that was some great music that Bernard produced. He had an ear for unusual people.

In your own musical itinerary, it's amazing the breadth of your activities. Starting with Harry Partch and John Cage, then in the mid- and late 1960s the Motown work, Barbra Streisand, Janis Joplin [musical director on her 1969 European tour], and yet you're also working on ESP projects. It didn't all make you a little schizophrenic?

Man, I did the Mingus concert, *Epitaph*, at Town Hall; I did the Cage retrospective at Town Hall. . . . I mean, all this music was interesting to me, and a lot of people weren't interested in doing other stuff. So, I guess my interest just led me to all these various paths. I'm an explorer.

As a listener, one can do that. But you don't see that many musicians who can think in so many directions.

It comes about from exposure. I mean, literally from birth every day I heard some live music somewhere, somebody was practicing or whatever.

Did you have a particular perspective, at the time or since, on the activities of the ESP label? Do you have a sense that it played a certain role?

Yeah, I must say I didn't think it was going to pay off right then. And I wasn't dependent on that, so I might have had a longer vision of how these things would evolve. But I just felt like some of this music was important, and some of it wasn't. Still, I'm more interested in what new is going to happen beyond that. Thank God I'm still active enough to want to do that.

Roscoe Mitchell

Saxophonist Roscoe Mitchell, an early member of the Association for the Advancement of Creative Musicians, recorded his first album in 1966, *Sound*, with its new approach to improvised music. The sextet he assembled for that session grew into the Art Ensemble of Chicago, which still performs occasionally, in modified form, more than forty years later.

I started listening to the first releases when they came out in 1965. Some I really loved a lot, especially Albert Ayler, *Spiritual Unity*. Also, the *New York Art Quartet*. I thought it was a very advanced move for ESP to do those recordings.

I met Albert Ayler when I was in the army, because he was in the Orléans, France, band and I was in the Heidelberg, Germany, band. Sometimes our bands would go to Berlin. We'd put three bands together and do these large parades and concerts. I didn't quite understand exactly what he was doing at that time, but as a saxophonist I did recognize that he had an enormous talent on the instrument. One time we were having a session, playing the blues, and Albert played the first three choruses of the blues straight ahead, so to speak, and then after he started to stretch the limits. That made a big impression on me.

[*On ESP's troubled financial history, not being an ESP artist*] I don't believe I ever talked to anyone about that, people who were involved in the label. It wasn't a point that I ever approached with anybody. I'm finding that out now.

Michael Snow

Canadian artist, filmmaker, and pianist Michael Snow, who has moved freely and with equal devotion among all the disciplines he practices, was living in New York throughout the 1960s and friendly with many adventurous musicians. On July 17, 1964, for his film *New York Eye and Ear Control*, he assembled a sextet in his downtown loft to record the soundtrack, with his neighbor, the writer Paul Haines, as recording engineer; the session was subsequently released on ESP. A decade later, after returning to Toronto, he cofounded the CCMC (Canadian Creative Music Collective), which continued to perform occasionally for the next three decades.

What did you know of the ESP label before you had contact with them?

All I remember is that Paul Haines called my attention to Albert Ayler, by telling me that there was this amazing tenor sax player that I should hear. We went to some place uptown in the '80s, where we heard the trio with Gary Peacock and Sunny Murray, and it certainly did knock me out. It was fantastic.

How did the New York Eye and Ear Control *session come about? What were you looking for?*

I had this commission from a concert organization here in Toronto, called Ten Centuries Concerts, which mixed music from various periods. At any rate, they asked me to make a film using jazz. This happened around the time that I heard Albert, and actually I chose the band. I had him, with Don Cherry and John Tchicai and Roswell Rudd [as well as Gary Peacock and Sunny Murray], and I simply said to them that I wanted to buy a half an hour of music. But it did have some stipulations, which were that I didn't want any previously played compositions, and I wanted it to be as much ensemble improvisations as could be with no solos. So, that's what they did. And then, somehow or other Bernard Stollman heard about it, I guess—because I didn't solicit this—and the idea came up after the film had been made and been shown and puzzled everyone.

So, the film had already come out by the time the record did?

I had shown the film, yeah, before the recording was issued. He asked me whether I'd be interested, and actually I had very mixed feelings about it, because it was precisely made to be used in conjunction with the images that I made. I was making a film with this music, and to separate the two, I really had to argue myself into it. Which seems a bit strange, I suppose, but the intention was to use it in a certain way with certain kinds of images. That was it.

As compositions, the pieces are attributed to Ayler. Did he actually write some kind of theme?

Oh no, absolutely not. It was completely free. Of course, he played some things that he himself considered his compositions, those little lines. And he really was dominant in a lot of ways, so I guess it was justified.

But certainly on that record, even credited as his compositions, the music is clearly different from any of his other records.

Well, it really was totally improvised, which is what I wanted. As I was being involved with so-called free jazz, I was always surprised at how everybody was still bookending, as in all of previous jazz where you play a tune, play your variations, then play the tune again. I kept feeling that I didn't want that, and particularly what I had in mind for the film, I definitely didn't want it. I wanted it as pure free improvisation as I could get.

Did the music come first, before you actually made the film?

No. It's like the music is a particular kind of experience, and the film is something quite different that you see simultaneously. That's why the title, *New York Eye and Ear Control*: it was actually being able to hear the music and being able to see the picture without the music saying, This image is sad, or this image is happy—which is a way that movie music is always used. I really wanted it to be possible that you could hear them. So, they're very, very different. It's as if the image part of it is very classical and static. In fact, most of the motion is in the music actually. So, they're kind of counterpointing and being in their own worlds, but happening simultaneously.

So the record came out of the project as a byproduct, in effect. Did you have any further relations with ESP, or did the record go its way and you went yours?

Basically, that's it, although by then I did know Bernard, and I was following up on what he was doing, and appreciated it, and saw him occasionally at gigs and concerts. But, other than that, there wasn't anything.

How long were you in New York?

I arrived there in 1962, and from '70 to '72 I was both in Toronto and there, living in both places, basically. After '72, I didn't have a loft anymore in New York.

Did you have a sense of ESP as framing a certain scene?

Well, I think what he was doing was daring and extremely valuable historically, because there was a lot of fear of free improvisation by jazz people. Some people thought somebody like Albert or Cecil Taylor was crazy. That's another thing: there was very little work. It was really incredible; hardly anything happened. So, what Bernard did was really wonderful, in that he did recognize some of the interesting things that were going on and recorded them.

The music that ESP was putting out, particularly the free improvisation, was it some kind of nourishment for your own music as a pianist?

Oh, very much. I heard some wonderful things. And also, Roswell needed some money, and he sold me his piano for a hundred dollars. This is probably in '64, on Chambers Street—we were in 123 Chambers [where the World Trade Center was later built], and he was across the street. So, I put the piano in my studio. And by then, I was starting to know a lot of people involved in that scene, and it seems they had very little opportunity to play. So, I made my studio available as a place to practice. Archie Shepp played there, and Paul Bley, Milford Graves, and the Jazz Composer's Orchestra started there basically; their first rehearsals were in my loft. So, I was listening. I was hearing a lot of amazing music and making it possible for people to play.

Was there ever an audience?

No, no, this was just for rehearsals, to play privately.

And did you play with them at all, any of those times?

Occasionally, yes.

Marion Brown

Alto saxophonist Marion Brown quickly became one of the bright young voices of the new music in the five years that he lived in New York during the mid-1960s. At the end of 1964, he performed both with Bill Dixon and Archie Shepp in the Jazz Composers Guild–sponsored series at Judson Hall, Four Days in December. Through 1965 he recorded with Shepp and on John Coltrane's *Ascension*, before recording his own first date as a leader for ESP (*Marion Brown Quartet*) in November; a month after, he played on Burton Greene's debut for the label. The following year he made his second album for ESP, *Why Not?* (recorded October 23, 1966), which was quickly followed by dates for Fontana and Impulse. Early in 1967 he played on Jacques Coursil's date for ESP (unissued), before leaving for Paris; in Europe he began his long association with Gunter Hampel.

During the 1970s he taught music at colleges in New England. In the '80s, often in Europe, he began to focus as well on painting, a longtime interest (in recent years, Marc Albert-Levin mounted a show in Paris of thirty-eight paintings by Brown: all of them sold). In the '90s a series of illnesses entailed the partial amputation of his leg and also brain surgery, and he lived for some years in a nursing home in Brooklyn, before moving to an assisted living facility in Hollywood, Florida, where he lived near his son Djinji, also a musician. In October 2010 he passed away there, a year and seven months after this interview.

You moved to New York in 1962, and the first person you met was LeRoi Jones. That led to Archie Shepp, Ornette, and Coltrane. But you also knew other writers there, such as A. B. Spellman and Ishmael Reed. What did that bring to you, being friendly with writers?

The writers who listened to me and liked my playing, they inspired me to be better, and I inspired them to keep listening. LeRoi Jones opened the door for me; he introduced me to the world. He was a very beautiful and very smart person. I've been reading some of his latest books.

We used to practice at 27 Cooper Square, and he lived in that building on the top floor. Archie Shepp lived on the second floor. So he knew what we were doing all along, because he was upstairs listening. And you know what, he was taking trumpet lessons. One day I was up to his house and he picked his trumpet up. I said, "Man, you sound like Don Cherry." He smiled, "That's who is teaching me."

How did you become aware of the ESP label? What records and musicians did you know?

I found out about them through working with Pharoah Sanders in Sun Ra's band. See, when Bernard Stollman came on the scene, he made an impression on everybody because he was really sharp minded. He knew there was a fortune in new music and new musicians playing away from the way they played in the past. And that's where he set his goal. He very seldom came to my gigs, but he had people coming there listening and telling him what they thought. They must have given good reports because he recorded me first.

How did Bernard Stollman hear about you?

Through his informers. Then he started coming out and listening, to see if what they said was right. Coltrane was the same way. He used to come to the gig, and I'd see him out there. I'd say, What is Trane doing here? He was listening to me. Because I had started out at a place where he was going. He was very interested in me. He treated me like a kid brother; he loved me.

Before ESP produced your first date as a leader, you had already recorded with Coltrane. You'd worked with Bill Dixon, plus Sun Ra, plus Archie Shepp. What do you recall about that first ESP session?

There was a Frenchman I knew named Marc Albert. He loved that music. He couldn't speak any English, but in two months time he was speaking it perfectly. He was there checking out the new music, because he started writing about music and translating books. He was sitting there listening to me play with his eyes like they were popping out of his head. He couldn't believe it. I've known him now for over forty years.

How was that ESP record received by the public?

Bernard used to give me copies of all the reviews. People would say, "This guy's got it. He's new—he's onto something but he doesn't know what it is yet. When he discovers what it is he's going to be a terror." Sonny Rollins liked my playing too. He knew everything about me.

A month after that date, you were part of Burton Greene's quartet on his first record, also for ESP. Had you been working with other piano players since Sun Ra?

That was the first time I worked with one who got recorded. I'd been with piano players who were so fantastic, you couldn't understand why they didn't make a record, especially down in Atlanta. Or like this guy Junior Harris, from Miami, he was as fast as Bud Powell. I met him on the Lower East Side, when I first came to New York.

On your second ESP date, Why Not?, *you had Rashied Ali again in your quartet, Stanley Cowell on piano, and Sirone on bass.*

Sirone was from my hometown, so I knew him a long time. He started out as a trombone player. He was so advanced the guys couldn't understand, so when he switched to bass he found his instrument, because he could push you. He'd make you go crazy.

Your cultural connection to the Georgia Sea Islands is evident in your later records, but how much of Gullah culture did you have growing up?

My grandfather was a conjurer. He knew about roots and all kinds of medicines, and he never went to school for it. He found everything all on his own. He was a genius.

And did that background come in at all when you were playing music in the 1960s?

Yeah, it did. And when I started playing with Rashied Ali, he brought all that stuff out of me. He knew it was in there.

In 1967 you went off to Europe and often worked there over the following decades. Your most frequent collaborator ever since has been Gunter Hampel. How did you meet?

He knew about all of the new musicians. Besides, he was going with Jeanne Lee, so he knew everybody. He was on a gig with me that Gérard Terronès booked. I liked Gunter's playing, and I liked him as a person, so we made a lot of gigs together and a lot of records.

He already knew of your work when he met you. Did you know anything of his playing by then?

I had already heard some of his playing on records that were being imported to the United States.

Between the two of you, was there any sense of family, say, being part of the ESP catalog?

Yeah, in that we were part of the new generation of musicians who were going to push things further away from where they were. We were going to cross into a never-never land!

In the 1960s, did you think in terms like "avant-garde" and "free jazz," or did any of those terms bother you?

They didn't bother me, because I knew what the people who used those terms were saying: that something was new, that something was changing, and it was going to be good. Kind of like Obama. He pulled a miracle, didn't he?

It was amazing, yes. Regarding the ESP label, what was your perspective on doing business with Bernard?

I knew the man was going to produce what he said he was going to do, so I just went along with his program and he came through. Because of him, I became a world-known saxophone star. Stollman, he was avant-garde himself; he's in the future. He's got some stuff of mine that he never put out, but I think he will.

A lot of people have said that your ESP records are among your best. Do you have any personal favorites?

Afternoon of a Georgia Faun [1970], for ECM. And *Soul Eyes* [1978], for Japanese Victor—Philly Joe Jones made me play my horn in a way I'd never dreamed I could do it. He was something else; he threatened to kill me if I messed up the music. When the gig was over, he came over to my booth with a smile and said, "Young man, I knew you had it in you. It just took me to bring it out." I said, "But you scared me." He said, "I was serious, I would have killed you if you messed it up."

Richard Alderson

Recording engineer and producer Richard Alderson, with his Impact Sound studio, was much in demand during the 1960s. He was the engineer on three dozen jazz titles for Prestige, and substantial portions of the Fania Latin music and ESP catalogs, while also working as a live engineer for concerts. Then and later, he worked as well for Nina Simone, Thelonious Monk, Bob Marley, and others, and engineered numerous commercials, film, and video projects. During the early 1970s he dropped out of the New York scene to travel through southern Mexico, exploring the highlands of Chiapas, microphone in hand. His marvelous recordings of indigenous music there were released by Folkways and reissued more recently as *Bats'i Son*. Since then, he has resumed his work in New York as a recording engineer, though less intensely, while developing an acoustic design business, building innovative sound studios and home theater systems.

How did you get started as a recording engineer? Didn't you originally meet Bernard Stollman when you were doing the sound for the Charlie Parker Memorial Concert in 1965 at Carnegie Hall, and he asked you to destroy the tape of Bud Powell's disastrous set?

That story is true in part, but I was also really good friends with David Hancock, who had previously recorded *Spirits Rejoice* for ESP. He was kind of a mentor to me, because I was pretty much beginning my career when I started working with ESP. David was the kind of engineer who recorded everything with only two ribbon microphones; more than that was a sin to him. So, his stuff was very diffuse, yet I kind of liked the way it sounded, though it didn't seem right for jazz. This technique was more appropriate for classical music.

He called me over to his place—he also mastered all the ESP and Prestige stuff that I recorded—and he played *Spirits* for me and said, "What do you think of this?" And I said, "Well, I rather like it." Albert Ayler was one of my favorites of all those free jazz musicians. And I became good friends with him, although I never did record him in the studio. *Bells* [concert at Town Hall, May 1, 1965] is the only thing I did record of him. He showed up at some of the sessions in my studio. We just bonded, and I really liked him personally. Anyway, David Hancock said, "Maybe you should be the one recording this kind of stuff."

At that point, I had also recorded some avant-garde stuff for somebody else, something at Town Hall [poet Ree Dragonette and Eric Dolphy quintet, November 20, 1962; unreleased]. I had started with live recording because I didn't yet have a studio of my own. The studio where I recorded all the ESP stuff was an abandoned warehouse on West 65th Street, which had been condemned. An artist friend called me and said, "Here's a great place for a studio, very low rent, but there's no running water and no heat." No matter, I just moved in and put up some sheetrock division walls, with egg crates on the ceiling, and made it into a recording studio for very little money. That's how my career really got started. Luckily, they didn't tear the building down for seven years and during that time we fixed it up and made it more secure and well-equipped. I began engineering by just doing it. I loved music but couldn't play it very well—so I recorded it.

Is that the studio that Harry Belafonte invested in?

That happened later. Initially, there was a young lady I knew from the Village, who had a little family money. She bankrolled me and became my first partner. I had been working for Harry Belafonte as a live sound man; that was how I supported myself. But I didn't like doing live sound that much. So, I started on my own with this person as a partner. We bought a piano and a couple of microphones, and it was basically two-track. I just kept investing in equipment and when Harry bought her out and became my new partner, he put another eighty-five thousand dollars into it. We bought a lot of microphones, and we acquired one of the first eight-track machines, a four-track machine, a couple of new two-tracks, an EMT chamber, plus a recording console I built myself.

Did you have all of this when you were recording for ESP?

Not in the beginning. Especially not when I did the first recordings for ESP, but the later stuff was recorded in a well-equipped studio.

Was Impact Sound a different studio?

No, it was the same studio. When Harry bought in, we changed the name from RLA to Impact. In those days, I had said both to Harry Belafonte and to Bob

Dylan—I did the world tour in '65 to '66 with Dylan—I would like to have my own recording studio; I don't want to be on the road. So Dylan said, "Well, go on the road with me, and I'll build you a recording studio." But by the time his tour was over, we were all burned out with each other, and Dylan didn't want to do it. Then Harry said, "Will you come back and do live sound for me some more?" I said, "Harry, I just want to have my own studio to make recordings. But I'll tell you what: you build me a studio, I'll do three months a year with you, and I'll train some other guy to do the other dates." And Harry agreed to do it. Belafonte recorded some really good tracks of his own at Impact, which were never released. I don't know why.

Why did you first say yes to working as a recording engineer for ESP?

Because he asked me, and I was intrigued. Besides, I didn't have that much business at the time. I had Don Schlitten from Prestige, for whom I recorded quite a number of straight-ahead jazz records, most of which don't get credited to me properly. As no one seems to really pay attention to the credits on a lot of the Prestige reissues, the session information often gets left off or they assume that Rudy [van Gelder] recorded it. I have a list of the stuff I recorded for Prestige [dates by Jaki Byard, Booker Ervin, Houston Person, Cedar Walton, Charles McPherson, Barry Harris, and more].

But the free jazz got to me. There was something about the raw emotion and honesty of it that I found compelling. A lot of the content was simply that an artist would come in for two hours and blow intensely through his horn and leave; there was not a lot of finesse to it. But I did other interesting sessions for Bernard, some of which were not so "free."

Let's go through a list of ESP recordings where you were the engineer. In each case, what was your part in shaping the music? First, the Sun Ra sessions for Heliocentric Worlds, *in April and November 1965. What were the challenges in recording a large group like that?*

Mainly it was just getting them in the studio. It wasn't a large room, and it was literally full to the doors with the band. They were all on top of each other. The studio was about thirty by twenty-five feet, and the recording booth was very small, six feet deep by twelve feet wide. It was truly overcrowded with a big band in there, but it worked.

Had you ever heard Sun Ra's music before?

I'd not heard of him at all. I had no idea what his music was like. I had no idea how big the Arkestra was. Almost no one whom I recorded for ESP was known to me in advance, nor was I given much information about the instrumentation or personnel in advance. How did I "shape" the music? I hope not at all. My whole intent was not to shape anything. I was just trying to capture the force and flavor of whatever the artists were doing without editorializing.

But how did you figure out the best way to place the microphones for that many musicians?

It was pretty much just trying to get all the instruments on the tape, because I didn't have enough microphones or channels or space to separate everybody. There were groups of horns on single microphones, the piano was separately miked, and the drums and bass were separately miked, but there was a lot of sharing of microphones. Capturing Sun Ra's music was challenging because they were practiced and disciplined up to the free-blowing section; they were playing careful arrangements before he turned them loose. I mean, Sun Ra is Duke Ellington on acid; it's very much like that to me.

With so many musicians, there wasn't a possibility of the sound getting over-saturated?

No, it seemed to work because the Arkestra was used to playing in small spaces. As I said, Bernard gave me very little information. He just said "Sun Ra's Arkestra." I knew it was going to be more people than usual, but I wasn't given any description of exactly how many horns, etc. I remember Sun Ra had a primitive little synthesizer that lounge singers used. When he played a few notes it would sound kind of ethereal and spacey—I was stuck figuring out how I was going to get a channel to record it. So, I just put a guitar amplifier on it and fed it into the room.

Did they help facilitate the recording aspect?

They just played and left it up to me to capture it. Sun Ra was kind of an imperious character, but he seemed happy with it. I mean, I did capture the emotional focus of the band.

What about the Milford Graves Percussion Ensemble in July 1965? Were there particular difficulties in recording the two percussionists with all their equipment?

There wasn't any particular challenge, drums and percussion being my forte. It was also relatively structured stuff. It wasn't as wild as the sax screamers.

Do you recall much about recording Frank Wright, the trio in November 1965 [Frank Wright Trio] or the quintet in March 1967 [Your Prayer]?

I remember that it was very vigorous, and there was a lot of energy involved in it. He was probably the most relentlessly abandoned of all the free jazz players I recorded.

Next in the chronology is the Paul Bley trio date [Closer] in December 1965.

That was completely the opposite, very tranquil jazz and totally different from the rest of the stuff on ESP. I became friends with Barry Altschul [drummer on that date]. He was very fussy about how he sounded. I did a bunch of stuff for him personally around the same time, such as a whole record of him just playing the drums. I don't have any copies of that, but I remember that a lot of work went into it and that I spent a lot of time with him making it sound special.

That same month, in December, you also recorded Patty Waters's first album [Sings]. One side is solo, and the other has a quartet with Burton Greene playing inside the piano behind her.

That was unforgettable. Burton Greene really had to stretch to figure out what she was going to do. The thing that was most interesting to me was how it was right on the edge of going over the top. I thought she was really unique, and many years later I communicated with her, thinking I would like to work with her again. She said, "I've recorded some stuff. I'll send it to you." She sent me something that was very bland. I didn't know what to say, because for me she had little to offer other than her complete abandon and emotional intensity. This stuff sounded as if Patty was on some mood stabilizer, and that was it for me.

I kind of shaped her stuff a little bit [the side with Burton Greene]. Exactly how, I'm not sure. She was very quiet before the storm. I probably encouraged her just to be loose and free and not to hold back.

Quite a different project for ESP, in 1966 you recorded Jean Erdman's The Coach with the Six Insides, *the audio version of her theatrical work, with Teiji Ito as the composer.*

Again, this was totally different from most of what was on ESP. It was very structured, based on *Finnegans Wake* by James Joyce. It was very challenging to record because there were a lot of performers, there were a lot of voices involved, there was the interplay of the percussion and the actors, and it's all in the studio simultaneously. Nothing was overdubbed. There was some splicing, but not a lot. I remember being quite proud of it.

Next is the Fugs, who had three records released by ESP but only one was recorded by you for the label. You also recorded them when they went to Sinatra's label, Reprise.

The first one I did, *The Fugs* [1966], was certainly the most creative thing I had done for anyone. I'm listed as the producer, and I'm well-credited by Ed Sanders elsewhere [from www.thefugs.com/history2.html: "One good thing happened as a result of the Fugs' relationship with ESP—we met engineer/producer Richard Alderson. . . . We wanted to get beyond tribal primitive in our recording techniques. . . . The second Fugs album involved many 4-track to 2-track to 4-track bounces to free up tracks for overdubs. Richard Alderson wasn't one of those 'don't touch the console' technobots, so that the Fugs could learn the art of recording simultaneously while we cut the tunes. He had good ears and good ideas, and he brought precision to our recording."]. I'm also called co-composer on "Virgin Forest," for the sound design. Aside from Pearls Before Swine, this was the most elaborate production I did for Bernard, by far. We spent a lot of time after the original sessions creating the sounds and mixing and overdubbing things. After this, I recorded two more Fugs records and was producer on one of them. This was all very exciting until Sinatra actually listened to what we were doing, was horrified, and immediately pulled the plug!

Did you know their music at all before you did that session?

I knew who the Fugs were, I was aware of the East Village scene because I had lived down there. I knew Ed's paper and the Peace Eye Bookstore. I probably had heard a little bit of the Fugs' music. I'm pretty sure I had heard the earlier stuff that Harry Smith did. So, yeah, I was familiar with them, and I immediately bonded with Ed Sanders and Tuli Kupferberg.

Their dispute with Bernard started soon after that record?

It started very soon afterwards, about financial arrangements that weren't honored. I don't know the exact truth of it, and I've never really cared to know the details. Often, after Bernard resurfaces in my life, calls me up, and starts to talk about all the great things he's going to do as far as giving me proper credit and paying royalties, etc., I communicate with Ed, who inevitably has a negative take on it. And Ed has, unlike Bernard, made good on paying me some producer's fees and giving me proper recognition. Up to the present day, absolutely nothing has materialized from Bernard's promises.

Didn't you perform with the Fugs at one point?

I was the CIA Man [in the song "CIA Man"], live at The Bitter End. That was at a Fugs reunion concert, and when it came time for that song I put on my spy suit and came out leering sinisterly. I would have made a really good spook.

You've mentioned that you should have gotten more credit on many of the ESP records that you worked on. Do you mean beyond being listed as the recording engineer?

On many of ESP's free jazz projects I should be credited as recording engineer/ producer, because there was no one in charge in the studio but myself. I suppose it's an arguable point, but nonetheless—you asked me how I shaped the recordings. Even though my uncredited role as a producer was not to shape it, I was alone making these decisions, allowing the artists freedom to do their thing. That was my whole point with Bernard. He should have acknowledged my role for what it was.

Another date you worked on for ESP was The East Village Other, *which was rather a curiosity. As I understand it, everybody just came into the studio.*

I was told to tune in the Luci Johnson wedding on a small radio, and the performers would just do whatever they were going to do; that's all there was to it. Andy Warhol was there and didn't say one word. He just walked in with shades on, stood still for twenty minutes, and left. That was his performance. There were a lot of people. I'm not really sure who all was there. Some members of the Velvet Underground, and Marion Brown, Tuli was there. This was as unscripted as anything I've ever heard of. It was truly a happening. The only planning was that they were all invited and that it was to coincide with Luci's wedding broadcast on the radio.

You were deeply involved with both Pearls Before Swine records, where you're listed as producer, director, and engineer. You weren't too happy, however, with the reissues.

The thing is, the original tapes sound marvelous. The original vinyl sounds right, as good as possible in that time period. So, in my opinion, what you would want to do would be to make the CD reissues sound as much like the original as possible. In the case of the Pearls Before Swine, the original sound was definitive. The fact that someone took it upon himself to change things around, just willy-nilly, EQ things—and then say, "Well, I thought I made it better"—well, excuse me. There seems to be a contagion of these remastering engineers, guys who get paid to mess up some great recordings and are considerably less talented than the original engineers.

I'm doing a lot of surround-sound installations, and I buy a lot of the high-definition reissues that have been tinkered with, such as the Beatles stuff that was remastered by George Martin's son for Cirque du Soleil. It's all very clean and inventive, but it seems totally misguided to me. It doesn't sound remotely like the original. They brought all kinds of things out of the music that are irrelevant as far as I'm concerned. Some people think it's marvelous—but it's certainly not what was originally intended! One would think that the correct thing to do would be to dust them off and make them sound as good as possible, using today's much improved digital mastering gear. I've just listened to some new *Tommy* remasters, where they did it in startling high definition sound, and yet it feels all wrong! If it really needed remixing, and you could make it better, that would be fine. But how can you remix *Tommy* and make it better? Can you really remix *Sgt. Pepper* and make it better? Anybody with common sense would know this is misguided. What should be done is just clean it up and polish it, like somebody would do with any art object that they're restoring, because after all that's what remastering should be—*restoring, not remixing*!

When you're hearing these, do you remember enough from years and years ago how you heard it back then? Or are you actually comparing them?

I have a lot of that stuff on the original vinyl, so I know exactly what it sounds like. Even if Bernard had come to me and said, "Remaster this stuff for free," I would have remastered Pearls Before Swine for free. I would have been enormously annoyed at not getting paid, but I would have done it, especially to prevent it from being tinkered with by hoodoos. I've written letters to Bernard that said, "Do you actually own the original vinyl? Do you have a good turntable? Have you ever put it on and listened to the originals? Do you have any idea what they sound like? How could you put this out and think that this is an improvement?" And then he's, "Well, we really didn't have the original tapes." But somebody told me that Tom [Rapp] has the multitracks, and he's been afraid to give them out for some unknown reason, so I said to them, "Why don't you just tell Tom to come to me? I'll be glad to remaster them just exactly like the originals but with more modern equipment." It was just whistling in the dark.

How involved were you on the Holy Modal Rounders record, Indian War Whoop?

I worked this out with Weber and Stampfel, and there was no one else at the sessions with much input. I should be recording engineer/producer on that, because it's a pretty elaborate record and I put a lot into it to make it what it was.

It's curious, even though you worked on much bigger things and went on tour with Bob Dylan, still you kept coming back to work for ESP.

Yeah. My interest was retained. ESP wasn't repetitive, the same thing over and over again, like the more conventional stuff that I was doing. I never minded doing it, and Bernard always paid for the recording. He didn't pay much, but he paid for all the engineering.

Roswell Rudd

Having already worked in the early 1960s with Cecil Taylor as well as Steve Lacy and Archie Shepp, who both became lifelong associates, trombonist Roswell Rudd was in the thick of the new music scene in New York. If that seems far away from his start in the Dixieland band Eli's Chosen Six, in the mid-'50s, for him it was all a continuum. He appeared on two albums released by ESP, both recorded in 1964: *New York Eye and Ear Control* and *New York Art Quartet*, which he co-led with John Tchicai. In later years, besides a stint in Shepp's band and leading his own groups, he collaborated on various projects produced by the Jazz Composer's Orchestra, Carla Bley, and related artists. Over three decades, he was also an intermittent assistant to ethnomusicologist Alan Lomax, and for a while he taught ethnomusicology at the university level. This led him to further explore non-European musical traditions, and in the past decade he has worked with Malian kora player Toumani Diabate, the Mongolian Buryat Band, and Caribbean musicians Yomo Toro and David Oquendo, among others.

How did you first become aware of Bernard Stollman and the ESP label?

I think it was the Jazz Composers Guild, somehow he was a part of that. I was in the October Revolution concerts, and Bernard was there. He came down to my place on Chambers Street and we had a meeting. I don't know if John was there or not, but I described to him what we were doing. John and I had been improvising with Milford and a couple of different bass players—at the end of '63 we started doing this, and we did it through the spring and summer of '64. Then it got down to the fall, and we were ready to do something. Because what it started off as was just three or four of us, two of us, whoever could make it, getting together and improvising. We didn't have any material or anything. We just liked the sound of what we got together. So, after a while the material began to emerge. In November we went in and pretty much in one session laid down that ESP record called *New York Art Quartet*. It got edited and mixed, and it sat there into '65 because the Jazz Composers Guild decided that nobody should release anything. Because we wanted to have a corner on this music. We wanted people to come after it. We figured: deprive them of it, and they'll come after it. That was one of the psychologies of the Jazz Composers Guild. Milford was not involved with the Composers Guild, nor was Eddie Gomez or Lewis Worrell, whoever was playing bass. I don't think any of the other people really had a record that was waiting to be released, so it was a hard decision to make. But we succumbed to the majority. So, it sat there until the spring sometime, when it actually got pressed and put out.

How did Amiri Baraka end up on that session?

John brought him in. That was my first experience of Baraka; I was not familiar with his work at that time. You know, there was a certain amount of rage in our music, and I thought that somehow it connected. It's not only rage with Baraka; there's a huge kind of humor that comes across. I think I identified with that more than I did with the rage, but I thought it worked.

At least for you and John, was the New York Art Quartet your main musical activity at the time?

Yeah, we kept on rehearsing, and there were these performances given by the Jazz Composers Guild. Judson Hall was where the main festival was, and that was followed by nightly performances in the Edith Stephen dance studio, on the top floor above the Village Vanguard. We all took turns playing up there. Sometimes Eddie Gomez was the bass player, sometimes a guy from Cambridge, Massachusetts, played drums [Lowell Davidson]—he was interesting, he was a pianist and composer, and he liked playing drums with us. If he happened to be in town, and Milford couldn't make it, then he would sit in. But it was mainly John and myself. We were in that guild, and we were utilizing the opportunity to perform. Judson Hall was the Four Days in December festival, and we played on New Year's Eve opposite Sun Ra.

That went on until the spring sometime, on a nightly basis. Four or five nights a week there'd be another Jazz Composers Guild group performing. Every so often we'd play; maybe every two weeks we'd do something. Not a big audience, but hard-core—artists, and other musicians, a nice Village crowd. It was ironic, though. The *Village Voice* never sent anybody over to review the concerts, and we were putting an ad in there every week!

When the ESP record did come out, was there much response?

Well, I expected more response. Speaking for myself, I think a lot of what we thought would happen was kind of wishful thinking. It just didn't live up to our expectations. We thought we'd sell a million records, and we were lucky to sell five hundred over a couple of years.

The Fontana record did more because it was being promoted from Europe. I think European jazz lovers were more enthusiastic about what we were doing than the hard followers over here. There was more acceptance in Europe of something called the avant-garde; here, the avant-garde is kind of the kiss of death as far as a sizable audience goes. In Europe, I had the experience of using the word "avant-garde" and getting a very positive response back then. That was hard to believe because it seemed repellant here.

How important, in retrospect, was the ESP date for you?

For me, it was very significant because I think it's some of my first writing being recorded, and some of my first what I would call original playing. Anything before this, what little there is, is very derivative, and I was kind of imitating my favorite trombone players, consisting of Vic Dickenson, Bill Harris, and other icons that I learned from. I was still working that stuff out. But this ESP record is definitely a leap away from that. That's because of the improvising that we did over that long period of time.

Also, on the previous records that you'd done, you were generally a sideman.

That's true, but there was something of a personality change, or a new feeling of not just freedom but that it's okay; this is where it wants to go, and it doesn't have to evolve logically from where I was. It was definitely some kind of a lifting up, a departure—and not a conscious one. And again, going back to these improvisations, usually up in my loft where people would drop in, a lot of them in this New York Art Quartet configuration, and just letting the sounds out, let the chips fall where they may.

Have you gone back in later years and listened to that ESP record?

Yeah! You know why? Because people keep sending it to me. So, I'll just wonder, why are they sending me this? I listen to it, and, yeah, it's kind of unique, kind of fresh—still. I listen to it every ten years or something, and it still holds up.

In terms of the band that was on the recording, something began to take shape. Something called a group sound may have been evolving. That's what I hear.

As the New York Art Quartet was taking shape, in the summer of 1964 you and John also recorded with Albert Ayler and others on the soundtrack for Michael Snow's film, New York Eye and Ear Control. *What was expected of you on that session? He did the film first, right?*

I got it differently from Mike. I understood that he had us just come up and jam, and then he went out and shot the movie.

That's what I originally thought I'd heard. But he said no. Did you ever see the finished film with the music?

I did see the finished film. I think Mike showed it to us on Chambers Street, because he was living right across the street from me. I thought it worked really well. I was kind of amazed.

You didn't have any clue what was going to be there visually?

No. I knew that Mike was working with certain symbolism, and he had these logos, the "walking woman." He was a man with a vision.

On the record, the pieces are credited to Ayler, although they're not like his other music. Yet technically there wasn't really any leader on that session, is that right?

Well, the times that I played with Albert, he generally led. It was just the force of his thrust. He had such a strong sense of purpose that the music kind of gravitated toward him. Then his dynamic would change, or he would drop out for a while, and then something else would happen. But by and large, when Albert was on the scene, he was blazing the trail, so to speak. He had a great quality that way. So, playing an accompaniment to him was like playing in a Dixieland band for me, with a strong trumpet player or something. It was kind of a natural reflex action that happened.

But Mike was shaping this thing; occasionally he was saying, "Okay, Don, would you play something kind of lyrical, and you other guys just play softly around Don?" I remember him shaping it at a couple of places, saying, "Okay, I want you to hit it, and then let it go for a while." Then something else would erupt, and then later on he might say, "Okay, we just need something a little more rubato, sweeter, toned down." So, we'd do a little of that.

Your 1966 album Everywhere, *for Impulse, was the only time Giuseppi Logan appeared on record outside of ESP. How did you happen to choose him to be part of that sextet?*

I had heard Giuseppi at one of the concerts that Bernard was putting on, and Milford gave me one of the ESP records, so I knew Giuseppi a little bit from that. And Giuseppi was at the October Revolution; I met him there. I really enjoyed what he did at his concert. That was probably in 1966.

How would you describe his contribution to your sextet record?

He played flute and bass clarinet. He didn't play any alto. Robin Kenyatta did the alto playing. So between Robin and Giuseppi, all the woodwind support that I wanted was there. And with Beaver [Harris] and Charlie Haden and Lewis Worrell, that was a wonderful outfit.

Did you ever play with Giuseppi after that?

No, I think that was it. I didn't work hardly at all. After that recording I sort of stayed with Archie [Shepp], because that's where the work was. I did have another band with Karl Berger and Robin, working infrequently.

Regarding ESP, how do you see the label's significance in its time?

The fact that he got in on this surge, this change of direction in the sound, the fact that Bernard was really the first one . . . I think that Bernard was the one that really got his arms around it, or his ears. A lot of it had to do with this Jazz Composers Guild, because we all happened to be there, except for Pharoah Sanders, Marion Brown; there were a few people. There was quite a bit of this new music right there that he took advantage of. So, ESP is unique in that respect. I know it went through changes in production when the archive was taken to Europe, and different people did different things with it, and I kind of gave up following on that. But that's how important it was, and how alive it was, that it would keep on regenerating itself like this.

Any comments on how the label went about its business back then? You don't sound like you harbor fierce resentment over the frustrations you may have had.

I would have to say that it wasn't satisfactory; that part of it could have been done above board, for whatever it was worth. But he paid us for the session. That's what I was used to getting my money for. I mean, royalties were something that I didn't really know anything about at the time, and I felt that we were lucky to get paid scale for the session. And to have that record come out, and to have it in our hands, that was the thing. That's where my head was at.

Montego Joe

A native of Jamaica and raised in New York, conga player Montego Joe (aka Roger Sanders) had recorded with Olatunji, Roland Kirk, and Art Blakey by the time he went to work for the Arts and Culture Division of HAR-YOU ACT (Harlem Youth Opportunities, Unlimited—Associated Community Teams) in 1965. The program had been launched in the wake of the Harlem riots to provide training and constructive guidance for local youth. (Jackie McLean also worked in the program around that time, and his son Rene played in the teenage jazz band.) Montego Joe's task was to teach Afro and jazz percussion, and when he felt the eleven teenagers in his group were ready, he decided they should record an album—as a reward for the kids as well as the organization, to show what they had accomplished. HAR-YOU Percussion Group's *Sounds of the Ghetto Youth* was recorded in 1967 for ESP and has remained to this day a perennial favorite. In June 2010 Montego Joe passed away, a year and two months after this interview.

*Was Milford Graves your original connection to the ESP label, since he had played on the records you did for Prestige [*Arriba!, *1964;* Wild and Warm, *1965—these dates also included Chick Corea and Eddie Gomez]?*

I don't think so, because he wasn't involved with ESP at that time. I heard about ESP records, but I don't know what influenced me to connect with them. Most of the records I heard were avant-garde—Marion Brown, Albert Ayler, all those people.

Why did you approach ESP for producing the HAR-YOU Percussion Group?

I felt they would do justice to it, rather than Columbia or Blue Note or any of those other companies. Because the other companies had strict guidelines, they were more interested in having groups or individuals who could really sell records.

What do you recall about the recording session? How did the kids take to that setting?

Oh, they did fine. As a matter of fact, I got together a few teenage kids at that time, including one of my daughters, and we got them all together for the clapping and background stuff.

So the studio was big enough to fit everybody.

Oh yeah. I knew the recording engineer [Richard Alderson], so I was very happy that he was going to do the engineering.

How closely did you plan the session? Were there multiple takes?

It was specifically planned out. I had rehearsals with the musicians, and if we did more than one take, it was no more than two or three at the most. We had to do some mixing; that wasn't a problem either.

The kids weren't overawed by being there? They weren't too nervous?

They were nervous, but not extremely. I think my influence over them helped, in the sense that this is something they were going to appreciate for a long time, even when they get older and they hear it, that it would be meaningful.

What were the kids' reactions when the record came out? Did they help to sell it at all?

They were very happy about it. There wasn't a lot of response in the community, because at that time the musical influences were rock and roll, rhythm and blues. There was some Latin jazz, but not a whole lot. So, they were able to sell it verbally and also monetarily.

Did the group perform much in public after the record came out?

We didn't do too many concerts, because a lot of them were in school. They were teenagers, and if they were to do any concerts it would have to be in the summer.

Was there any response from the organization that oversaw the program?

Yeah, moderately. I mean, they were satisfied by what I did with the young men, and overall they were satisfied with what the whole department did—departments like music, acting, because some of the kids that were in the acting did some roles. A couple of them were in *Shaft* and other black films at that time. And then there was another gentleman who had the music department. He was my supervisor, but he had a big band and a lot of good guys came out of that band.

Were any of the kids in the percussion group playing in that band?

They did a couple of performances with them, but not all the time.

After this record, was there ever a possibility somewhere of doing a second record with them?

That never came up. What I'm planning to do now—I teach at a cultural organization called Ifetayo, in Brooklyn, I teach percussion and traps there. We've got two young men who are about fifteen years old, very good on the trap drums, and I've got a couple of others around the same age who play the conga drums and the bongos. There are two other young men who are not involved with Ifetayo, but their father is a musician and also teaches in the school system. Whenever I can, I try to set up something where they can perform publicly. But the overall picture that I'm trying to paint here is that I want them to record. This would be a new group, a new era. And Bernard is for it.

Would this be about the same size as the HAR-YOU Percussion Group?

About the same, ten kids or so. We've got a young kid who's thirteen years old; he's a very good guitar player. And then you have the two boys that I'm talking about: one plays piano and one plays bass. The two trap drummers, if all goes well they would split the date between the two of them. I've got to look for horn players.

I've got all my work cut out for me. I've got to get to the parents, the parents have to agree, and once they agree then I have to have a meeting with Bernard and the parents and the kids. So if they all agree, then we can go ahead and record.

Back then with the HAR-YOU group, was there much parent involvement or response?

Yeah, not as much as I would have liked. But, you know, they'd say, "Yeah, we trust you. You go ahead and do it [*laughs*]. You babysit for me."

Did any of the HAR-YOU kids continue to work in music, and did you stay in contact with them?

Oh yes. There were only two of them that I was not in touch with: the piano player David Edmead—we used to call him Mousie; he's up in Canada so I never really got a chance to see him—and one of the boys died around that time; he was murdered. The piano player [Nick Kirksey] who wrote those tunes where there's a lot of clapping and he was singing the blues, he died several years ago. And the bass player, John Moody, died—they were in their forties at that time. Nelson Sanamiago died; he had a heart attack. I stayed in contact with as many as I could.

Well, Samuel Turner was with Lionel Hampton for twenty years. Nelson Sanamiago was in music. John Moody, the bass player, he stayed in music. Andrei Strobert became my protégé, so he was working all the time.

Do you have a sense of the life of that record? It seems that people have known about and made reference to it all through the years.

Yes, I do. The premise on which I got the idea to do that recording was a little different from the premise that I'm using now. The difference being that the HAR-YOU thing came out of more of a political aspiration, meaning that at that time the powers that be who oversaw the action wanted to make sure that the government money allocated to Harlem to help the youth in the ghettos was being put to good use. So, I wanted to do my share in showing that. Now, the premise that I'm using is more or less to influence other young people who are interested in music to become aware that this is African American classical music, that there's more than just hip-hop, or that hip-hop was born out of this music.

Over the years, after the HAR-YOU record came out, were there any music world people or record companies coming to you about the record? Were there any echoes?

Yeah, there was one company called Ubiquity, out of California. He heard it. There was one tune they were playing a lot in California, so he found me and we negotiated a deal, and the record was on the Ubiquity label for a while, in the 1990s.

Since ESP reissued the record at the beginning of 2009, have there been any new responses?

According to Bernard, it's been getting a lot of airplay on the college stations and also abroad.

Evan Parker

British saxophonist Evan Parker was an early proponent of the new improvised music in London in the 1960s; with Derek Bailey and Tony Oxley, he founded Incus Records there in 1970. Though not recorded by ESP, he clearly was of a like mind with many of the artists found on the label.

It must have been *Spiritual Unity* that made me aware of ESP. We were already listening out for Albert Ayler. After that, I heard most of the records as they became available. It clearly required a paradigm shift to accept that this was an inevitable next step in the evolution of the music.

As I started to get more established, I wanted to start a label myself. At that point, the lessons from ESP had been learnt both musically and practically. The documentary style of some of the key ESP records was an influence. I remember that Bernard Stollman came to London and was at the inaugural meeting of what became the Jazz Centre Society—an important occasion—and his practical advice to the musicians present was to start documenting their work. I think I already knew that and had started the process with Incus, but it was good to hear him say it.

The broader significance is tied up with the exponential growth of interest in "free music/free improvisation/free jazz," whatever you call it, and the growth of independent labels in the music business across the board. Although ESP was not the first such label, it is a historic part of a grand tradition of independent thinking that continues to grow at an amazing pace.

Alan Silva

Bassist Alan Silva worked with many of the prominent figures in the new music of the 1960s—Sun Ra, Bill Dixon, Cecil Taylor, Albert Ayler—and he appeared on Sunny Murray's 1966 record for ESP. In November 1968 the label produced his first date as a leader, *Skillfulness*. Soon after, he went off to Paris, where he took part in a busy community of free jazz players, American as well as French (Frank Wright, Anthony Braxton, Sunny Murray, and the Art Ensemble of Chicago were all there in the late '60s). He recorded extensively for the BYG label; performed at the Pan-African Festival in Algiers in the summer of 1969, and also that October at the equally legendary festival in Amougies, Belgium, produced by BYG/Actuel; and was central to the many musical activities held at the old American Center in Paris throughout the '70s, which had a strong impact on French audiences.

In 1972 he made the conscious decision to develop his career in Europe, living around Paris in the decades since. "I don't consider that an expatriate position," he says. "It was like we were on loan. People were interested in our music over here, so we stayed." From the start there, he formed the monumental and long-term Celestrial Communication Orchestra, though his main group in the '70s was the Center of the World collective, with Frank Wright, Bobby Few, and drummer Muhammad Ali. Concurrently, for some two decades, he was the founder and director of the music school IACP (Institut Art Culture Perception). In recent years, he relocated from Paris to Le Mans.

What were your origins in the New York music scene that brought you into the sphere of ESP?

I was involved with the Jazz Composers Guild, with Bill Dixon, when he did the October Revolution. Burton Greene and I had a group called the Free Form Improvisation Ensemble [a 1964 recording of the group was released by Cadence Records in 2000], and we were playing some small concerts, including the Music of Our Time series that Norman Seaman was doing at Town Hall. Bill came to our concert and suggested that we play at his festival. The group was myself, Burton Greene, Clarence Walker, Gary Friedman, and Jon Winter. So, we played there, and that's where I first came in contact with Bernard. What I was interested in at the time was improvisation—I was looking for a broader base than jazz, which was the Afro-American base and which is still part of my base. But during the '60s I felt that Afro-American music was segregated in America. It had a second-class relationship in the music—and me being a foreigner, in the sense that I'm not born an American. I'm Portuguese and African; I was born in Bermuda, and I came to America when I was five or six years old. I lived in Harlem, so I was raised in an Afro-American music community, a Latin American community. I was not really trained to be a musician—I was a jeweler, designing jewelry for high-fashion companies—but I loved music, and I took music lessons early in my life and developed that and became interested in painting. So, I come from more of an artistic background.

But getting back to Bernard, when the Jazz Composers Guild was formulated he was at some of the meetings. It was Bill Dixon's idea that musicians need to organize themselves into some kind of guild, which was different than a union, because we had the 802 Union. My interest in Bernard was that he was a lawyer, dealing with artists' estates. I was wondering why when Charlie Parker died, he didn't have any money—because fundamentally, I found out, his publishing was fucked up. In terms of the legality of the situation, I thought all the Afro-Americans were being deprived of performance opportunities because of their national origin. But Bernard was there at the beginning of the Jazz Composers Guild, and he helped us with some legal aspects, such as, should we be a business or should we be a nonprofit organization? I was more with Sun Ra's idea that we should have been a music business.

Though the guild was short-lived, what were your particular responsibilities there?

The guild fell apart through internal griping. The focus was the problem. In the Jazz Composers Guild, we set up into different committees, and I was in charge of discovering what the aspects of the record industry were. So, I did a lot of research looking into how much it cost to make records. We looked at the Jazz Composers Guild primarily as a place for musicians to come together and do everything themselves. When I was presenting my briefs, I said, "If everybody in this group gives me a hundred dollars, we can produce a record." I was aware, after working with Bill Dixon, it was not that difficult to make a small label. Another thing was that most musicians never really invest in themselves, which was different from my point of view because I was an artist, so I knew how to invest in myself. Bill Dixon and I come from artistic backgrounds, so it's no different to go out and buy some paint. Sun Ra was the only man who seemed to be really aware. He taught me a lot, because he was the only one documenting his music.

What was the guild's attitude toward musicians working with different record labels?

First of all, what was interesting about the bylaws of the Jazz Composers Guild was you couldn't do a contract without bringing it to the guild. Number two, we were selling ourselves as a group to any label. John Coltrane was interested in the Jazz Composers Guild as a group, because we asked him if he would be interested to join us. He said, "I can't because I'm under contract. I support your idea." We asked Ornette Coleman to join us, but Ornette wanted to do his own thing. We were trying to make a real tight organization. That might have been the problem with the guild; the bylaws were really strict—you couldn't do a gig unless you brought the gig to the guild. The idea was a kind of closed group that's committed internally to a certain collective goal. But Sun Ra was really the key to my thinking, because he had already set up several ideas that I thought were absolutely ahead of the game. He had his own Illinois corporation. I learned everything about the recording industry from Sun Ra. But we just couldn't get all these things together. In fact, the guild was against Bernard's ESP Records, because we were involved in organizing control. If Bernard was going to be our lawyer, then that's different.

Even so, a certain number of the people connected with the guild eventually recorded for ESP. But weren't you involved with the label before making your own record?

I worked for Bernard in his office. In the '60s, I was doing a lot of different jobs in the music business. I worked in record shops—I was a record collector for a long time anyway; I collected jazz records. Before I met Bill Dixon, I was working with Donald Byrd as a trumpet player. I studied with Donald Byrd when I was fifteen. I went to a lot of recordings. I was absolutely fascinated by the record industry. I was in the studio with Donald and Jackie McLean, a lot of sessions for Blue Note. These guys were my friends. I used to go out and get coffee for the guys. I had worked with Sun Ra too, selling his records, Saturn Records. I would go to shops and sell his records. So, I was doing like a journeyman trip. After Bernard made the label, I talked to him and said, "Allow me to be a salesman." So, I worked trying to sell Bernard's product in the United States. I was in charge of Chicago and the whole Midwest area for a while, but it was difficult times. He had a big struggle trying to get distribution for the records. I was working there as a district sales representative, trying to get radio time for our records, and the whole problem was the rise of rock and roll. This is a big issue that a lot of people do not come to grips with, the invasion of rock music into the American scene and how it affected guys like me who didn't buy into that at all.

Were you working there long? How did you end up doing your record, Skillfulness?

It was not too long, about three or four months. He had problems paying me [*laughs*]. It was late '68 when I did the record for Bernard, *Skillfulness*. I didn't really want to do this record, but I did it anyway. And it had to be a studio date, in a certain way, because I had no band. I said, Well, okay, I'll put together something, a conceptual record. *Skillfulness* was done based on the Lotus Sutra, which is on the original album. It's the Buddhist concept of enlightenment through music. That's why I call the name of the piece "Skillfulness." And I didn't play bass in this group at all. I played my violin, and I played my cello, and piano. I was allowed to do my first orchestral piece ["Solestrial Communications Number One"], which was based on my free-form concept where the improviser creates his own music—the composer is different.

This was my original contention when I joined the Jazz Composers Guild. I said, Well, you guys want to be composers; I want to be an improviser. It was a matter of, how do you define American music without improvisation? If you didn't have Duke Ellington in America as a composer, you don't have American music, orchestra music. Everything else then is individuals. So, my idea was the orchestra that Sun Ra was proposing was the final concept for any music. What made great European music great is the orchestra, not the individuals. The composer was the central element in European music, but the orchestra was the vehicle for the composer to reach a higher level of organization of music. Ellington developed an American idea that the improviser plays a strong role in the development of orchestral music. So Sun Ra, for me, was an extension of the Ellington idea. Most people figure you have to abandon all the old elements in music just to play improvisation, and I don't agree with that.

At the time, I think Bernard had the idea that the record was a form of publishing, a way that artists can have some way of expressing themselves. See, the people in the '60s were fighting just to use their First Amendment rights—the right to publish, the right to distribute. So, I really respect him for taking the challenge. You can control your own history. That's what I liked about Bernard's idea.

With regard to Skillfulness, *that record came about at a curious point in your musical trajectory.*

I was working with Bernard there in the shop, and he was having a rough time trying to sell his records. He said it was about time that I should do a record. But I was already thirty-something years old. I mean, I had recorded my major works when I was in my twenties, when I played with Cecil Taylor. I had already played on a major label. And I had played with Albert Ayler, on Impulse. So, my recording history with those people was already documented. But as far as me making my own record, I didn't really think that. So I said okay. The idea of that record was my duet concept and the large orchestra, and these interactions between the players that I was working with at the time: Karl Berger, the flutist Becky Friend—she was unbelievable, Dave Burrell, and Michael Ephron.

How do you consider Skillfulness *in relation to your subsequent work?*

For my career, this particular record was something I had on my mind for a number of years, of an orchestra music. As I said before, I didn't see myself as a leader. I always saw myself as part of a group. So, I made a thing called the Celestrial Communication Orchestra, which came later, when I did two records with BYG. But *Skillfulness* is like the beginning of that, especially the flip side, the orchestra side where I do my first conductions.

Why did you decide on that record not to play bass?

Because I play them all! People didn't know I played violin and cello and piano. I studied them all.

What do you recall about the recording session itself?

It was great, because Onno Scholtze did the recording, using a couple of microphones that were interesting at the time. With ESP, the engineering aspect was interesting too—Bernard was really not a producer in that sense; he's more or less a coproducer of these records. So, the next person who comes in very strongly is the engineer. The idea that Bernard was interested in the sonic aspect, that was good too. Because there were a lot of problems that this music had, I saw that early in the game, how to record this music. The first problem I had was when I did *Unit Structures* [Cecil Taylor date, 1965, for Blue Note] in the studio with Rudy Van Gelder. Of course, he had the piano, bass, and drums concept, how to record that; he was very well known as an engineer, and he built his own studio. But when it came to *Unit Structures*, how do you handle that kind of music? Ouf! Or how do you handle [Coltrane's] *Ascension*? So, I had been recording myself long before, because I had my own four-track stereo system. When the engineer came in, and we discussed the sonic idea, that was great. Because these are the problems all of this music was having—Sunny [Murray] would be playing too loudly, simply because he didn't have any concept of the recording studio. A lot of problems that Albert and them had were primarily because he didn't have any recording chops. They had performance chops, which is different than working in the studio.

So, with Onno Scholtze we discussed how to keep the volume at a textural level. For example, we didn't have any saxophones. I wanted to keep it at a high level of twenty minutes where the solos were not even present. I was interested in a maximum of improvisation density. It all just happened right in the studio, captured right in the moment.

Did the record come out before you left for Europe in 1969?

No, it took a while. And the original cover is a little different. The first one was a profile of myself, like a silkscreen picture; the second one, he used a photograph of me on the violin, but that came in the '70s. The first is really the one I like, because the back cover had the Buddha on it—I consider it a Buddhist record, because it had the text of the Buddha on the flip side.

Were you sent copies of the record at a certain point in Europe?

I never received anything from Bernard, actually. As far as the business was concerned, I never received anything after that, and to this very day.

So you never received copies of the record?

Nope. Even the reissues, and Bernard would always tell me, "I don't know where you are." That's not true. I'm on the Internet since 1992. I'm all over the place—I was one of the first jazz musicians to have his own website, me and Frank Wright: center-of-the-world.de.

Have you arrived at some kind of historical perspective on Bernard and the ESP label?

I don't take the "beat on Bernard" story. He is whoever he is. He's got a heavy case, because a lot of people feel they've been exploited. If you ask, Did he send me a record, did he send me a royalty statement? No. But I look at him as a lawyer. He should know better. I always saw that as an honorable profession. A musician is a composer; he has to have these business ideas. So, a lot of guys who entered this business, especially a lot of young people, have a very bad antibusiness attitude. Which is not good for the business. A lot of rock musicians entered this and got ripped off simply because they had no business idea. Anyone says they're exploited, I say, "Hey, man, you exploited? No, you should have known better." A lot of people put that on Bernard, "Oh, yeah, he exploited me." I say, "Well, I don't know. What do you mean by exploitation?" Some people were thinking that this music was selling a lot. I said, "No, it's not. Why don't you just accept that? You go to a record shop one day and just standing there you'll see what people buy!"

You have this especially among my generation. To a lot of guys I say, "Hey, look, just get a job in a record shop, five days; find out what people really buy." The problem is they're blaming Bernard for not being successful, when in fact what they don't understand is there are so many different people in between— the distributor, the shopkeeper, and so on—before it gets to the public. And then the record sits there for two years, and nobody's sold it. I learned that at Bernard's place. He allowed me to go with his brother to a disc jockey convention. We were down there and had all our records we were going to sell, like Sun Ra, to these disc jockeys—they were not fucking interested at all! We were a bunch of idealistic people. I thought that Bernard was idealistic, and this was a black disc jockey convention. Imagine that Bernard Stollman was trying to sell records to Atlanta, Georgia! Sun Ra, man—who the fuck is that guy?! But then you wake up. You say, Well, yeah, it's a real big country, and then you realize. I sat there and I said, Yeah, man, this shit ain't what you think it is. Bernard and I kind of agreed that America needs to have a much broader base in the music industry.

Those documents that Bernard recorded and the way he shaped the record label is genius. If every record label were as diverse as his, then maybe we'd be in a more interesting point of view. Why was Albert Ayler not invited to Woodstock? We had three thousand record shops in America in the 1960s; in '67 when I worked for Bernard we had a list of them all. And we had a telephone line that we didn't have to pay. So, I got on the phone and started calling all these places around college areas—this was white America, all these small shops. Wisconsin, "You know about Sun Ra?" "Oh no, where's that?" And then you look at the playlists of the local radio stations. . . . So, these were the things that Bernard was confronted with. He didn't have a million dollars to sell Albert Ayler. I mean, he was struggling. All the independents were struggling.

Giuseppi Logan

After a disappearance of nearly forty years, multi-reedman Giuseppi Logan resurfaced in New York in 2008, and the downtown scene was abuzz. Always a singular figure, with a sound and approach like no other, in the early 1960s he had lived in Boston, where he sat in at Connoly's with Sonny Stitt, Roland Kirk, and Eric Dolphy, who inspired him to pick up the bass clarinet. Arriving in New York in 1964, he quickly fell in with the new music folks, and after the October Revolution concerts he recorded his first date for ESP, *The Giuseppi Logan Quartet* (on November 11, 1964). Six months later, he made his second album, *More*, at the same Town Hall concert (on May 1, 1965) that produced Ayler's *Bells*. The next year, he was part of ESP's college tour through upstate New York, and further opportunities followed. But by the beginning of the '70s, he was nowhere to be seen.

Family and personal difficulties led to a very long eclipse, and despite occasional sightings no one really knew if he was still in this world. With his return to New York, he has struggled not only for survival but to regain his ability to play. Musicians donated instruments—Matt Lavelle gave him a bass clarinet and helped find an alto saxophone; Alan Sondheim gave him a flute. Videos of him playing in his regular spot in Tompkins Square Park appeared on YouTube (shot by Suzannah B. Troy) and support grew: in February 2009 he performed onstage for the first time in all those years, in the ESP-sponsored series at the Bowery Poetry Club, with a quartet that included Lavelle, bassist François Grillot, and Warren Smith. Aided by the Jazz Foundation, he managed to play other concerts with the same group, and in the fall they recorded a new album with pianist Dave Burrell, an old friend. *The Giuseppi Logan Quintet*, for the Tompkins Square label, features five new original compositions and three standards ("Over the Rainbow," "Blue Moon," and "Freddie Freeloader").

You returned to New York just a year ago, in 2008, and certainly it's been very difficult working your way back into music. You've been long gone, so far gone it's a wonder you managed to come back at all. Where were you?

I had been in a mental institution for three years straight, and the next time I got caught they put me in there for two years. And the next time, I had to stay in there for eighteen to nineteen months. I lost my wife, my family, everything. Everybody left me. I was homeless. I had a home. It's still in my name, but she got it. That was in Virginia.

Isn't your son a musician?

Yeah, Jay Logan, he's in California. I'd like to know something about him. I don't know what he's playing. I never heard him play, but I started him off. I wish I could hear him. They tell me he's good.

What do you recall about meeting Bernard Stollman?

I know he was good to me. He gave me a piano. I only had a saxophone and a flute; I picked up those instruments at a music school in the Village.

How did you decide on those particular pieces for your first ESP record?

I wrote the pieces for that session.

Milford Graves brought in Don Pullen and Eddie Gomez for that date. Were you familiar with them?

No, we never played together before the session. And it was the first time I played with Milford Graves. He heard me play in Boston; that's how he met me. I had been playing with many other people for a while, so I decided to go back to school. And from going to school, my concept changed.

At the New England Conservatory of Music, you began to think more about modal possibilities.

Yeah, I went through a lot of modes: the Phrygian, the Lydian, the Mixolydian, the Dorian. I learned a great deal from that school.

You had been doing a certain amount of writing by the time of your first record.

Yeah, but it got burned up and I lost it, so I've got to write them over. There were some beautiful tunes. I'm going to try to remember some of them.

One of your tunes, "Dance of Satan," you reorchestrated for Roswell Rudd's session on Impulse two years later. One can recognize the tune, but it's still quite different. Did you have other opportunities to reorchestrate your pieces?

No, I was just messing with different kinds of instruments. I was playing everything, violin, all kinds. I was just playing music. I was doing concerts on them, too.

On your second ESP record, you offer quite a strong performance on piano with your solo piece "Curve Eleven." Had you studied piano much?

My father used to play spirituals on the piano, and I learned how to play boogie-woogie; that's how I started messing with the piano. I mastered the piano for myself. I never really tried to be a piano player. I should practice—if I had one, I would practice. But when I started going to school, I took up the saxophone. So my father got me a saxophone, down in Virginia, God bless him. And I'm still trying to learn how to play it. There's so much.

Back in the '60s, there were only certain people that you usually played with. Do you think there was something about your own music that was challenging or difficult for others?

I don't even know. Maybe I play different. I don't know. I haven't heard too much of myself. I've just been trying to play.

Your two ESP records impressed many people over the years. Is there any way to say what those records meant to you?

I never really had a chance to listen to them. I've heard them a little bit, but I haven't been able to sit down and just concentrate on following the innovation and the melodic contour, and things like that. I would like to hear it.

Do you have much of a sense of your records' existence out in the world?

Well, one of my sister's children was stationed in Germany, and she told me she heard it over there. That was about four or five years ago. But I was out of touch with everybody, with all music. A bomb fell on me.

You were also part of the college tour that ESP sponsored in upstate New York in April 1966. You even appeared on most of Patty Waters's College Tour *record, backing her on flute.*

I had a new group: Scobe Stroman on drums, Dave Burrell on piano, and Perry Lind on bass. We were rushing around. We'd play, then rush to another place. We never had time to really get together with people.

You wrote music as well for a chamber ensemble that was performed at Judson Hall, which Marzette Watts recorded.

Yeah, I'd like to hear that. I don't know what happened to it.

Bernard said that originally Marzette Watts told him the recording didn't work, then years later admitted he had lied to him, worried that Bernard wasn't going to treat you right. Bernard has been trying to recuperate that tape from Marzette's son.

I remember the Judson Hall concert. Those were new pieces; I wrote them just for that concert.

Through the many years that you were gone, were you thinking at all about music?

I lost everything. That kind of shocked me, you know. And I guess I was out for a while. I was abusive to myself too. I was incarcerated and everything, not being able to play. They shook all that out of me.

Didn't you also play on the street sometimes?

Yeah, I played on the street, and I got put in jail, got put in a mental institution for doing that.

For playing on the street?

Yeah, in Virginia, it was terrible.

When you played on the street, or even now when you play on the subway platform, what sort of music did you play?

Just anything that came into my mind. That's what I'm doing now. I'm trying to stay in shape by playing.

Have you started writing again at all?

I wrote some changes for a tune that I haven't written yet. I wrote the chord structure of it. I did that for two or three tunes in the last six months. I'm going to try some new kind of tunes.

Is there any way to describe your musical thinking now?

My thinking goes one way, and when I get to play it something else happens [*laughs*]. I don't understand, but I think I'll leave it up to God. I hope I can play, that's all.

What are you doing now musically that's different from the '60s?

I listen to a lot of concert music, and the type of intervalic relationships they're involved in. That's given me a new approach to playing.

a. ESP 1028 *Fugs*. Cover by Howard Bernstein   b. ESP 1030 Sonny Simmons, *Staying on the Watch*. Cover photo by Sandra Stollman   c. ESP 1032 *Sunny Murray*. Cover photo by Ray Gibson   d. ESP 2001 Cromagnon, *Cave Rock*. Cover by Howard Bernstein

Pharoah Sanders. Juan-les-Pins,
France, 1968. Photo by Guy
Kopelowicz

Paul Bley. Comblain, Belgium, 1968.
Photo by Guy Kopelowicz

Ornette Coleman, with Charlie Haden and Ed Blackwell. Bilzen, Belgium, 1969.
Photo by Guy Kopelowicz

Burton Greene. At Albert
Ayler's *Spirits Rejoice* session,
with the harpsichord that
Call Cobbs played on date.
New York, 1965.
Photo by Guy Kopelowicz

Gato Barbieri and Don Cherry. Recording session for Krzysztof Komeda's
soundtrack of Jerzy Skolimowski's film *Le Départ*. Paris, 1966. Photo by Guy
Kopelowicz

Charles Tyler. New York, 1967.
Photo by Guy Kopelowicz

Albert Ayler's *Spirits Rejoice*
session. New York, 1965.
Photo by Guy Kopelowicz

Donald Ayler. At Albert Ayler's *Spirits Rejoice* session. New York, 1965. Photo by Guy Kopelowicz

Sirone. In Pharoah Sanders's group. Juan-les-Pins, France, 1968. Photo by Guy Kopelowicz

Barbara Donald and Sonny Simmons. Central Park, New York, 1966. Photos by Sandra Stollman

Sonny Simmons. Krakow, Poland, 2005. Photo by Piotr Siatkowski/www.slojazz.net

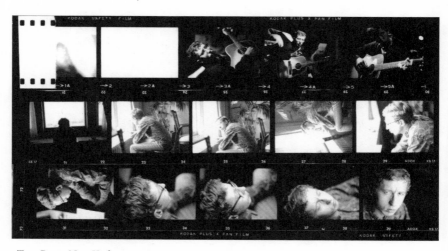

Tom Rapp. New York, 1967. Photos by Sandra Stollman

James Zitro. Big Sur, California, 1975.
Photo by Roland Hall

Cromagnon: Brian Elliot, Austin (Bob) Grasmere, and Sal Salgado. Staten Island Ferry, New York, 1969

William Parker. Krakow, Poland, 2009. Photo by Piotr Siatkowski

Frank Wright and Muhammad Ali. New York, 1969. Photo by Sandra Stollman

Booker Ervin, Jacques Coursil, and Frank Wright. New York, 1967. Photo by Guy Kopelowicz

Jacques Coursil.
New York, 2004.
Photo by Ramez Elias

Peter Stampfel

As half of the original Holy Modal Rounders, with Steve Weber, fiddler and banjo player Peter Stampfel showed a remarkable grasp of American old-time music and popular songs. The pair kept the music ever alive by having an uproarious time of it, plying mischievous twists in their delivery and providing new lyrics and new songs in the spirit of that noble strain of weirdness so prevalent in the tradition. They made two records for Prestige in 1963–64 and then joined the Fugs for that group's first Folkways album in 1965. In their brief second phase, with playwright Sam Shepard as drummer, in 1967 they made their only album for ESP, *Indian War Whoop*, their most far-out record (the relaunched label later issued the unreleased *Live in 65*). They regrouped again at the end of the decade, before the augmented band moved to Oregon in the 1970s without Stampfel, who stayed in New York but worked with the Rounders occasionally. In 1980 he took a full-time job, which he has held ever since: as submissions editor for the science fiction publisher DAW Books, founded by his wife's father. He has remained active as a musician, forming various bands, playing with guitarist Gary Lucas, and lately concocting the loosely tethered Ether Frolic Mob, with John Cohen (of the New Lost City Ramblers), Annabel Lee, and sometimes Sam Shepard.

How would you differentiate what the Holy Modal Rounders were up to from the New Lost City Ramblers and other folk revivalists? Didn't you also draw on Harry Smith's Anthology of American Folk Music *[1952] records?*

I heard bluegrass in '56 when I started college. I first heard the Ramblers in '58. I recognized what they were doing as what happened before bluegrass, and that suddenly seemed a lot more interesting than bluegrass. When I heard the Harry Smith anthology, I felt it was on me to keep all those—I assumed—totally dead people and the amazing tradition alive. Thousands of other people my age had precisely the same idea—like I needn't have bothered, it was well in hand. I first heard the anthology when I came to New York in '59. I went to the Café East, north of McSorley's, and somebody put volume 3 on the turntable. I, like, shit a brick. And the booklet that came with it was as cool as the music was, which was phenomenal.

Anyway, what made the Rounders different from the Ramblers is in 1963 I had the epiphany that what if you could bring the Smith anthology guys to the present, and they would still be the same age they were in the 1920s, and then what if you exposed them to rock and roll circa 1963? So, the idea of what those guys would do given the possibilities of rock and roll certainly seemed *way* more interesting than "let's do it like 1936 perfectly."

Were there any other cultural elements that contributed to the Rounders' style? Surrealism, the Marx Brothers?

Well, I try to steal from as many people as I possibly can. The Marx Brothers, definitely. And listening to the 1965 record, my voice while introducing a song is like I'm doing Dave Van Ronk doing W. C. Fields. We got it from the ancestors, like Dionysus, or Hermes—he invented the flat pick, the plectrum. And Krazy Kat. And Pogo. And Spike Jones. Like all the guys in the anthology. There was a mother lode of ancestors to follow in the footsteps of.

Were you at all friendly with Harry Smith?

He was the producer for the Fugs. But I met him once before that. It was like, Look, Harry Smith is over there. I was expecting this godlike human; he looked like a drunken Bowery bum basically. Long hair that hadn't been washed in God knows, and glasses with tape in the middle. I'm ashamed to say how off-putting I found his appearance, ashamed and embarrassed, but I wish I would have had some conversation with him. He had this whole system of recording. I didn't realize how into recording he was. I planned to write a series of songs that depicted the life of Harry Smith, which would be called the "Harry Smith Anthology." I did a lot of research, and I wrote one song, which is simply about his recording: "Harry recorded with a wire recorder back in World War II, / Harry recorded with a reel to reel when the reel to reel was new."

The musical orientation you describe, did you share that outlook with Steve Weber?

Antonia, my old lady, used to give me these Weber stories, and he sounded like this scary speed freak guy. Then I met him, in May '63, and my immediate thought was, this is my long-lost brother. And the first time we played music together, it was perfect. Then we took a bunch of speed and played for about three days, but I had gigs, so we'd go perform and then go back. Antonia's idea was for us to play together. She envisioned it; basically she planned to keep Weber off the streets. Weber had a lot to teach me, and I had a lot to teach Weber. By the third day of being up, Weber would go whack. We were on stage, and I played a bad note. He grimaced like I'd poked him in the eye and played this really bad discord. He played four more discords, each one worse than the one before, right on the beat, then screamed, leaped off the stage, and ran through the door. And as he started doing that, I just pushed my chair back, and so instantaneously he was out the door, and I was flat on my back on the stage, all in the space of a few beats. I thought, this is truly magic. So, a lot of it was automatic in terms of our styles.

How did you end up joining the Fugs?

Weber came over and said, "You should hear what Ed and Tuli are doing—'Coca-Cola Douche,' 'Bull Tongue Clit.'" Yeah, let's go! Only Ken [Weaver] had drums. So, it was like, Hey, you need a backup band! It was like a big playpen. It was really fucking great. But Weber started getting really crazy, and he missed three jobs in a row. At which point I declared, fuck it, I don't want to play with them anymore. So, I stupidly quit playing with the Fugs at the same time; it was an extreme reaction. I had been playing with them for about eight months, between the fall of '64 and July '65.

Do you think you and Weber affected the Fugs' sound at all?

Not that much. It was basically like watching what was going on. If we would've played with them longer, we would have. But it was still just so interesting to watch by itself that I really didn't have any inclination toward offering any direction yet. I was totally in backup mode and enjoying it thoroughly.

How did you first become aware of the ESP label? Was it through the Fugs?

Well, me and Antonia stayed up most of the summer of 1966 taking shitloads of speed, and we were three months behind on our rent come September, and

Bernard Stollman called up out of the blue and said that this ESP record that I was on, the first songs [*The Fugs First Album*], was on the charts. He wanted to give me $180, which was exactly three months rent. So, that's the first I heard of Bernard.

That money was the royalties for your part on the first Fugs record reissued from Folkways?

Yeah, royalties or whatever. That, however, was the last money I ever saw from any of those albums. Then, in 1967, Stollman said he wanted to record the Holy Modal Rounders. One of the reasons that we broke up was, after Weber realized that we had some sort of a chance at a relative degree of success, he refused to work out new songs. He would go into tirades about it on stage. We had rehearsals, but he refused to do anything. I was playing with Sam Shepard at the time, and so the three of us went into the studio and basically made the record cold, which is why it's kind of a mess, *Indian War Whoop*.

Since the Rounders had already split up, what made you two decide to do a record for ESP?

Because I wanted to make another record, and he offered the three of us $150 apiece. That was like two months' rent. What happened was that he stiffed Sam—he paid me and everybody, but he never paid Sam. And he wouldn't let Sam be on the album cover, because it was the Summer of Love, and Sam had cut his hair into a crew cut, as a gesture. So, Bernard wouldn't let Sam be on the album cover because he didn't have the right hair. Can you imagine how cool it would have been to have a picture of a twenty-four-year-old Sam Shepard with a crew cut in 1967? Anyway, the years went on, and the album got released in Italy and Switzerland and all over the place, and years later we said, "Gee, how come we never got any royalties?" And he said, "Well, didn't you read the contract? The contract says that all rights belong to me. You have no royalties ever, ever, ever. The publishing is mine. You don't own the songs anymore. We don't owe you anything." And then he explained that he had to do that because whenever you get a hit record, the Mafia would make bootlegs of them and ship their bootlegs instead of his. And therefore it was "too bad, guys, but because of that I have to rip you totally off."

How long did it take to make the record?

About a week. I stupidly didn't go to the mixing session. I didn't realize at the time that it was really necessary to do that, and he [Richard Alderson] got the idea of no grooves between the songs, which was just to make it extra easy for the DJ, if anyone does have an inclination to play the record. When we made the Elektra album [*The Moray Eels Eat the Holy Modal Rounders*, 1968], I played them the ESP record and said, "See what a mess this is? That's because Weber wouldn't rehearse. You've got to force us to rehearse or else it's going to sound like this." And he [Frazier Mohawk] had the same idea of a record with no grooves between the songs!

But listening to the CD version of the ESP record, it almost sounds like a concept album, because of the radio theater elements to it. Whose idea was that?

Basically we recorded a bunch of shit, and a lot of it was improvised fucking around, and then Richard just sort of ran with it.

And the radio theater aspect, was that done during the record or after?

Weber was doing some speed rapping, along with the music. Like spoken word and music, him talking with an attendant musical accompaniment.

Bernard wrote that you were dismayed by the results, whereas Steve Weber felt differently.

"Dismay" is an accurate word. Although, I heard a bit of the album a couple of months ago—I'd only listened to the album a handful of times—and I found it a lot more tolerable than I had considered it. There's a number of cuts that are really okay, like "The I.W.W. Song" and "Bay Rum Blues."

What was the response from listeners?

The consensus was "Oh God, these guys have really lost it. Off the deep end, too bad."

I read that Weber was taking speed and that you had taken acid during that recording session.

No, I never recorded on acid. Performed at Carnegie Hall on acid with the Rounders, in 1970. Not the brightest idea, but it was fun. During the ESP recording, both Weber and I were on speed and pot. Sam was clean. By the way, the first two Prestige albums were recorded on speed and pot.

Did people warm up to the record in later years?

Yeah, a lot of people would say, "But I like that record! What do you mean?" One guy said some mornings, when he didn't want to go to work, he would get up and play that record and then not go to work, and it was great! Music to not go to work by.

How did the Rounders end up playing with Sam Shepard at that time?

Carol Hunter, who played banjo and guitar, had just been to this university in Illinois in 1966, and she said they would pay the Holy Modal Rounders three hundred dollars and plane fare if we'd play there. That was a lot of money. So I asked Weber whether he'd do it for the money. Yeah. I'd pawned my fiddle to buy speed, so I had to get my fiddle. I went to the pawn shop, and I'm there with my fiddle. This guy said, "Hey, are you a bass player?" It was Sam. He'd been playing drums behind this guy called the Heavy Metal Kid, and they needed a bass player. So that's how we started playing together. We played together until 1969, with Antonia. I wasn't playing with Weber except for that one gig in Illinois and making the album in 1967, until the Elektra guy wanted to make the album, and I said, "Okay, if I can play with my band," which was the Moray Eels. And then after, we decided to all get together again.

Did any of this work mix in with Shepard's playwriting?

Oh yeah. He wrote *Operation Sidewinder* when we were in California, and he thought that a lot of the songs really fit into the play, so we actually performed when the play was at the Vivian Beaumont Theater in 1970. By that time he'd been offered a gig writing a movie for the Rolling Stones, so he quit the band.

But Robin Remailly did music for one of Sam's plays, and I was friends with Lothar and the Hand People, and some of them wrote music for his plays as well.

How did the record Live in 65 *come about, which ESP released just in recent years?*

The way that came about is my mom died. I was looking through her effects, and on a reel-to-reel tape—one of my regrets about the Rounders in the early days is that there were no extant recordings, and here was a live performance taken from the radio in Detroit in early 1965. We owed Gene Rosenthal, of Adelphi, an album because Rounder was going to record the Holy Modal Rounders in 1976 when they were on the East Coast for a funeral. My manager lined it all up and then Rounder reneged once we started recording. Adelphi agreed to release the recording with the stipulation that we make an album for him, just me and Weber. So we owed him an album. And there was a party, at which he was there and Weber was there, and Weber's girlfriend, Judith, was there. I brought a rough of the CD that a guy made of the recording and played it there, and then Weber and Judith said, "We didn't hear it. Can we take it with us?" And like a total fool I said sure. This is like '02—my mom died in '01. So, what happened was they took the album to Bernard Stollman, and Stollman said, "It's about time that you give Weber a turn. Because you're always the guy that's arranging things." So, they stole the record. I went to a lawyer to see if I could stop them—they stole my dead mother's tape!—and the guy said if there aren't any original songs that haven't been recorded before on it, then no one legally owns it and finder's keepers. I found out that Runt, a West Coast distributor, paid Bernard seven thousand dollars to print up a bunch of copies, and they took a bunch of albums for their cut basically, and sold them. Weber and I never saw a single penny. So, I am deeply upset about all this.

Burton Greene

Raised in Chicago, classically trained pianist Burton Greene arrived in New York in 1962 and quickly found his way into the new music scene. A member of the Jazz Composers Guild, he made his first record (*Burton Greene Quartet*) for ESP in December 1965, with Marion Brown. Around that time, he also played on half of Patty Waters's first date, the startling "Black Is the Color of My True Love's Hair." The next spring, his new trio was part of ESP's New York State college tour, resulting in another record, *On Tour*. In 1969 he went off to Paris where he recorded an album for the BYG label and worked on dates by Jacques Coursil and Archie Shepp and played the festival in Amougies; the next year, he settled in Amsterdam, where he has lived ever since, mostly on a houseboat. Among his many projects in improvised and composed music, he began to explore his Eastern European Jewish roots and in the late 1980s cofounded the band Klezmokum; still active, and including his old friend clarinetist Perry Robinson, the group draws on klezmer, Sephardic, Balkan, and jazz traditions.

How did you first meet Alan Silva, with whom you created the Free Form Improvisation Ensemble in 1963?

He put an ad in the *Village Voice*, "people looking for a cosmic solution to life and artistic pursuits," etc., etc. I was staying, at the time, on 72nd Street and looking to get out of there any way I could. I saw the ad, and there was a piano on the upper floor—that was all I had to hear; I was over there in a minute. We worked out with the Free Form group continuously. We practically lived together; the other guys were over at the house [419 Cumberland Street, in Brooklyn] all the time. So, we really got to second-guess each other. It was second nature.

How long did that band exist?

We did it for two and a half years. We only had maybe ten, twelve concerts, that's all—for maybe fifty people—but we got some recognition. And a review.

He came all the way up to Harlem, to a coffee shop, where there were five people including the waitress, and he loved it. He compared it to really contemporary music; he didn't put us in a jazz bag. He was an important *Voice* classical critic actually—Leighton Kerner. He gave us half a page. The thing about that band was we all came out of different disciplines. We didn't have a bag; we were just open for anything to come out. So, he caught that right away, that it was just an open thing. It was as much classical forms happening, European stuff—which I've always had a penchant for in my music—as jazz or folklore. There were no boxes; we had a stream of consciousness.

Had you yourself been doing anything like that before?

No. I felt like that direction. What happened was we met in a church basement where they had an old grand piano down there. It was Alan's concept in the beginning because he already had a band. We were going to discuss about living in the apartment. I told him I was a pianist and I like improv, so he invited me down, and I saw what those guys were doing. I looked at them and smiled, and I said to Alan, "I guess we don't need a script, do we?" That's how it all started. We never talked about the music for two and half years. What's interesting is, we were looking for some new directions and Gary Friedman composed a piece, so-called graphic simple stuff (and he always felt a little guilty about that). He said maybe that was the beginning of the end of the band, because he brought in an actual composed piece ["Eat Eat," third track of 1964 perfor-mances later issued by Cadence Records in 2000].

How did you come into contact with Bernard Stollman and the ESP label?

The grapevine was very clear in those days. As soon as somebody said some-body was recording this crazy music, everybody knew who Bernard was. He contacted me, because he thought I would be a good accompanist for Patty Waters, so that worked out. That was actually some months before he recorded my quartet. Patty came up to my loft, and she was doing a kind of Nina Simone thing at the time; she kept doing these ballads. Then at one point—I had this garbage can cover that I found in the alley behind Katz's Delicatessen on Hous-ton Street—I thought, Why don't you do it with the garbage can cover? It's got a nice warp in it. What would that sound like on the strings? I was already putting in golf balls, bottles of water, all kinds of shit, to see what the sounds would be like in the piano.

Anyway, Patty kept going on with the ballad routine. I thought, this chick is sitting on a big egg; this egg is going to be some kind of monster, and I've got to help her hatch that egg. So, at about the fourth or fifth ballad, I dropped the garbage can cover. "My God, Burton, what are you doing?!" I said, "Well, what are you going to do with it?" She was playing around with the idea of "Black Is the Color," this old minstrel song, and then she got galvanized somehow. She just went out on the word *black* and curdled everybody's blood. Artists are the real newspaper. You don't get it in the *New York Times* or the *Village Voice*; you get it from the artists, and she curdled everybody's blood with her primordial scream on "Black Is the Color." It was *things to come* right around the corner, six months before Watts, Newark, the riots, Detroit; this was heralding the whole thing.

Did you play that piece together a number of times before recording it?

Yeah, we practiced a few times, as I recall. We got a kind of shape to it. Because she was quite shy and reticent, I just pushed her a little bit, and the inside the piano stuff certainly helped. It's the first extended free vocal solo on a record.

How did you choose the musicians on your first ESP record?

That was my first quartet, just after the Jazz Composers Guild, with Marion Brown, and Henry Grimes. I was working with Rashied [Ali] on a few gigs, but Rashied got busy with Coltrane at that moment, so I used Dave Grant. We all knew each other; we played jams and different things. I thought Marion was a brilliant alto player. It was a pleasure to work with him. And after all this time, Porter Records is putting out a quartet from that same period, a gig we did in Woodstock with Rashied, before he went with Trane [*Live 1965* was released in March 2010].

How long did you work with Marion Brown, and where did you go from there?

From '65 to '66 maybe, then I did some trio stuff. Then the New York State Council on the Arts tour. In '68, I started working with Byard Lancaster, on the record we made at Columbia Records, and after that, with Sam Rivers before I left the States. We did a bunch of gigs with Sam.

What do you recall about the recording session for that first quartet date?

We just went in and did it, one or two takes. That's all there was time for. There were three-hour sessions in those days; that was it. Richard Alderson was the engineer; he was on the case. The last piece was totally spontaneous, with Frank Smith, that was a ball—"Taking It Out of the Ground."

How had your music developed by that time since the group with Alan Silva?

The quartet was the first time I had a venue where I could really present my own compositions. The Free Form Improvisation Ensemble was exactly that; the whole thing was collective, and it was all spontaneous. Now I was finally getting a chance to notate some basic stuff and have it played. I've always been a composer, but in that first period I just let all the notes go, and I was grateful for that. Because when I was a kid, a whole bunch of piano players of my generation who had classical training got hit in the hands when we didn't read the music fast enough. After the twentieth time that the Prussian teacher I had hit me in the hands with the ruler, I thought, I'm going to use my ears from now on if I want to play music. So, of course my option was jazz.

How did it affect your composing after having done the completely free stuff?

Everything helps everything else. Years later in Europe, I had kind of a nervous breakdown after all the tumult in New York, and after that I couldn't play the screaming stuff anymore. I started noodling ragas and working in a group called East-West Trio, ten years before they called it world music: piano, a bongos and conga player from New York—Daoud Amin—and Jamaluddin Bhartiya, a great Indian sitar player; we all met in Amsterdam. And I realized, playing these five- or seven-note scales continuously, but with all kinds of variations or sliding off the minor ninth to get the so-called quarter-tone feel, I realized that when I was younger doing all this free stuff, a lot of it was collage. I was jumping from one thing to the next without really "milking the cow," so to speak, or milking a phrase. With the sitar master from India, I had to milk the phrase. He would sometimes try to get me to do five notes for two hours if necessary. But after I stopped rebelling with my ego and went along with it, I started hearing the way the spaces really worked. So, working with the microcosm I understood the macrocosm much better. And how to get much more out of a phrase, how to sustain things. And you would hear that. When we were young, we were full of testosterone and piss and vinegar, and we just let it all out in this healthy scream. But we could have said a lot more with a lot less if we were pacing ourselves. I remember hearing Pharoah [Sanders], for example, with Coltrane in '67. Pharoah would get up and blow for twenty minutes. It was fantastic, but then Trane would quietly get up and do the same thing as Pharoah did in eight minutes, instead of twenty. He encapsulated the whole thing. That really made an impression on me.

On the ESP college tour in the spring of 1966, what schools did you visit? Who was there?

They were six or seven schools upstate—Syracuse, Ithaca College, Utica, I don't remember them all. That was the first State Council of the Arts tour that Bernard helped organize. He asked me to emcee it. We traveled on a bus: Sun Ra was on it, and Ran Blake, Patty Waters, Giuseppi Logan. I was so happy to see Giuseppi the other night. The feeling was mutual; we hadn't seen each other in forty-two years [April 6, 2009, at The Local 269, on East Houston Street in Manhattan: the Burton Greene/Perry Robinson Duo played on the same bill as the Giuseppi Logan Quartet].

What was the audience response at those college tour concerts?

Well, kids are much more open than adults. They really enjoyed it, I think. People were astonished, because they had no idea what they were going to get into. It was all so new at the time, shocking to some people. But kids are more resilient. They don't have preconceptions; they're less judgmental. Today it's still that way. The younger they are, the less judgmental they are. If they don't feel aggressive and angry vibes, they go along with all kinds of stuff. I had a workshop two days ago at the Longy School of Music, with Perry Robinson. We did some pretty way-out stuff and they were right there with it.

How soon did the relationship with ESP begin to sour?

In the beginning, everybody laughed and realized Bernard was just as nutty as we were to do this music. Nobody expected anybody to get any money out of the deal. So, I personally cut him some slack for twenty or twenty-five years, but it just went on. Every time I heard he leased or rereleased the stuff to half a dozen companies like ZYX and Abraxas, I wondered about royalties. I said, "What's going on?" He said, "Well, they burned me, they burned me." I said, "Look, Bernard, you were not born yesterday. You're Jewish, you're from New York, you're not from Podunk, Iowa. Give me a break—you're a lawyer on top of it. I mean, I can understand you've been screwed a few times, but after that, screw them! Now we're getting screwed." So, I guess around 1990 or '95, I just ran out of patience. And I'll be honest about it, I was even thinking of a class-action suit because he kept ignoring me, saying, "Well, I never made any money on it." I said, "Bernard, you paid me sixty-four dollars for that record date. Give me a break." When I got high-speed Internet, and I looked my name up on Google, I said, My God, man, there's twenty pages at least on Burton Greene. How's it possible? I didn't have a gig at the moment, but there were twenty pages on me. And nineteen pages were about all the rereleases of ESP! I said, Oh, come on now. And here, I finally got a check thanks to Tom Abbs. He turned Bernard around, I guess. There were some other people who were getting irate too, but a lot of people were apathetic—it happened forty years ago, forget it. So, it's starting to happen. People are getting paid, and I appreciate the intention.

The fact that the ESP label has been relaunched in recent years, and that your first record was reissued, what does that mean for you?

Of course, it's always flattering to an artist to know his music lives on, that his music is still in demand. There is a basic value to what we did forty years ago, and there's a value to it now. That transcendental kind of timelessness, I think every artist tries for that if he's serious. Real art should have endurance, as far as I'm concerned. So, in that sense it's great that it keeps coming out again, that it showed there was validity in the first place that would renew itself.

After all these years of living abroad in Amsterdam, do you have a sense of something gained for you musically or personally remaining at a distance from the American music scene?

All experience that you have—wherever you are, Timbuktu, I don't care—if your eyes and ears are open, if your heart is open, you just gain so much. You enrich yourself. It's not a particular place or location. It's the enriching process. It makes the bouquet just that much brighter. And as you mature, you pace yourself more, and you use all of it. A painter gets a richer palette, that's all.

I come back at least once a year. Maybe you're asking about the rough edges, the things that drove me out of America in the first place. They don't bother me so much anymore—the big hustle in America, and the greed and the avarice. I just bypass it.

When you do come back, do you feel any cultural gap?

No, not at all. Even if I'm not playing very much in Holland because of the mafioso kind of atmosphere over there at the moment where they're just giving work to the same guys, I have all the time I need: I own my houseboat. I'm not hassled. I have a grand piano. I can practice when I want, and I have a lot of time to write music. If I was continually hustling and bustling in New York, who has the time to do that? I have time to nurture these things, and grow with them, because I'm not under the gun. The music is not harried or rushed, and I bring it over here when it's full-blown and play it, even if it's for twenty people in a Lower East Side bar. It works for me.

But I would like to get another place within half an hour or so from Manhattan. My problem in Holland is I've become a local schmocal. I've got to get out of there more often to perform my music. A lot of people in Holland (or Europe for that matter) don't have a clue what I've been doing in the last twenty-five years. Ideally, I'd like to spend half the year over here, half the year over there.

The Coach with the Six Insides
Jean Erdman and Van Dexter

A comedy in three acts, *The Coach with the Six Insides* premiered on November 26, 1962, at the brand new Village South Theater (now the Soho Playhouse) in Manhattan. Inspired by James Joyce's *Finnegans Wake* and adapted, staged, and choreographed by Jean Erdman, with music by Teiji Ito, it ran for 114 performances, then toured the world: the Spoleto festival in '63; Paris; two weeks in Dublin; British Columbia; and Hawaii. Invited by film director Hiroshi Teshigahara, it spent four weeks in Tokyo in '64, where the cast was feted at every turn. In a newspaper review, Yukio Mishima praised the performance as a "miraculous happening," calling it "an endless flow of beautiful movement and an elaborate work of fusion of dance, music, words and mime." Between 1964 and '67, the show did three tours of the United States, mostly at colleges and universities.

A sound recording of *The Coach with the Six Insides* was made for ESP in 1966, with its original cast: Jean Erdman as Anna Livia Plurabelle, Anita Dangler as Wife and Charwoman, Sheila Roy as Daughter, Leonard Frey as Elder Son (Shaun), and Van Dexter as Younger Son (Shem). Its final run was in 1966–67 at the East 74th Street Theatre in New York (where a still-unknown Peter Max offered to design a poster for the production). The show was later revived twice at the Theater of the Open Eye, cofounded by Erdman and Joseph Campbell, starting with a year-long run in 1979. The cast was different, and Erdman shared the role of Anna Livia Plurabelle with dancer Leslie Dillingham, while Teiji Ito again performed the music along with accordionist Guy Klucevsek and violinist Fumiko Wellington.

Jean Erdman

Though best known for *The Coach with the Six Insides*, dancer and choreographer Jean Erdman already had her own company by then for twenty years, after five years in Martha Graham's company. She had often worked with John Cage and other modern composers and taught extensively as well. Married to Joseph Campbell for forty-nine years, they moved part-time to her native Honolulu in the 1980s, where she has lived exclusively since 1995. At the time of this interview, she was ninety-three years old: I had sent her a copy of the ESP recording to help refresh her failing memory, but we could not get very far.

Why did you decide to adapt James Joyce's work for the stage? Considering how difficult the book is, what drew you to it?

It was one of my husband's favorite books, and when he was writing [with Henry Morton Robinson] *A Skeleton Key to* Finnegans Wake [1944], he would read to me out loud everything he was writing. So, that's how I found out about *Finnegans Wake*. I probably couldn't have understood it if I had read it by myself. That's the book you need: then you have an enjoyment instead of a feeling of desperation trying to figure out what it's all about.

How did you make your selections from the text in building your theater piece? Did he help you?

I would make the choices, and then I'd ask him if they fit right. He'd sometimes say yes, and sometimes no, so he'd help me out whenever I needed it. It's so long ago that I can't remember the details.

The composer Teiji Ito did the music on a number of your pieces. How did you work with him on The Coach with the Six Insides?

Oh, gosh, it happened so long ago. All I know is that whenever I wanted to have advice, I would ask him, and whenever I was trying to find out how to get what I wanted, I would ask him.

It must have been tricky taking a work that was so multidimensional, with actors and dancers, and then go into a recording studio and just do a sound version.

Well, of course it was tricky, but we did it. And that was lucky.

Van Dexter

Arriving in New York in 1945, Van Dexter studied acting at HB Studio on Sixth Avenue with Herbert Berghof, Eli Wallach, and Lee Grant; musical comedy with Charles Nelson Reilly; and later mime with Etienne Decroux and Jacques Lecoq. By the time he met Jean Erdman, he had been working for years in Off-Broadway theater (and in the early '50s, while working his day job at Whelan's lunch counter, he steered a young Steve McQueen into acting). After The Coach with the Six Insides, he formed his own nine-member Commedia dell'arte company for three years. During that time he produced, directed, and booked the shows, along with helping to design the costumes and scenery and understudying the lead. He remained active in theater from 1955 to 1985, took a twenty-year sabbatical, and then returned to acting, doing commercials, light opera, and background work in film. He also ran a vintage toy store, Second Childhood, in Greenwich Village, which closed in 2008 after nearly forty years. He was eighty-nine at the time of this interview.

How did you get involved with The Coach with the Six Insides?

I looked in *Billboard* one day, and there was a notice for actors and singers who had some dance training and mime. That was perfect for me. I went to audition. They were on 14th Street between Fifth and Sixth Avenue. Jean Erdman said, "You were our very first choice." They hired a young actor, Leonard Frey [later famous as Motel the Tailor in *Fiddler on the Roof*], his very first professional engagement. They had Sheila Roy, Anita Dangler, and later on Gail Ryan and Michael Prince, but they jumped in as understudies. Equity gave her a dispensation to hire four people at thirty-five dollars a week, and we took about a year to get it together. We never had a complete script. She would bring in a few lines, and we would improvise. There's a complete script somewhere. But have you ever tried to understand James Joyce's writing? Since Jean Erdman was married to Joseph Campbell, he explained everything to us. "Van," he said, "don't worry about it. Just get your mind blank up there, because one word can be four or five different things." So we were always ad-libbing it, to keep the performance fresh.

Were you all involved in developing the piece?

Yes. I did most of my work myself, with Jean. I'm a mime. We did about ten different people, animals and whatnot. Each actor had a number of parts. I played the younger son—and I was older than Frey. He was twenty-two and I was forty-two, but he played the older son.

Didn't you also have a hand in other visual elements?

I made all the props. And I made Finnegan's costume.

How did the sound elements come into play? How did Teiji Ito develop his music?

He improvised a lot too. He followed the lead of what we were doing, what she was doing. We were all involved.

Just listening to the audio version of the piece, the orchestration of voices is very striking and there are a lot of different sounds. How did that develop?

From the very beginning, Jean said, "Do some kind of animal voices, crickets, insects." We helped her with that. Bird calls. And it worked out very well.

In developing the work, were you all drawing on a common theatrical tradition?

You could do anything you wanted to do. You were free to improvise and create.

Was this piece much of a departure for you, with regard to your theatrical background?

I did a lot of Off-Broadway work in the early '50s. I also toured in *Stalag 17* in 1954, in the Catskills, with Shelly Berman and Martin Landau. I had a hell of a time getting my Equity card. I've done everything but grand opera, and Broadway, and vaudeville. I've done Shakespeare too.

The ESP recording of Coach was made in 1966. The show had toured extensively since its first production in 1962. Did you do much else in those years?

I was working part-time for Whelan's drugstore as a soda jerk. I was studying voice, studying mime, and acting. But I never missed a performance. I missed one rehearsal in all that time; I slipped a disk in my back.

How was it decided to end the show at the time of its last production in 1967?

It had started to fall down, because Jean left. Her understudy took over, and I couldn't believe that. She was like the mother figure, and she went to California.

We felt like we were being abandoned! It started to trickle down, trickle down, the performances and the audience. Then one night, between the first and the second act the manager came over, and I said, We can't do that. This should be our final performance. I refused to go any further. We had an understudy ready to go, and my Commedia dell'arte troupe was about to open its own show.

Do you recall much about the actual making of the record for ESP?

It was a new experience for me doing a record. It had the original cast. We just jumped in and did it. We were so adept at the dialogue; we could have done it in our sleep. Maybe a dozen copies of the record sold, I don't know.

Leo Feigin

A Soviet émigré to London in the 1970s, Leo Feigin founded Leo Records in 1979, a label for "the inquiring mind and the passionate heart." By now, it has released more than five hundred titles of improvised music, introducing to Western audiences innovators like the Ganelin Trio, Sergey Kuryokhin, and Sainkho Namchylak, while offering significant work by Western artists such as Cecil Taylor, Sun Ra, Anthony Braxton, and Evan Parker.

I first became aware of ESP when I lived in the USSR. At the end of the 1960s, a friend of ours showed us an LP that was pressed on transparent vinyl with music on one side only. That record was *Bells*, by Albert Ayler. The music was absolutely shattering. By that time, we were listening to Impulse and Blue Note records, but this was something else, absolutely shocking!

At that time, you could buy foreign LPs on the black market. An LP used to cost about half a month's salary, but the main source for getting records was foreign friends who would bring LPs into the Soviet Union. We had a pretty wide circle of record collectors, so we used to exchange and swap LPs with each other.

There were rumors that Stollman did not pay musicians for their recording. However, I honestly believe that musicians should erect a monument to him. It was difficult to sell those LPs, because nobody wanted to buy them. Bernard Stollman was investing and losing his money on producing the recordings, and he deserves a lot of credit.

Erica Pomerance

For many years now, Erica Pomerance has been known as a documentary filmmaker based in her native Montreal. But in the '60s and '70s, she was just as active working as a singer-songwriter. In December 1968, on one of her extended visits to New York, ESP produced her only record, *You Used to Think*, a stylistic amalgam of folk, jazz, Eastern inflections, and rock. Fresh from a stay in Paris during the student uprisings, she was attuned to movements for change both at home and abroad, along with the hopes and disappointments of a generation.

Were you aware of the ESP label before coming to New York?

These friends of mine made a record for ESP before I did, Bruce Mackay and Tanya Mackay—both eventually became filmmakers as well. Then I went down to New York and somehow bumped into Bernard Stollman, who heard me sing at a café in Greenwich Village. I ended up becoming a member on staff at ESP. I would work in the office; at the same time he was preparing me to make an album, because he thought that the stuff I was doing was original. I had been performing for years. I was a Joan Baez clone and actually was friendly with Joan Baez. I had seen her in California and met her in Montreal because a friend of my father's was an impresario here who brought in many famous folk and other performers. Because I sang her songs so well and looked so much like her, he arranged for me to meet her after a concert that she gave here. So, when I was in New York, I was sort of hooked into the folk and blues scene.

As office jobs go, working at the label must have been a little unusual.

It was a way for me to keep living in New York, because I had this cockroach-infested apartment in the East Village. My friend Richie Heisler, who was on the album with me, we were hanging out together and playing music and doing hippie things in those days. So, I was on some kind of stipend for a couple of months working at ESP, classing albums and shuffling papers and taking phone calls, basically being an office girl. The office was in a building downtown, and I used to go there every day. Musicians would breeze through, and we'd meet all the jazz musicians. It was really kind of an exciting place to be for me. That area was the heart of the folk music scene too. I met Izzy Young. He had the Folklore Center and a radio program on WBAI, and I would be on that program occasionally. Eventually my recording date came up, and we went into the studio.

Had you visited New York before?

I was like an adopted New Yorker. I had started coming down to New York on vacations when I was about thirteen or fourteen. I'd gone to a summer camp for progressive Jews and met some friends from New York.

Was music your main artistic outlet in the '60s, or were you already interested in film?

I was developing both interests at the same time. When I was in Montreal, I worked for a film company and after Expo 67 the money died down for small independent production companies. When I lost my job, I went to Paris. A lot of the songs on that ESP record reflect my stint in Paris during the student uprisings that became May '68. I had a very exciting time in Paris. I was actually holed up in the Sorbonne with all these students and singing. They considered me an anarchist, because the place was dominated by sort of left-wing communist trade union people who didn't like anarchists, people like me who were part of that new generation. My song "The French Revolution" was about that, because I was right in the thick of it. I was there when young people would go out at night—they called them the Amazons—women and guys that used to go throw cobblestones at the CRS, the police. I came back for a short while to Montreal, then I went to New York and started to work for ESP. I had been singing and involved in filmmaking, and I painted. I was one of these all-around artistic people who couldn't find one true vocation. In those days, there wasn't so much pressure on you to professionalize immediately, to start earning a living. So, I was kind of an eternal bohemian, and I just kept doing things that interested me.

When you were doing folk music in Montreal, did you know people like the McGarrigle Sisters?

The McGarrigles were actually quite close friends of mine. We don't see each other that much in Montreal now, but my daughter and Kate's kids, Rufus and Martha, kind of grew up together. Kate and Anna, and the musicians they played with, that whole group was part of my McGill experience. I was part of the McGill Folk Music Society. We used to host people like Sonny [Terry] and Brownie [McGhee], the Fugs, Frank Zappa, and we'd hang out with them. And of course Leonard Cohen, who was still not really well known for his music until '67. But he was sort of a star in the bohemian circles that I hung out with in Montreal; he was a good friend.

Wasn't the French-Canadian music scene also beginning to blossom in Montreal at that time?

Exactly. With Gilles Vigneault—I know him because my girlfriend dated him, and he was an influence, as well as performers like Claude Gauthier and Monique Leyrac. There were lots of *chansonniers* who were coming out with a very *québécois* message and style of music, and that influenced me to start performing in French. After that record, I performed almost uniquely in Quebec, French songs in French coffee houses. I really switched my career into French.

Was there much overlap culturally between the two linguistic communities?

In those days, there was a movement, *McGill français*, to open McGill up to French reality. The divide in the city—created by the religious school boards, Catholic and Protestant—had kept the French and the English separate. The Jews were stuck in the middle because most of our parents had grown up in French-Canadian neighborhoods, but there had been a love-hate relationship in a way, because of Catholics insulting Jews. And then during Nazi Germany there was a whole anti-Jewish wing of fascist French-Canadians. But my father, who'd been a left-winger, my parents had lots of French-Canadian left-wing intellectual friends, so I was disposed to be open.

Did ESP's troubles with the bootlegs affect your record when it was made at the end of 1968?

See, I never knew anything about that. I was living such a tumultuous personal life, breaking away from my family to establish my own identity. The minute after the record was pressed, I with my little group of friends, most of whom had played on the record, off we went to Mexico and stayed there for a few months, so I had no idea what was going on. The record actually was released when we were in Paradise Island, at a yoga camp, then we went to Mexico from there. I remember being at Bernard Stollman's farm in Woodstock the next year, and he was talking about Jimi Hendrix coming up to do some kind of session. It all sounded very exciting. But I did get the feeling that he was trying to start something new and move the focus out to the farm.

Another artist from the ESP catalog whom I became friendly with is Marion Brown. He was in Paris when I was there, so I got to know a bit about the jazz side of ESP through him. We had common friends. He and I ended up going for a weekend to visit François Morellet, who was a famous French artist and a friend of my parents; he was also a friend of Marion's, so they invited us both to their château *sur la Loire*. We didn't talk too much about ESP, because he was an exiled American jazz musician in Paris. He was doing quite well and playing a lot at the American Center. The poet Lee Bridges was also there, who was a friend of Marion's. I put one of his poems to music, "Burn, Baby, Burn."

For your ESP record, how did you choose the other musicians besides Richard Heisler?

Some were people Richie or Gail Pollard knew; some were people I knew in New York. There were some takes with Sonny Greenwich, which we didn't end up using; he was a friend of mine from Montreal. Basically, the whole record was just a jam session, although Richie and I, and Gail to some extent, had practiced the songs. Gail played sitar, and Richie played guitar and sang with me. He had a big influence on me in those days. Some stuff I just improvised. It was a horrible night when we did the recording. There was a sleet storm, and we almost didn't make it because we were out looking for a taxi to get there. We finally made it to the studio a bit late.

How much did you plan the material for the record?

I had prepared most of the songs. There had been a previous session where I recorded two songs, and then we redid them that night. Just a couple of things were improvised, where there was the basic lyrics and then I'd take off, like on "We Came Via." "Koanisphere" and "Anything Goes" were totally improvised—the lyrics too, we just made them up as we went along—but everything else was songs written that I'd been performing in Paris and in the States, and in the coffee houses in Greenwich Village. On that record I was looking for something very experimental in my style—and I had a huge cold as well, so my vocals got a little growly.

On the record you acknowledge Alan Silva and Becky Friend, among others. Why?

Because we had done a first take of "You Used to Think" and "The French Revolution" with Sonny Greenwich and them. Then we didn't use those takes. It had a different feel; it was much more controlled. We went with the second versions, so I thanked them for their work.

How does the record relate overall to your work in music?

I sang for a long time publicly, mostly in Quebec. I was sort of well known regionally, but mostly in French-Canadian circles—there are a lot of people in Quebec that remember seeing me. But nobody knew about this record. It was never played on the CBC; it never was distributed in Canada. I've done a little recording with Radio Canada singing French québécois songs that I composed, and quite a few Acadian musicians have recorded one of my songs—"Pêcher aux Iles de la Madeleine" [Fishing on the Magdalen Islands], which is an adaptation of a song I learned when I was living there, sort of a folk song that I made into a regional hit. It's in the Cajun style of music. But then I gravitated toward documentary film, because I've always been doing the two, and this is basically what's taken off for me. I've made quite a few films involving music, a lot of which is African or Haitian music, documenting the experience of the diaspora musicians who've moved to Montreal. And I go frequently to Mali and to Senegal. I'm now developing a film about a Haitian musician and dancer connected with voodoo culture. She goes back to West Africa looking for the roots of her own musical inspiration, by looking at the music and the dance and the cult to Mami Wata, who is the goddess of water and who is prevalent in many West African cultures. So, a lot of my interest now is still in music, and I manage to incorporate it into some of the films I do. But I do mostly social issue films. I've been working a lot in the Canadian Native communities for many years; most of my stuff goes on APTN [Aboriginal Peoples Television Network].

Joe Morris

Mostly self-taught, Joe Morris took up the guitar at the age of fourteen, in 1969, and gradually developed a very personal aesthetic as a free improviser. Along the way, living in Boston, he became friendly with the radically original pianist/composer Lowell Davidson, whose only record (*Trio*) was made for ESP in 1965. Through the 1980s, Morris worked extensively with Davidson, whose ideas had a lasting importance for him; this can be heard most directly in the record that Morris made in a trio with John Voigt and Tom Plsek (also longtime Davidson collaborators), *MVP LSD* (2008), based on Davidson's graphic scores. That date was released by Morris's own label, Riti, founded in 1983, though he has recorded for many labels and with a long list of improvisers. On October 4, 2008, playing bass (which he took up in 2000) as part of the Flow Trio, with tenor saxophonist Louie Belogenis and drummer Charles Downs, he made *Rejuvenation* for the relaunched ESP. A week after this interview, on May 12, 2009, back on guitar with his own trio, he also recorded *Colorfield*, released by ESP in the fall of that year. He subsequently made *Camera* for ESP, recorded on April 3, 2010, playing guitar and leading a quartet that included violin, cello, and drums.

What was your first exposure to the ESP label?

The first thing was the Fugs, because when I was a kid in New Haven, in the early '70s, I had a lot of friends who were into Frank Zappa and edgy kind of rock. The Fugs played in New Haven a couple of times. And from that, I heard Albert Ayler, probably around '71. *Spiritual Unity* was the first thing I heard. I remember thinking it was kind of crazy, but very intriguing.

Did those lead you to other people in the ESP catalog?

Well, somebody I knew had a copy of *Ornette at Town Hall*. Gradually as I got more into free jazz, from '72 on, I knew about a lot of them. I had the Sun Ra record, *Heliocentric Worlds*. I got that from my brother in about 1973. And I knew Giuseppi Logan and guys like that. That's really what formulated my musical identity, if I have one: I saw free jazz as the thing after Hendrix and psychedelic rock.

How did your perception of the label affect your own approach to music?

I really did aspire to play the guitar like Albert Ayler, and Trane on *Ascension*. That's what I worked to do for a long time—I still do, in a lot of ways. The texture of those records is still important to me. The kind of culture around independent jazz records, of which ESP is like the earliest version, has always been the thing that interests me the most. My limited LP collection is made up of mostly cut-outs from Arista-Freedom and things like that, do-it-yourself records, things that were pressed in five hundred or a thousand at a time. I don't have a Blue Note collection; I don't care about that. I'm a hard-core ESP/free jazz kind of guy.

How did the Flow Trio happen to record for ESP? Did joining the label's roster count for you?

Tom Abbs, the label manager, just asked Louie Belogenis if he wanted to make a record. Louie and Charles and I really have a lot of fun playing, and we'd been looking for opportunities, so we agreed to do it. I guess knowing about Lowell Davidson and his ESP record . . . just to interject, I was a disc jockey on WMFO at Tufts in the early '80s, and I played a lot of the records then. In the past, I would have had serious reservations about dealing with a label like ESP. But these days, there aren't many situations that are better. I have a lot of respect for Tom Abbs, who is a nice person and a very good musician. I think he is really sincere about trying to give people a chance to do things. If I didn't feel like I was in a pretty good position, from my business point of view and from my awareness of what things are, I might not have made a record for ESP. They have a good distribution network, and considering that most of the free improvisation records are either do-it-yourself or limited in their distribution, distribution is an advantage over a small advance. The trick is to always try to reach different segments of the audience. I think ESP offers some things that some other labels—that might consider themselves to be of a cleaner reputation because they've been around for less time—might not offer.

What is the nature of the Flow Trio?

It's a collective. The Albert Ayler kind of platform that comes off of the ESP records is attempted a lot, and from my viewpoint most people can't control the energy well enough. To me, the deal with Ayler's music is that it's very melodic, very bluesy, and it's very deep and soulful. A lot of what's happened in, say, the last ten years by people who emulate Albert Ayler is what I would call the demolition derby version of it. Like, let's all scream together. And I never heard that in Ayler's music. I always hear people listening and people playing melodic things, who are playing in response to melodies and dealing with the energy in this very swirling collective way. I think that's what Louie and Charles and I are really able to do. Individually, we all have our idea about that and degrees of commitment to it. Collectively, it all comes together and makes something else. If there's a resemblance to an ESP kind of tradition, it's by coincidence and also the fact that we hear those subtle things in that sort of library of records.

Regarding Lowell Davidson, how did you meet him originally?

He was playing solo piano at a poetry bookstore and gallery in Boston called Stone Soup. This was in the summer of 1980. My friend Jack Powers ran the place. He used to have a lot of music there. Jack said, "You should hear this guy, Lowell Davidson." I said, "Who is he?" And he said, "He played piano with Ornette Coleman." I went to the concert and Lowell was playing on their old upright piano. He had little index cards with these scores that had like one note on them, one circle and a bunch of lines, strange suggested sort of scores. I told him I would love to play with him. He said, "Oh, sure, sure," which is what he used to say all the time. So, I let it go and then I went to Europe for a while. When I came back, I called him up and I went to his house, and he didn't show up. Then I went again, and he did show up, and we started playing. That would have been in '81. I worked with him pretty regularly for about eight years. He was really losing it in early '89, or late '88, and I had to sort of keep my distance from him.

Did he just burn out in the end?

The best way to clarify that is to read the notes on the Calibre [Dutch] edition of Lowell's record on ESP. I wrote the liner notes for that. Lowell died of tuberculosis in '89. He had a sort of psychotic disorder, and he had lived in a house in the south end that his parents owned. He had a crazy girlfriend, and he started losing it, so his parents kicked him out of the house. He moved to Dudley Square in Roxbury and was hanging around homeless shelters quite a bit. He got tuberculosis and it went untreated, and he died. He didn't die from a lab accident [as reported elsewhere]. [Bassist] John Voigt told me that while Lowell was at Harvard he was playing jazz and going down to hang out with Ornette and stuff like that, but he started doing a lot of psychedelics and crystal meth, and it basically fried his brain out and probably brought about whatever psychosis he had. But also his family, who were pastors of a church, were pretty far out too. So, according to a bunch of people, his regular demeanor wasn't so far out, but he'd have episodes where he was pretty out there and pretty inappropriate.

Through all those years that you played with him, was there a particular setting?

He had a couple of things with him on piano, but he played aluminum bass and also drums with me. And we had a trio with [drummer] Laurence Cook, with him playing bass. And then I did a group that I have a recording of, with Butch Morris, Malcolm Goldstein, and Lowell playing bass and percussion on it, which I hope to get released. It's pretty amazing. In the meantime, Lowell had his piano trio with either John Voigt or Mario Pavone or another guy, and Laurence Cook. He also had a group with [drummer] D. Sharpe and Leon Maleson, a bass player who lives in New York, Lowell's close friend with his family. So, he kept his piano trios separate, and then he did other things with me, mainly because I played guitar.

What did you recognize as special about his ideas?

His music was much more about sound. He used to talk about the upper partials clashing together. It was very slow moving, it was much more about sounds slowly morphing into other sounds. It was not like Ornette Coleman's, it was not like Anthony Braxton's, and it was not like Cecil Taylor's. It was more like what you would call electroacoustic improvisation now. His trio music, even though it had bass and drums, moved at a very slow pace. It had a sort of groove, but it was very different. And he operated differently. His rhetoric was very different. I don't think he ever thought of himself as a jazz musician; he just saw himself as a musician. He was a very dignified, incredibly brilliant guy. He would never lower himself to some mere label.

Did he ever talk with you about his ESP date or other performances in the past?

Lowell was fairly disengaged from some of the business end. He told me one time about seeing Stravinsky at Symphony Hall, and Stravinsky went up and shook hands with his bass player, who was the concertmaster—who was, of course, Buell Neidlinger. Lowell said he was sitting in the front row studying for an exam and he had all these placards. Then Milford got him a gig at Vassar, so he went down to Vassar and it turns out the bass player Milford got was Stravinsky's bass player! I'm pretty sure it was something he just went and did; there wasn't any rehearsal for it. He didn't reminisce about it. He was very much into his current stuff.

Why didn't he make any other records commercially?

I blame that primarily on the free jazz scene being a pathetic joke, from a business point of view. There are a lot of musicians in Boston who liked Lowell, and he was a difficult guy to deal with. They would all praise him, but very few had the connections outside of the city to do anything with him. The kind of attitude there was like, "Lowell is a crazy guy, but I'll be happy to hang out and play with him." I never thought of it like that. I always thought it was like, "Lowell is a brilliant guy; it's too bad he's crazy." But I had a different connection to the scene. I was really involved in free jazz, so I tried to get Lowell heard by those people. I put him on a concert with Billy Bang that I organized. I always tried to get him out there. John Zorn gave me and Lowell Davidson a gig, in '84 or '85. Lowell and I went down to play at the Club Chandelier, which was a squat theater where Zorn curated a series, on Avenue C. I organized concerts at Tufts University, and Lowell played there. I did a lot to connect him to other people, knowing full well that he almost didn't have the psychological capacity to handle a lot of it.

Your own label just released MVP LSD, *based on Lowell Davidson's graphic scores written on index cards. In the notes you say he made some private recordings. Are those still in existence?*

There was a bookshelf at Lowell's house, about five feet high and five feet wide, full of reel-to-reel tapes. Those are completely lost. There were stacks of cassettes all over the house, Lowell used to record everything he did with his tape deck. There are a few rough piano trio tapes that various people have, and I gave a few to Lowell's daughter Sara—because I didn't think they were my property; I wanted her to have them. She was talking of posting them on a website that her husband was going to build, but that hasn't happened. The reel-to-reel tapes seem like they're lost for good. I don't know what happened to them. They had people like Billy Elgart, Kent Carter, probably Michael Mantler, lots of people from the '60s and '70s.

Lowell was an intriguing character, but Boston was and still is virtually disconnected from the music scene. And the people in the music scene never paid any attention to what happened up there. I did have Peter Brötzmann and Peter Kowald in my car, in 1983 maybe, and I had a poster in it from a gig I was doing with Lowell at the time. They saw the poster and said, "He lives here?" And I said, "Yeah." They go, "Why here?" I said, "You guys live in Wuppertal—what's up with that?" They knew him from the ESP record.

How did the experience of his playing affect your own approach?

Lowell was not interested in line so much. He played church organ and made these subtle dissonances that sort of blended together. That's something I did with Lowell. He really got on me for playing too many notes. I had to deal with the partials of the tone, and I didn't want to do that à la Derek Bailey and play harmonics, so I drew inspiration from spike fiddle music, from West Africa, and started bowing the guitar. A lot of stuff that Lowell and I did was him on the bass and me on the guitar, and it's totally the clashing of partials. I have a couple of recordings with him. If I can get those out, that will make the point. They'll be out eventually. The things on *MVP LSD* where the guitar is bowed and there's a clash of partials, and then it slowly moves to the next pitch, and slowly moves to the next one, that is more the way we all played with Lowell.

Has your thinking about his ideas changed much over the years?

Yes. I couldn't really understand what he meant when he referred to the biochemistry of the brain. I figured he was always trying to reconstitute the biochemistry of his brain. The story of him staring into a lightbulb for three years is something he actually did. This chrome painted lightbulb, with little dots on a piece of aluminum foil, he stared into it so that the shapes, as he said, would burn into his synapses. There were a lot of things like that which are really far out, but considering he was a biochemist, he was kind of like a mad scientist. He was so brilliant in the way he spoke about things; it was impossible to dismiss it as just crazy talk. Even though at first it sounded like that, over time I understood what he was talking about, and we could have conversations. He used to say it was about evolution, that if we play things we haven't heard before, it will alter the biochemistry of the brain. He said that's what evolution is about. So, what I understand now is that it works like language: if we learn what the function or meaning of something is, and we come up with a word for it, it changes the amount of information we have as people, and that's evolution. I understand that what he was really trying to do was to move humans forward. And in my own way, I'm trying to do the same thing.

William Parker

Bassist William Parker was just twenty-one when he played on what became one of the last records in ESP's original catalog, tenor saxophonist Frank Lowe's explosive *Black Beings*, a concert from March 1973. Around that time, he was also one of the house bassists at Sam Rivers's nightly loft sessions at Studio Rivbea. Throughout the 1980s he was a regular member of the Cecil Taylor Unit, while also working in many other ensembles, including his own, and he has kept his busy pace ever since. A prominent figure in what might be considered the second wave of the new music, he has played in both lead and supporting roles, while also being an active arts organizer. He has been on the board of the Vision Festival since its start in 1996, which has featured many artists who recorded for ESP.

What was your first exposure to the ESP label?

Around 1969–70, we used to go down to Sam Goody's record store in Manhattan. They were selling all the monaural records for ninety-nine cents—or forty-nine cents. And Sam Goody's had the entire ESP catalog. I didn't have much money, but I would buy what I could, and at one point I did have the whole catalog, including two or three ESP sampler albums. What was intriguing about the presentation of the record was that you'd see a black-and-white cover with just the face of the musician on it, and then the information was on the back. Each cover was different, and all the music was different. There was a mystique about the label, especially compared to the other jazz labels at that time.

Were you discovering these records with other musicians?

Mostly by myself, or with my brother. At that time, we were studying music, and we listened a lot. So, that was all part of the experience. You would read in *DownBeat* magazine a review by Kenny Dorham of Albert Ayler. It's a famous review: Kenny Dorham says that Albert Ayler sounds like the Salvation Army band on LSD, and that's *Spirits Rejoice*. So, it's very intriguing—what does this music sound like? We went out and they had Frank Wright, Charles Tyler, Sonny Simmons, Ornette Coleman, etcetera, Gunter Hampel, even Willem Breuker, recording for this label. So, they had European music and also American music. I bought *Closer* by Paul Bley, *Barrage* by Paul Bley, the Lowell Davidson trio; everything was really hip, the Fugs. They had a record by Timothy Leary, of him speaking about mind-enhancing experience. So, all of these things were good. It was all part of the awareness principle of the music.

At that point, had you started playing the bass yet?

I was studying, and I had been playing music. I played cello. I played the trumpet, the trombone, and around that period I was beginning to switch from cello to bass.

Just a few years later, your first appearance on record turned out to be part of Frank Lowe's quintet [with Joseph Jarman] on Black Beings. *Wasn't that from a concert?*

Yeah, it was at Artists House, 131 Prince Street, Ornette Coleman's performance space. We did four sets of music, two nights there, Friday and Saturday. It was all recorded. I think Frank might have said that Bernard Stollman was interested. I'm not sure. The performances were much longer, and everything was edited to fit the record [on the CD reissue fifteen minutes of music were restored to present complete versions of pieces]. If I had known it was being recorded for a record, I might have used a bass amp. But the music at that time was very powerful, and it had some really strong people in New York playing. Everything was on fire.

The label was practically out of business by the time that date was recorded. Was it released fairly promptly? Do you recall if the record got around much?

Within that year it was released. I remember you could get it at certain stores. When it came out, they played it on WBGO. Michael Anderson had a show [he later did the research, restoration, and transfer for the CD reissue]. And it was played on WKCR. But I think that's all.

Becoming part of the ESP roster, did that have even a small bit of meaning for you?

I was happy to do the music, and then the fact that it was going to be a record . . . At that time, I thought ESP was out of business. Then Frank said no, they're still in business. It became part of the legacy of that label, maybe the last record they did.

Despite Bernard's reputation among musicians by that point, it's interesting that some people still wanted to work with him. Did you perceive any of that tension?

We were young, and Frank wanted a record out. So, he gave them the record, they gave us the money, and that was basically it. Did we even have to deal with the record company? Not really.

Somewhere you mention one of ESP's mystery people, Byron Allen, who recorded an early date for the label [and one other title elsewhere, years later]. Did you know him? Is he still alive?

Yeah, I know him. He's in California. I got some recent tapes of his that someone gave me. The last time I saw him, and Alan Shorter together, was in 1989. We were there at Yoshi's playing, and Byron walked up. I think he's still alive. But he was one of these musicians who kind of fell to the side of the road, getting involved with a lot of nonmusical things and being homeless or off the main track of business and music. He was a guy who was out there, who had talent and would be ready, but there'd be something from getting him started to really move.

Has the label's revival in recent years helped to reinforce the positive aspects of its history?

The way a lot of people feel about ESP Records, it was good because they recorded the music. Maybe if they didn't do it someone else would have, but *they* did it.

Ken Vandermark

Based in Chicago since 1989, tenor saxophonist and clarinetist Ken Vandermark has long maintained a busy schedule. Born the year that ESP began and mostly self-taught, he has become a leading figure among a newer generation of improvisers cognizant of the innovators who preceded them while offering living proof that the new music continues to renew itself. Working in multiple groups, he has recorded extensively (though not for ESP) and organized many concerts in his adopted city, notably the weekly series that he codirected for a decade (with John Corbett) at the Empty Bottle.

When did you first discover ESP and under what circumstances? Which records did you hear?

Probably when I was in college, in the early to mid-'80s. In Montreal, I had a professor who found out that I was a musician and interested in jazz and more experimental music. He played me Albert Ayler's stuff, and that was the first time I had heard Ayler. I'm pretty sure that *Spiritual Unity* was one of the albums he played for me, so that would have been the first ESP record that I remember hearing. I was studying film and communications, and he was an English professor. He was a huge music fan, so we spent more time talking about music than English.

Did you develop some consciousness of ESP as a label after that?

The LPs were super hard to come by. He had worked at a record store in Kalamazoo, and he brought that stuff up to Montreal. It wasn't really until the CD market started reissuing back catalogs that I got all the albums I have now from ESP, which are quite a few. When that started happening, it motivated me to find out more about the label and the connection with the scene, particularly in New York.

Did you have a sense that the records from ESP framed a kind of identity?

That was a legendary label. When it came out again, pretty much all the people I worked with were trying to get the albums. It had a reputation for covering an essential period in the music, particularly that group of musicians at that time. There really aren't a lot of other documents of that specific period in the '60s. In many cases, some of the best work these musicians did was on ESP. There were a bunch of people I wasn't even aware of until I got the albums, people like Sonny Simmons, and that was because of my awareness of the label and the quality level of the albums. They sounded good, but also the performances were so strong. So, if it was on ESP, I'd check it out. The success rate in aesthetics of ESP is pretty astounding in that period.

How significant were ESP recordings for your own work as a musician?

The music was so forward thinking that it still affects the way I think about the music I'm trying to make now. Like all great recordings of improvised music and jazz, they're timeless in a sense. So, they continue to inform what's happening now. There's more information there about ideas that affect me than other periods in the music. For a small label to have the awareness about the artists, how to get them to record in a way that made them feel open to play at their best level, it's extraordinary. As far as the way the music has affected me, it eliminated a lot of the structural foundations and opened up a bunch of possibilities that may have been suggested previously but weren't pursued strongly until those albums came out, in some cases. And that breakdown or explosion away from conventional thinking in the music, even based on the breakthroughs of Ornette Coleman or John Coltrane—I mean, *Spiritual Unity* is unbelievably significant as an aesthetic revolution in dealing with playing the saxophone, but also in terms of rhythm and the expression of time. So, that sense of possibility that you hear on those albums totally informs what I'm trying to do now, because that's what I'm chasing.

What other musicians did you discover through ESP?

I didn't hear Frank Wright until I got the ESP recordings. For me those were super important, because he was this legendary figure, and I wasn't able to find any recordings of his. He would always get associated with Ayler, but he's a completely different artist.

What is your perception of the ESP echo on the European scene?

I know that people around my age—Mats Gustafsson and Paal Nilssen-Love, guys like that—have the same feeling I do. Those albums are like a source of inspiration and information. As far as people who were playing at the time those albums were coming out, I know that Peter Brötzmann, for example, is extremely passionate about Frank Wright's music. And I would think that with Frank Wright, it's more that Peter knew him. So, in a lot of cases the relationships people have with the music of their peer group, so to speak, is more through the actual participation in the live experience. They were seeing those guys play live. Guys my age weren't there, so the records are the only thing we've got.

What is your assessment of the ESP label now that it's been given a new life?

There's no question that there's a lot of feeling that the artists didn't get compensated for their work for the label. That's one of these problematic relationships that happen with lots of small labels; usually it's like a one-person or two-person business. They're passionate about the music, and if it wasn't for the label—ESP is a perfect example—that whole block of history would just not exist. The concerts would have happened, but for people like me, I never would have heard some of those artists. So, there's this weird relationship where as a person interested in the history of the music, it's priceless what they did. On the other hand, it's an ongoing thing with musicians being ripped off by small labels who promise them a lot and then they never get their due, which is why invariably these things fall apart after a certain point. And the truth is, these records, I'm sure, sold very, very small numbers.

But that's a common story. It's a situation where the people running the label believe in all the stuff and can't believe that they're not going to sell enough records to keep the system afloat. They want to pay the artists, they want to make more records for the artists, and then the money just keeps going back into the label and doesn't get distributed to the people making the music. So, what we're left with, from an objective standpoint, I would say the contributions of ESP outweigh the penalties. But I wasn't one of the musicians that didn't get compensated!

What do you think of the new groups that ESP has produced in the last few years?

To be honest, I haven't listened to any of those. It appears they're trying to record contemporary musicians that fit into whatever aesthetic ESP developed in the '60s; that's my impression. But the problem is, now it's almost 2010. We've got almost fifty years of change. That also is a problem with this music, because in a sense it's always changing. It's like a musician. If you develop something you're known for, then it's almost a penalty because either you continue to do that and meet people's expectations—which is contrary to the nature of the music, because it's not supposed to be about that—or you keep changing and moving, and then you have people complaining all the time because you're not meeting their expectations. With the label, it's a similar problem. In a sense, to be true to what he was doing at the beginning, to find another let's say so-called Albert Ayler, would mean he'd be finding someone completely different from Ayler, playing completely different music than Ayler played. So, it's interesting that it's moved beyond reissuing the material and to actually recording new things. We'll see where it goes.

Gato Barbieri

Argentine tenor saxophonist Gato Barbieri began to develop his signature sound once he left his native land for Europe in the early 1960s. In Italy he met Don Cherry, who was influential in his thinking, and soon became a member of Cherry's group for a few years. They recorded two albums for Blue Note in 1965–66 and played an extended engagement at the Café Montmartre in Copenhagen, in March 1966 (ESP released these club recordings in three volumes in 2007–9). That same year, along with Cherry and others in Paris, he recorded Krzysztof Komeda's soundtrack for the Jerzy Skolimowski film Le Départ. On March 15, 1967, he made his first album as a leader (besides an early record before leaving Argentina), In Search of the Mystery, for ESP; with an unusual quartet that included cello, bass, and drums, it was the freest music of his entire career. Two months later, back in Milan, he recorded a trio date, and he continued to work steadily until his soundtrack for Bernardo Bertolucci's film Last Tango in Paris (1972) made him an international star. He settled in New York definitively in 1971, moving to his home on Central Park South some years later, where he lives with his second wife, Laura, and their son.

How does your free jazz period in the 1960s fit into your overall musical trajectory?

I started professionally with an orchestra playing bebop in Buenos Aires when I was sixteen. I am seventy-six now, so that was sixty years ago. Later I had my own group there. We played every Monday, made a small record. I've worked with a lot of different people, different kinds of music. I was a very good sight reader—in Italy, when I didn't have money, they asked me to play a concert of Stravinsky, so I did. But after, I said I wouldn't do that anymore, because the people who play in symphonies are fast. I had played symphony music in Buenos Aires, when I played alto. I learned everything. In 1960 I went to Brazil and stayed for six or seven months, then I went to Cuba, and from there, I said to [his wife] Michelle, "We should go to Europe." In 1962 we went to Italy, where nobody was playing. So, I taught a lot of people, not by talking but playing. Because I don't like to talk too much about music. You can explain something but, for instance, with Don Cherry in forty-five minutes we played fifteen tunes—because he jumped from here, to there, to there. And I learned to be attentive, to listen to the leader. It's like a basketball team, or in soccer, when they are good they have this kind of intuition, they know each other very well. Music can be like that. With some musicians, everything just flows. On *The Third World* [1969], I picked up Lonnie Liston Smith, Roswell Rudd, Beaver Harris, and Charlie Haden. I gave them the music, and we didn't do rehearsals. We just went in and played. But when you are young, you go and you don't have anything to lose.

*How did the duo session with Dollar Brand [*Hamba Khale*] come about? That was a beautiful record.*

That was in 1966, in Milano. I had played with his drummer, Makaya Ntshoko. And I had seen him play, but we never played together except this one time. We both happened to be in Milano, and someone said, "Why don't you do a duo?" So we did. We just started playing. It was incredible.

When you made In Search of the Mystery *for ESP, your first record as a leader, how did you approach the occasion?*

My concept was don't use piano, and use Calo Scott. I had two melodies. They weren't very clear but they were there. Unfortunately, while we played, the drummer seemed to think he was playing solo. Besides, we weren't there for the mixing. We made the record and then we left.

How did you choose the musicians, particularly Calo Scott on cello and Sirone on bass? That made for an unusual combination.

Well, I was around, and somewhere I saw Calo Scott, and I immediately thought of the tenor and cello together. I called musicians I knew, more or less. Before this I had been playing with Don Cherry and Carla Bley, so it was a mix of things I had in my mind. I asked Sirone and the drummer Bobby Kapp because we had played some things together.

What was the response to the ESP record after it came out? Did anyone seem to notice?

No. I went so many times back and forth to Europe, and my English wasn't very good. For me, New York was a new city, but we knew where the musicians were.

Like at the Five Spot, we were always around there, and nothing. But Archie Shepp was aware of the ESP record. ESP was the only label to put out such things. You didn't make anything from it. But everybody did it because they wanted to do something different, to have a new experience. You always learn something.

Do you see any sort of musical evolution from your work of the mid-1960s to the '70s, when you were exploring a particular kind of fusion between Latin American traditions and jazz?

I had played so many things—with Carla Bley, JCOA [Jazz Composer's Orchestra Association], Charlie Haden's Liberation Music Orchestra—when the Brazilian director Glauber Rocha said, "You are Latin, and you have to make the Gato Barbieri orchestra." So, I went to Buenos Aires, and they offered me concerts. I played for more than a month, and there I started my new fusion with the Latin American instruments. This was in 1970. We didn't have a cent. I brought in Nana Vasconcelos, with his berimbau, and I used an Indian drummer who played with five *bombos indios* on the floor. He was really superb. And something new started to happen. After that came *Last Tango* in 1972—it's strange, a beautiful film can make you feel completely different. I played like I was starting to see something. A lot of people said, "How can you play jazz if it's called *Last Tango in Paris*?" Anyway, the arrangement was by Oliver Nelson. I wrote all the music, but he did the orchestration. He was fantastic.

Though you still give concerts, like at the Blue Note club occasionally, I understand you have had health problems in recent years. Of what sort?

What happened is with my eyes. I can see you, but it's blurry. I have macular degeneration. All the time, I used to fix my saxophone. I always said that when I got old, I would like to fix saxophones. I can only manage to watch television from two or three inches away. But I use my instinct to imagine things. For instance, I like to see old movies because I understand better what they are saying. The films that are made now are so difficult, my goodness.

But now you have an eleven-year-old son.

Yeah, he helps me. It's incredible.

Is he a very American kid?

Yeah, he's American. He's a Yankee fan. It's amazing how they're playing. They've won seven games in a row, and with new people.

You're a Yankee fan too?

Oh yeah! I played soccer until I was twenty-five. I was good, but I was afraid of some of the bigger people. Baseball is easier for me to see because in soccer they move all the time, and in baseball they use so many cameras, you know everything. I used to watch basketball a lot. I saw the Knicks championships, with Frazier and Monroe, in 1970, '73. But now, it's too fast for me.

Are you able to read at all? How long has your eyesight been deteriorating?

I can't read newspapers anymore. I can't read music. For nine years I've had this, and it's gotten worse. Besides, I have insomnia. It happened because sixteen years ago I had a triple bypass. And I take a very strong pill that also affects my eyes. After Michelle died, one month later I had the surgery. Before Michelle I was already having pains. Then I went to play in Washington and by the last set, the pain was terrible. An hour later, I was being operated on. And I was alone, because she didn't have family, and my family was in Argentina. For them to come, it would take a month to get a passport. So, I did everything myself, with a woman who came in the morning and the afternoon. It wasn't easy. But after three or four months, I started to play. Plus I owed taxes, and I had all the medical expenses. I just tell you these things because it was tough.

And so, how do you assess your experience with ESP in the end?

At this point, ESP is part of my music—because you never stay in one place; you always move. Even if they didn't pay much, ESP made a real effort for musicians to have the chance to play. And I consider that a good thing. They gave a lot to musicians.

Amiri Baraka

Poet, playwright, essayist, music critic, Amiri Baraka (LeRoi Jones) was a proponent of the new music from its start, as a writer, polemicist, concert organizer, and even record producer (his short-lived Jihad label in the mid-'60s). He can be heard reading his poem "Black Dada Nihilismus" on the *New York Art Quartet* album produced by ESP, and poetry has often accompanied his passion for the music. In 1965, after the assassination of Malcolm X, he left behind the Lower East Side and moved to Harlem, launching the Black Arts Movement, which advocated the creation of black-owned publishing houses, journals, and arts institutions. Some years later, he returned to his native Newark, where he continues his work as a cultural and political activist.

Was it true that you ran a series of concerts in your loft at 27 Cooper Square in 1964?

They weren't regular, but we started a series. Actually, I was writing for *Down-Beat* at the time, and I started calling for concerts in nontraditional spaces, because the club owners were not ready for what had developed, the new music. So, we held concerts in the loft there. We all lived in the same building—Archie Shepp, myself, and Marzette Watts, who was the last person to come in. He had the actual loft space. It was the apartment under mine; he had a big space because he wanted to paint. So, the concerts started to be given there, but also at the same time in coffee shops and other people's lofts. There's an essay in my book *Black Music* about that. There was an art gallery called the Nonagon, a coffee shop called the White Whale, a cluster of places in the neighborhood that had these concerts.

How long did the concerts continue at the loft on Cooper Square?

That continued even after I left. Marzette Watts was giving concerts there after I moved up to Harlem in 1965.

Were there any particular criteria regarding who performed in the loft?

It played out based on the taste of the people who were setting up the concerts, and the people who were in need, because it was that combination. The people who weren't actually in need of those kinds of concerts—that is, they could appear in the traditional clubs—were automatically not considered because they didn't need it.

There is a private recording of the New York Art Quartet playing at a Halloween party in 1964 at Marzette Watts's loft. How much did all of you document these performances?

I can't tell you about that. I didn't start really documenting stuff like that until the late '60s in Harlem, and then in Newark. There might be documentation of those concerts then, but I'm not sure there are. One thing that I know I documented was in 1968, Albert Ayler and Pharoah Sanders, up in Harlem.

At what point did you become aware of Bernard Stollman and the ESP label?

I knew he was operating. I mean, word goes around. I knew what he was doing but, except for the New York Art Quartet, I wasn't that clear on just who—I could see the albums popping out in that circle of young musicians that I could relate to as being close to that Lower East Side kind of thing, but that was it.

Who brought you in on the New York Art Quartet date?

Probably Archie.

How much was your performance of "Black Dada Nihilismus" planned, or did you just go in and hit it?

Well, Archie and I were closest of those folks, and it was a question of just "do something." We probably discussed it a little bit, but it wasn't any grand plan. It was simply, look at this poem; this is what I want to do.

Did you have any overall perception of ESP as a label in those first years?

I knew it was the label that was trying to capture the people who were the most advanced in the kind of music not already caught by the major labels. It seemed to me ESP was trying to record a trend in the music, what was happening not necessarily in the clubs, but in the actuality of the music.

At that time, there were many writer-produced small presses, such as your own Totem Press. Why weren't there a comparable amount of artist-produced labels among musicians?

I don't think they had gotten to that point. Certainly there was, by that time, Max Roach and Charlie Mingus [Debut Records]. There were a couple around, but not as many as the writers. You talk about writing, and then getting that writing published; it's a little more direct. And the little magazine thing has an older tradition than self-produced records. That's a prototype of whatever avant-garde supposedly existed. I came to New York, and there were already hundreds of little magazines, not to mention the academic ones. And we always thought of that as a traditional nontraditional way, if you will.

How did you view ESP's widening the frame of its catalog? Pretty soon it began to include folk rock and spoken word and even a little bit of theater.

By then, I had gotten a little distant from them. As they evolved into that, I was less interested because it seemed to me the most impressive thing they were doing had been the music.

As the decade moved on, were you aware of the label's disputes and financial problems?

I had talked to Bernard every once in a while, but I wasn't really on top of what was happening with that. Actually there was a long kind of pause between our discussions. I think I talked to him as he began to put the label together again, about five to six years ago.

With the label's revival, does it suggest in your mind any particular commentary on the continued importance of the music from forty years ago?

If you can listen to Gregorian chants and Bach, you can certainly listen to something from forty years ago. The question is, at any time, what is valuable. But I'm sure that there's a great deal that remains and will remain.

For people who don't listen to this music, what was created in the 1960s still sounds challenging, I think.

Oh yeah, without a doubt. Because certain people were raised in a different framework. I mean, Bartok sounds challenging to people who only listen to pop music. So, it's the same thing. It always will be in that frame what it proposed that it was—experimental, something new—and for people who never took to that as an acceptable continuum, then it will always seem a little weird.

Michael D. Anderson

Jazz producer and researcher Michael D. Anderson was the drummer for Sun Ra's Arkestra in the late 1970s to the early '80s and remains his longtime archivist. He has spent thirty-seven years in radio broadcasting, including Sirius Satellite Radio (2000–2003); coordinated the Apollo Hall of Fame's Legendary Artists Photo Gallery; and worked as the prerecorded musical consultant for *The Cosby Show* sitcom on NBC-TV. He helped Bernard Stollman relaunch ESP and produced important archival releases for the revived label, including the Don Cherry Quintet's *Live at Café Montmartre 1966* (three volumes), box sets of Billie Holiday (*Rare Live Recordings 1934–1959*) and Charlie Parker (*Bird in Time 1940–1947*), in addition to performances by Bud Powell, Lester Young, and Sun Ra. In addition, he assembled over two dozen potential titles of archival recordings from the '60s onward (Charles Gayle, Braxton, Ornette), a project that mostly ran aground. Even so, in the fall of 2010 he was back working with the label on still more historic productions.

When did you first become aware of ESP?

It was the summer of 1975. A friend of mine, Russ Musto, was the program director for radio station WRTI-FM at Temple University in Philadelphia. One afternoon while I was visiting Russ at his home, he played me Pharoah Sanders's first recording, then went to Sonny Simmons, *Staying on the Watch*, and then to Noah Howard. I said, What is this label? The music was incredible. This was my introduction to ESP: while in my teens, when everybody else was listening to current pop music, I was listening to Sun Ra and Frank Wright. I heard everything the music was saying, and from that day I was on a mission. I collected every ESP-Disk' recording I could find, including multiple copies of some. At the same time, I was doing a show at WRTI and would play ESP records as I found them.

ESP was out of business by then. Were you able to find the records?

Oh, heck yeah. As a matter of fact, Jerry Gordon—who ran Evidence Records—had the best jazz record store in Philly, called Third Street Jazz. He was liquidating the excess in his collection, so he sold me several ESP and El Saturn records that I was looking for.

Were you already a musician at that point?

I started my first band at the age of nine. Later, when I met and performed with the Sun Ra Arkestra, that was a musical experience all its own. I already had a sense of musical direction, and after joining the Sun Ra Arkestra, it confirmed my intuitive feelings in viewing all types of music without prejudice.

How did you meet Sun Ra?

The funny thing about all this is, Sunny was listed in the phonebook under Sun Ra. Russ Musto said I should call him. At that time, I only heard the way-out side and was unsure of what he was trying to do musically. So I called him, and what really caught his ear was my knowledge of early jazz: Fletcher Henderson, Coleman Hawkins, Jimmie Lunceford, Luis Russell. The radio show I did focused on the swing and big band eras. With the WRTI library, I was able to have hands-on learning experience in teaching myself the history of the music chronologically. I also put emphasis on finding lesser-known artists, with the inclusion of Duke Ellington and Louis Armstrong. It was a wealth of music at WRTI, and I did my homework.

Early April of 1977, Sunny invited me for a visit and requested I make him copies of various songs. I had access to top-of-the-line equipment and ended up doing this for him for many years. The copies enabled him to write out arrangements on songs for the band.

Again, I was unsure of who this man was and the rumors that they were from outer space didn't sit well with me either. Upon meeting Sun Ra, I felt a kinship like father and son, and he saw where I could fit into his program by supplying tapes of songs he needed to transcribe, as well as by playing drums. So, two weeks later, I found out that I was in the band. Yes, my Space Daddy was a real—excuse the term—humanitarian. Sunny saw that I had a sense of direction at a young age and became my guidance counselor, teaching me things about music that will be with me for the rest of my life. Even children in the neighborhood would stop and talk with Sunny.

When you first began listening to ESP records, did you perceive a coherent identity to the label?

It gelled pretty quickly with me as something beyond special, musically. There was nothing like it. I also discovered other avant-garde record labels like America, BYG, and Fontana, which were documenting the founding aspect of the new music era of the '60s, with ESP as the front-runner. It was rowdy and beyond adventurous, and everybody had their own voice.

Did you hear any of the nonjazz material from ESP?

I basically focused on the jazz side, although I also dug rock music. In the '80s, I began collecting copies of the ESP rock series starting with the group Octopus and then the Godz. By the late 1980s I had collected most of the catalog. To me, the Charles Manson album is an incredible work of musical art, regardless of what he did shortly thereafter. I couldn't find any Fugs albums during my searches, for some reason.

When did you become aware of ESP's troubled past?

I was unaware of the trouble ESP had until hearing a statement from a musician on college radio station WXPN-FM in Philly in the '70s. After moving to New York in the mid-'80s, I worked for jazz station WBGO-FM, and musicians began to tell me more of the story. Many were the actual ESP performers involved. I had to find out for myself how independent record companies work. Most musicians assume that a company made millions when the bulk of the vinyl LP product sat on shelves, was dumped, or could be found at Sam Goody's and other music cutout bins for 99¢ or less a pop—let alone that the music wasn't widely distributed at the time. Keep in mind that an album only cost $3.98 then, and independent record companies only pressed five hundred to a thousand copies of a record. Not a lot of money.

To get back to Sun Ra, how long did you perform in the band?

From April 1977 to late 1983 I performed with the Arkestra. During this time, I was able to live among a communal family of musicians sharing in the conditions that came to be. From daily rehearsals to being on the road, that became my regular gig for the next six years. After I moved to New York, I worked as a public relations representative for the band, making sure radio stations had copies or knew of the new Sun Ra recordings.

How did being with the Arkestra affect your overall perspective on the music?

I'd always been different as a child, and as a young adult I knew there was more to explore in life. Being with the band reassured me of many things I was already aware of. I always looked for something different, something deeper that I could learn. I enjoy meeting different people who are on the same level of consciousness, and Sunny became number one in my book.

With my exposure on radio and as a performer, I took my job seriously. I saw the importance of documenting and exposing the history of the music, and I have spent my entire career doing just that.

Did Sun Ra cause you to think differently about how you played?

I was a drummer since I was seven, with an influence from bebop. I would incorporate all I knew into Sunny's music. Sunny would say, "Don't play correctly; you gotta learn to play it incorrectly." My mind said, Play it wrong; how do you play it wrong? Then I realized what he was saying: by taking what you have musically and utilizing it in another way. For example, even though I'm a drummer I had to learn to play the drums like a piano or do a riff like a saxophone.

When did you start becoming Sun Ra's archivist?

On the second floor was Sunny's room, where piles of tapes and records were lying all over the place. A part of my discipline was to study Sunny's music, so I could become familiar with his repertoire. One day I decided to clean up his room so I could be comfortable and started rolling tape back onto reels and placing them in the right boxes. Sunny commended me for my initiative. On October 18, 1977, Sunny went into his room and saw everything was a wreck and bawled me out that it was my job to keep things in order. I didn't know it at the time, but I damn sure knew then. Things were happening fast, and I was ready for it. I had to figure out how to use what I was being taught and how to take it to another level.

After that, you were in charge of his recorded documents?

Every member of the Arkestra had a specific discipline or job. In using the term "The Shadow World," and under specific instructions from Sun Ra, I worked with the 5626 Morton Street music archives, beginning October 1977. Again, it's because I had access to professional studio equipment at the radio station; I would make copies and compilations of things for Sunny in the two-track WRTI studio. It was an honor to work with the tapes at such a young age. I also had a grueling job as tape saboteur, or "Hatchet Man," meaning Sun Ra directed me to cut up tapes onto various reels because of the tape thefts that were occurring in the house at the time. I hated that job but would later reassemble everything in chronological order, discovering many hours of unreleased material.

When did you first make direct contact with Bernard?

In the late 1970s, I wrote to Bernard. Tenor saxophonist Elliott Levin had a loft on Germantown Avenue across from Vernon Park in Philly, and we would let tapes roll while we played for hours. One day I said to Elliott that we should find Bernard Stollman to see if he wanted to release some of the stuff we were doing. Byard Lancaster, Keno Speller, Sunny Murray, and other members of the "Out Crew" would come by and jam at Elliott's loft. Elliott and I would do a tenor and drums thing that had a real intense high energy we wanted to record for ESP—I was unaware that it had been out of business for a few years.

One strange day in 1997, while I was working as the jazz, blues, and new age department director at HMV Retail at 86th and Lexington Avenue in New York, a hippie-looking guy came in as I was setting up the ESP section. I began helping the gentleman, and while looking at an ESP CD, said I would like to meet Bernard. Then the gentleman said, "You want to meet him?" I said, "Shit, yeah." A few days later, he took me to meet Bernard, who had just moved to Walker Street Studios in the Village. After conversing for some time, Bernard seemed amazed that I had played in the Sun Ra Arkestra at such a young age and had been on radio professionally.

At this same time, Bernard was in negotiation with Calibre for a new licensing deal, supposedly ending his association with the Abraxas folks in Italy. I happened to be there when Bernard signed the Calibre contracts. The whole thing became another nightmare for Bernard, just like the Abraxas licensing deal. This is due to Bernard trustingly leaving everything in the hands of the licensees and not being more involved with the process of the negotiation and operation. He looks to give people the opportunity to do the right thing, but when things don't go right as planned, he gets left holding the bag of responsibility.

The reason why I came into the picture was to assist Bernard with my professional skills in getting control of the ESP-Disk' operation under his direction. My responsibility would shortly thereafter be more directed in the production area. I successfully established the first functional PR department the company has ever had, even though I had no prior PR experience working with radio and press affiliates.

His licensing deals always gave him trouble. Wasn't it their responsibility to pay the royalties?

Whoever buys the license to issue a recording becomes the responsible party to pay all royalties and fees as a part of systematic protocol. Bernard was not releasing the ESP catalog on CD. It was Abraxas or Calibre who released the CDs, and they are the responsible parties as the licensees. It became evident that, along with Bernard, sadly, the musicians would again be taken advantage of, leaving Bernard to answer for something someone else was supposedly responsible for. He licensed the recordings, and that was that, legally.

Regarding your own radio work, besides all the histories you've compiled—of the bebop era, for instance, and of various artists—for thirty-plus years you have interviewed many musicians. Some of these interviews were included as bonus material on ESP reissues in recent years, as with Pharoah Sanders, Frank Wright, Sunny Murray, Sonny Simmons, Burton Greene [although these were not sufficiently credited in the liner notes]; the Charlie Parker box set that you produced for ESP includes portions of other interviews you did. You also interviewed a wide variety of other musicians, like George Clinton, Bernie Worrell, and the last interviews with Leon Thomas, Ike Turner, Bo Diddley. A certain amount of this material is archived at WFMU. But do you have a sense of where that entire body of work might go eventually?

I would like to establish a learning mechanism utilizing my archives in a private website I hope to build. I have over forty-four thousand hours of my radio programs and artist interviews on tape and CD going back to 1974, including my WRTI shows, the overnight show I did six days a week for WBGO, some Sirius Satellite Radio airchecks, and most of my WFMU radio broadcasts.

When you compiled and produced the Billie Holiday and Charlie Parker box sets, you drew on Boris Rose's collection. What was your connection to him?

I knew Boris before I knew Bernard, from doing my *Bebop City* program for WBGO [1984–95]. Boris was another person who had a bad reputation about the way he did things, although he had documented the most important music era in jazz history captured live, the bebop era. With his sixteen-inch disc cutter, he would sit all night and cut discs of radio broadcasts from the Royal Roost and Birdland, with Charlie Parker and many others. I respected Boris for his willingness to document the music historically, whereas others stated he made large sums of money by later selling copies overseas and in America on various pseudonym record labels. This particular area of his archive covered a period from 1948 through the late '60s, with many hours of unreleased material. Bernard and I were talking about getting the collection from him and putting it out legitimately, with all the conversation unedited—because the bootlegs edited out announcer Symphony Sid Torin or Bob Garrett's conversations, which to me is vital to the flow of hearing the original broadcast.

Wasn't there supposed to be an ongoing effort, as part of the revived ESP, devoted to that kind of material?

I compiled a series of CD projects utilizing the vinyl recordings from the Boris Rose archive, along with other historic material in my archive, for packages like the two-CD sets, *Lena Horne Live—The Wars Years (1943–1947)* and *John Coltrane with Dizzy Gillespie at Birdland 1951–1952* [both sets remain unreleased]. In 2007 ESP did issue the Lester Young recordings *Live at Birdland 1953 & 1956*.

Near the end of my association with Bernard, we were discussing the establishment of an alternate label we had started in 1998 called Haven Disk, for the issuance of more rare historic jazz recordings. I maintain my set of the incorporation documents. In 2009 there was talk about finally putting out the John Coltrane with Dizzy Gillespie, but it never came to be.

Sal Salgado

The band Cromagnon existed just long enough to make one record, *Orgasm* (reissued as *Cave Rock*), recorded for ESP in 1969. A project conceived by the late Brian Elliot and Austin (Bob) Grasmere, it eventually developed a minor cult following and was hailed as a pioneer in sound collage experiments. But there were other musicians involved, mysteriously listed as the "Connecticut tribe," and they too made the regular trips down to New York through the months it took for the album's gestation. Drummer Sal Salgado was one of these musicians, and most of them—including the two principals—had previously been members of the Boss Blues for several years, a teenage band with a steady regional following that resisted the pull to become just another prefab pop act. Instead, they invested their efforts in something utterly different on the ESP record (with Howard Bernstein's psychedelic cover). Salgado is the only one of the so-called tribe to appear in the album photo alongside Elliot and Grasmere.

Who were the unnamed musicians involved on the Cromagnon record?

There was myself, the bass player Peter Bennett, another guitar player, Vinnie Howley, also Mark Payuk, Peter's brother, Jimmy Bennett, and Gary Leslie. They were on pretty much all of the record. We all did overdubs, different things—handclaps, chanting, different sound effects.

Why did Bob and Brian use that term the "Connecticut tribe" instead of naming the rest of you?

I think maybe they came up with that to expedite things in an interview, instead of trying to name the rest of the members of the band. They wanted to have a certain mystique to the group, so they just said the Connecticut tribe. In their original formula, this record was like some of the earliest sounds that people were going to listen to. Early on, Brian said, "If Elvis in '59 was shaking his hips, and people were freaking out; and ten years later, Hendrix was putting lighter fluid on his guitar, and people were freaking out; thirty years after that, in '99, what are they going to be doing?" So they said, "Let's say there was some horrific, cataclysmic event that occurred. People would be starting out in a tribe in the woods somewhere. And when they got together to make music, maybe one of them would have a guitar. There probably wouldn't be any electricity—they'd have to just do whatever singing or chanting or humming, that sort of stuff." So, it was a real primeval thing.

Were you aware that you would all be lumped together as the Connecticut tribe?

We didn't know anything about the tribe. We thought they'd say they used everybody that was in the Boss Blues, plus a couple of others.

How would you describe Bob Grasmere and Brian Elliot's roles in the Cromagnon project?

They were instrumental in taking the idea and really fleshing it out. They presented it to a couple of more traditional music labels who didn't want to hear it. Then they went to ESP-Disk' because of the nature of the label; it had a lot of avant-garde people—Sun Ra, the Fugs. They figured, sound collage, let's go there. But they asked us for ideas. Brian wanted me to work on some storylines for certain tales. He called them tales more than songs, because we were telling a tale— like how storytelling throughout the ages has been one way of having community with people. So he asked me to write up some stories, about what maybe the day's activities would be in the tribe. And then try to tell that story and have background sound effects. We were just trying to work on these ideas, because it was totally new to us. It wasn't about boy meets girl, fall in love, sing the song, girl leaves boy, breaks heart, whatever. It was unfamiliar territory; we were experimenting.

What was Bob's and Brian's relation to the Boss Blues, and what was the nature of that band?

Brian was the producer when we, as the Boss Blues, had a record contract with Buddha Records in New York City. In 1967 we signed a three-year deal with them. We released a couple of 45s, and we were about to start working on an album when they fired Brian. Bob was not too happy with the staff and the A&R guy they brought in. They were changing our sound. It was starting to sound real bubblegum; we didn't want to be like that. So, the rest of us—being seasoned veterans, all of sixteen and seventeen years old—figured we'll show them. What the hell do they know? But then they breached our contract because we didn't show up for a couple of sessions.

When we started with the band, we had more of a rhythm and blues background. We did a couple of statewide releases, 45s, with an independent label from Hartford, called Globe Records. We had some pretty good regional success, so they put us on these tours: we opened up for Smokey Robinson and the Miracles, we were on television with the Temptations, and we opened a festival with the Commodores and Marvin Gaye. It was really weird; here's five white kids coming out to a five-thousand-people crowd of mainly African Americans. So, they're like throwing things at us and booing us. Talk about baptism by fire, my God!

How long did the Boss Blues exist?

We signed with Buddha Records in the fall of '67 and by the winter of '69 we were pretty much ending it with them. We had been around for a couple of years before that. Originally, we were called the King B's, then we became the Boss Blues. We were trying to hone our craft, and to that end Bob Grasmere, Vinnie Howley, Peter Bennett, and myself were writing songs, and Brian was our producer. So, it was just a natural progression that once he was ostracized from the group in our business deal, we said, Hell, we're going to go with Brian.

Had you guys finished high school?

No, we were all still in high school. And lots of times we'd be on the road. If we were in Chicago or the Midwest, we'd come back from a Saturday-Sunday trip out there and wouldn't get back here until late Monday. Then we'd sleep in on Tuesday and wouldn't get to school till Wednesday. So, we started racking up a lot of absenteeism.

Were you all friends from the same town?

Actually, three of us came from Bethel; that's a little town next to Danbury. Bob came from Redding, which is the next town south, and Brian came from Ridgefield, to the north. And then Vinnie came from Danbury.

So, how did the band come together in the first place?

Just playing in our garage—Peter on bass, his brother Jimmy on guitar, and I played drums. And Mark would sing; we had this little quartet. Then we heard of another guy, who was in the Air Force but a good keyboard player, and when he came home for a week or two he would play with us. He said, "You've got to get my cousin Vinnie into this." So he came, and he was a really good rhythm and blues guitarist who could play harmonica at the same time. We brought him in the band. And then my mother was working with Bob's father at this electronics firm, and she said, "My son's putting this band together, and they're looking for a lead guitarist." Bob was playing with a soul band, and he came to our first rehearsal driving this pink Cadillac with a pack of Marlboros rolled up in his T-shirt. So, we went from there.

By the time you all worked on the Cromagnon concept, that was quite a radical turn.

Totally. We used to have arguments in the beginning, How can you expect us to just transform into cave dwellers and think that way? But they were trying to get us to think outside of the box. It was not verse, chorus, verse, chorus, lead, chorus, out—that kind of formula. They said, "Let's just really work with no rules," and that's what it was like. One day while we were recording in July, we were having pizza out on the street there in the West 90s and we saw this guy. He had this long coat on and a vacuum cleaner under his arm. We walked up to him and said, "Hey, man, you want to come and do a recording?" He said, "Will you buy me something to eat?" So we bought him a slice of pizza and a soda, and we brought him back into the studio. That was just a freak thing that happened, but lots of times we would be sitting there working on a tale, and one of us would say, "You know what would be cool? Let's blow through reeds of grass, like when you're kids out in the yard." And it just led to other things—having crickets in the background, and then the Jew's harp, that whole beginning of "Caledonia."

Was Cromagnon conceived just as a special project or as possibly a new band?

It was more of a project at first, and then after we did the final product, that's when they started talking about doing a stage show. We would go to Amsterdam; that would be a good place to start a European tour. Brian and Austin's idea of the first show was that it was going to be on a barge in the canals in

Amsterdam. It would be like an illegal thing, because we wanted to psychedeli-cize anybody within a four-hundred-foot radius of the stage. We wanted to put such a barrage of sound to completely overload their senses. That's what we were thinking, because it was going to be a womb trip. We were going to have an embryo on stage, and we were going to come out with flamethrowers, ex-plode it, and there would be a whole bank of electronics behind it, and then we would just go into the show. We wanted it to become illegal. We wanted people to freak out, to have a Woodstock experience again, only the whole three days all in a one-hour show.

Was there any particular meaning for you guys in being part of the ESP label?

We just felt like we were the low man on the totem pole. I mean, who's going to buy this record, first of all? And it's weird, who does buy this record? People that are into sound collage, sound painting, different audiophiles who can listen to it for a while—because it's hard to take, some of it. And it was meant to be that way.

What do you recall about the recording experience itself, working with Onno Scholtze?

He was very easy to work with, and one of the quickest guys at the controls. I was amazed how we'd go in there in the morning, and in three hours we'd have a song done. He would bring in certain electronic effects, whether using a Leslie speaker from an organ to sing through or double-tracking things. He could work with a click track and build off of that; he could really multiply tracks quickly.

How long was the period in which you were recording?

We ended in November, so it was about six months. In the beginning, we went down there [from Connecticut] at least once or twice a week, for maybe two months. We got the body of all of the tales together, and then for the last three or four months we would go down there once a week and work on overdubs. By then, we'd be there only an hour or two, maybe three hours. But it was more Brian and Bob that spent the lion's share of time in there, with Onno mixing things down, compared to the time that we spent. I really think if we spent eight hours a day in the studio, the album would have been done in three weeks.

Was this his own recording studio?

It's a mystery to me [in fact, it was Herb Abramson's A-1 Sound Studios, off Broadway and 72nd Street]. We were in the dining room of an old hotel. It had French doors with old curtains on them, and the booth had been built in an area that might have been a room where they prepped salads. The rest of the dining area was void of anything except for a set of drums and some congas, and they had a big fishnet hanging in the corner with maracas, tambourines, claves. And of course there was a piano, and an electric piano, but it was a makeshift studio. I thought it was ESP-Disk' that rented this room in the bottom of the hotel.

What else were you all doing during those months that you were making the record?

Well, we had been a really popular group in the area for years. As The King B's, back in '64, we had a fellow in the band who started a teen dance association and we had fifteen hundred members in Fairfield County. We would put a thousand people on a Friday night in a hall here in Danbury, or we would go to the convention center in New Haven and play with another band there, the Shags, and have fifteen hundred people. So, even after we became the Boss Blues, we still had a large following. In 1969, when we made this album, we were kind of coming to an end, because we could see that maybe it was time to do other things. We'd been together almost five years. I was trying to finish high school. I went back and I did finish—because I'd been expelled for missing too many days in my junior year—and a couple of the other guys did that as well. Some of us were working part-time jobs. My dad had a business; he asked me to work sometimes for him, but I was very lazy, lackadaisical at best. We weren't quite teenagers anymore; we were about to turn twenty. But we were being asked to join other bands. There was a lot of opportunity at the time to play in the area. Every single weekend there were like eight bands playing in town.

I was making so much money in those years. I walked into the local car dealer here when I was sixteen and just laid out $3,800 in cash. I bought a brand-new super sport Chevy Malibu. We all would be making two or three hundred dollars apiece on a night. And sometimes we would do that two nights out of the weekend. It was a crazy time.

Were you around in the area by the time the record was released?

No, unfortunately. Something happened to put things on hold at ESP, and the record took at least a year to come out. By then, we had all gone different directions. I went to California and stayed there for twenty-five years [where he even did gigs with Skip Spence of Moby Grape]. I didn't hear anything until Bob came out to California in '85, and that's when he told me there'd been a reissue. He said people loved it in Norway. This was the first I heard it had come out at all! We never signed anything, so we weren't getting any royalties.

In retrospect, how do you see the record in the historical context of rock/experimental music?

I am really stunned that so many young people have listened to this thing. Like Curt Wargo, the DJ at WXCI in Danbury, who said on the air, "I've never seen the Connecticut tribe. Anybody out there know the tribe?" And my domestic partner was listening to this. She calls him up and says, "Hey, I live with one of those guys." That led to a whole radio show [on December 10, 2002, Wargo hosted Salgado, Howley, Peter Bennett, and honorary tribe member Nelle Tresselt for a live interview]. But when we first talked, he was saying this album is almost like a cult classic to him and some of his friends who listen to these other types of groups that do this, whether it's the Residents or Test Lab. And then Ghost, from Japan, closed their show at Terrastock with "Caledonia." It was on YouTube! To think that forty years later it would have any impression on people, that's really amazing! I never in my wildest dreams thought that bands would be using it as a template. That it's given them any kind of inspiration musically, I think that's payment enough for me.

Lindha Kallerdahl

Her first solo record, *Gold*, coproduced by ESP in 2007, recalls such uninhibited vocal experimentalists as Patty Waters and Diamanda Galas—and yet Lindha Kallerdahl had never heard them. In the 1990s she studied at Swedish jazz schools and has since collaborated with many adventurous musicians in her native Sweden and beyond.

I did the CD for me. My husband put it out on the label he runs with friends in Sweden. Then we came to New York for two months; that's when Bernard called. He heard me on Myspace, and asked if he could sell my CD! The first I heard of ESP-Disk' was when he called.

I never chose to sing, in a way. In my voice I feel free, so I do a lot of different kinds of music. I don't sing to be somebody. I think of music as a mirror of my heart. In every gig as a solo singer, I feel the room, look at the people in the room, and hope that the spirit of music will flow through me. I never make music to fit in.

[*On* Gold.] I sing in English and made-up language! No Swedish. No Esperanto. I sing from sounds that run through me.

I am very happy to be on ESP-Disk'. They've had my CD out in more places than I could ever dream of by myself. Bernard and ESP-Disk' helped me understand that my music will live.

Sirone

As an adventurous bass player grounded in rhythm and blues, Sirone (Norris Jones) was a highly versatile force in the new music even before he settled in New York. In 1966–67, he appeared on four ESP recordings as a sideman: on second dates by Marion Brown and Noah Howard, and then on Marzette Watts and Gato Barbieri's first dates as leaders. Later, in 1972, as a member of the newly formed Revolutionary Ensemble, the collective trio released their first album, *Vietnam*, on ESP, recorded in concert in March of that year. After several more albums (including one on the A&M label), the group disbanded in 1977 but reunited for one last record in 2004. Over the years Sirone played with many of the leading figures in the music and occasionally led or co-led his own groups. In 1989 he moved to Berlin, Germany, where he died in October 2009, a few months after this interview.

What brought you to New York when you came in 1965?

When I arrived in New York, it was on an invitation to do a concert with Marion Brown. At that particular time, it was a theater on Second Avenue called the Village Theater, which was very productive for the music. There was a series of concerts, and it was quite an honor because all the main people were doing these concerts—Trane, Albert, Ornette. During that period, it was a relationship of a family that was happening with the music, in the sense that it wasn't so divided as we have today, that it's grown into, in other words, focused on individuals. You had individuals, but you had the essence of the music—which is, as far as I'm concerned, coming from a group. We had a collective power, and the industry had to deal with the musicians.

Was that your first time working in New York?

No, I had been to New York many other times because of my musical experiences. In '57 I was working with Sam Cooke, Jerry Butler—these guys were very much in tune, especially Sam, with what was going on. They knew I was hearing other things, but they needed a bass player. Believe it or not, during that time with them I played contrabass, the upright. So, I had the typical touring thing, the circuit that those groups went through. Jerry was coming out of Chicago, so it was interesting to see the Chicago scene at that time, because Chicago had another musical thing happening. The musicians who were going in the direction of jazz were not so focused on the format of piano, bass, drums, and saxophone, and trumpet. They were omitting the piano. This is where I met Rafael Garrett, and we hung out. But in '65, coming to New York, on this series of concerts at the Village Theater, it was very impressive to see how the energy of the music was going to the public. People were diving for tickets—we're talking about a theater that had seating capacity for at least 2,000 to 2,500 people. Later, it went in the direction of pop music. [Previously a movie house and Yiddish theater near East 6th Street, in 1968 the Village Theater became the Fillmore East.]

What was your connection to Marion Brown originally?

That went back a long time; we had a group in Atlanta. Music was very strong in Atlanta. We had a sextet with George Adams, Willie Wilson, and Percy Connolly, and we used to be the opening act for the groups that would come from New York. We were teenagers, and we would be burning, so the cats might have thought they would come to Atlanta and have an easy day, but that was not true. We would leave the stage on fire. And they would say, like, "Damn, what are you all doing here? You should come to New York." And the most wonderful thing happened—we didn't go to New York as a group, which was unfortunate—but we finally came together in New York as a group and were able to do some performances at the Village Gate.

During the years you recorded as a sideman for ESP, were you dealing with the label yourself?

Being fresh in New York, I was using it as an experience of just seeing how the guys were dealing and how groups would be planning. Eventually I knew for myself that I wanted to settle in with a group and really develop the music.

On the Gato Barbieri date, you worked with cellist Calo Scott. Had you played together before?

Gato and I and Calo had worked together. Calo was an incredible cellist. I did not know this until later but I heard that he had played saxophone and had some health problems—I don't know how true it is—and this is why he switched over to cello. But the concept of the way he would go with cello, it was like he was playing a horn. His phrasing was completely taken in a different direction from the cello. But, in fact, when Gato first came to New York, I was one of the first people that played with him.

You and Calo Scott make a nice combination on that record.

It was wonderful. For two string players, we were very much accompanying one another. We were never in each other's way. And when we made the individual contribution, the contribution was made toward the whole. This was one of the most incredible things that I shared with the Revolutionary Ensemble, with Leroy [Jenkins].

With all the changes in music by the end of the 1960s and into the 1970s, with musicians like Miles going electric, were you ever tempted to take up the electric bass?

I touched it, but I never did really spend any time on it. It's a different instrument, and to me it was just limited. When you take the double bass, you have two instruments. I love bowing, and the electric bass doesn't give you that, of course. Later they developed some where you can, but it's just a different feel. You don't really feel the wood, you don't get the vibration of the tones coming back into your belly. There were a lot of double bass players who switched over for a moment—because we're talking about a money thing, possibly you could get more work, it would be easier to carry around, all that.

You and Leroy Jenkins were both in Paris in 1969, but you didn't meet until later, is that right?

Yes, it was after that. In 1969 there was a series of concerts in Paris, a festival really, and Leroy was there. In fact, I was over playing with Dave [Burrell]. Anyway, during that BYG festival, many musicians from the avant-garde were there. But I left, because to me it was really humiliating how the musicians were treated. Many people know the incident that I went through personally, and maybe my rep might not be so good in certain areas. It was an incredible story. Leroy was there, Marion, Braxton, anyone that's on that label was there. Originally the festival was supposed to happen in Paris. But they moved the festival because, during that time, the peace talks were going down between America and Vietnam, and all of a sudden the promoter, Mr. Karakos [Jean Georgakarakos]—I never will forget that, he's a gangster—moved the festival outside of Paris because they figured there would be heavy protests, or it would interfere with what was going on with the peace talks. They moved it to Belgium [in Amougies, just over the border], to a big open field there. He had all of the musicians in a circle. He got in the middle of the circle with his interpreter and shouted out what the change was going to be and so on. Afterwards, he said, "You can take it or leave it," and walked away. I was not in the circle, but it was interesting to see how the revolutionaries of the music swallowed all of this shit this guy was saying, and no response. So I responded to it. After my reaction, they said of me, "Well, they're taking him to the guillotines." But they weren't. They were taking me to my hotel and giving me everything that I'd asked for [*laughs*]. Everything that I'd asked for. They all saw that, and I guess nobody reacted. Anyway, we played the festival. It was my first time playing with Steve Lacy. I played with Dave and Steve Lacy and Louis Moholo. It was interesting, with Irene Aebi playing cello.

How did the Revolutionary Ensemble come together and end up doing its first record for ESP?

We needed a recording. Bernard being still open the way he was, it was not a problem. You did not have to go through a whole lot of negotiating. He heard the music, he knew of the group, and he said, "All right, do it." We brought him a tape that we had recorded, a live concert in the Peace Church on West 4th Street, near Washington Square Park. It wasn't the best sound, because the church had this echo a lot of times, but if you were into the music, you could hear the instruments. Of course, Leroy wanted the audio to be clearer than it was, but I said, "Let's go with it," and it was not a problem for Bernard. It was fitting for the moment, and it led to the second recording of the Ensemble for India Navigation—that was not one of our compositions ["Manhattan Cycles," by Leo Smith], but again we needed a recording.

But I must say that the Revolutionary Ensemble was really a revolutionary group, because when we came together many of the musicians in New York said, "You must be crazy. Violin, bass, and drums!" There have been a lot of different combinations in new music that involved other instruments, but very few of them stay together long enough to develop. This was one of the foremost

things with the Ensemble. We wanted to stick together; that was the main purpose, to develop our music.

When I first heard Leroy, he invited me to one of his rehearsals with a group
that he had, and without being derogatory, I heard the group but it just wasn't
happening on that same level musically as Leroy. After the rehearsal he asked
me what did I think of the group, so I told him, "I wouldn't have any problems
playing with you, but those guys, it's not happening." It was a strange group. He
said, "Well, what do you think?" And I said to him, "Why not have violin, bass,
and drums?" He almost turned white! I knew exactly what was going through
his head at the time. I said, "Look, wait just a minute now, everybody has to
hold their own ground. We're not talking about no leaders here." That cooled
him down. He said, "What will we call it?" I said, "I don't know, man. You give
it a name." He said, "What about the Revolutionary Ensemble?" I said to myself,
the guy must be crazy! "Okay, if you like it, we'll go with that." The next thing
was to find the missing link, which would be the drummer. We had Frank Clay-
ton at first, then eventually Jerome came, in '70 to '71. Leroy brought Jerome to
me, and we talked about music and what we were thinking.

We were rehearsing down at Ornette's place on Prince Street, Artists House;
even before Jerome came in we were talking about Mondays, Wednesdays, and
Fridays. That's the kind of dedication we were talking about with the music. So
I said, "Okay, let him come to rehearsal tomorrow." This was on a Sunday afternoon. I remember it very vividly. Leroy said, "Yeah, but you've got to have an
amp, Sirone." I said, "I don't need no amp." Because I was kind of slow getting
an amp. But we went there, and it was no problem. We played acoustically, and
we knew he was the cat. Jerome made the commitment, and that's when it took
off. We spent a lot of time together because, besides the three days of rehearsing, many times we would be out looking for jobs. It took a long time for our
following to build, but it did; we finally got through. It was a hell of a lot of
work. But to think of violin, bass, and drums, that was just unthinkable in a
group.

*Whose idea was it to go to ESP? Didn't you have reservations about that because
of the money?*

Yeah, I just knew that money was going to be short. But as I said, we needed a
recording, and Leroy knew that I had had connections with Bernard. I'd worked
with him, so I should have some kind of influence in getting us the recording.

That was the reason—we would probably have less complications. So, I approached Bernard. Of course, Bernard had his ear to the ground with what was going on in the musical world, and he had heard about the Ensemble. He was very receptive to the music, to new ideas. One might say whatever they might about Bernard, but Bernard was very instrumental in bringing a lot of artists to the forefront. I mean, it wasn't the best deal in town; the money was not the best money by any means, but ESP had established itself as an innovator to the music, and it had some incredible artists coming through.

Did the ESP record come out promptly?

To my recollection, it came out pretty fast. By me being in New York before Leroy or Jerome, I had made connections with some people that were in the production world, graphic artists and photographers. The ESP album had a very new creative layout, with photos by Matthew Klein and Larry Fink. We had some good press, and from known writers—Nat Hentoff, Bob Blumenthal, Chris Albertson. It was a strong recording, and a good representation of the group.

Sunny Murray

A pioneer of free jazz drumming, Sunny Murray first became known from Cecil Taylor's seminal groups of the early 1960s, which led directly to his tenure as Albert Ayler's drummer throughout 1964–65, appearing on all of Ayler's original ESP recordings. At the end of '65, he made his first record as a leader, *Sonny's Time Now* (for LeRoi Jones's fledgling Jihad label), with Ayler and Don Cherry in the group playing Murray's compositions. He then led a date for ESP on July 23, 1967, *Sunny Murray*, where his quintet included Alan Silva, trumpeter Jacques Coursil, and alto saxophonists Byard Lancaster and Jack Graham. He often led his own groups after that, and in 1968 went to Paris for a few years. There he recorded various albums under his own name, for BYG and other labels, and played on dates by Archie Shepp, Dave Burrell, and François Tusques; he also played the Pan-African festival in Algiers and the festival in Amougies.

In recent years, he has again been living in Paris, and in 2008 was the subject of a spirited documentary with a familiar title, *Sunny's Time Now*, made in Europe by Antoine Prum. Among the contemporary sequences were concert footage of his British trio with saxophonist Tony Bevan and bassist John Edwards and rehearsals of a seventeen-piece band assembled for the occasion, with an impressive array of players doing mostly his music. The next year, he visited the States again where he was featured at the Vision Festival in New York.

How did you get started in music? When did you leave Philadelphia?

Before I got busted [as a teenager, he did some time in prison], I got into rhythm and blues, going to concerts, dancing with the music. It was the only outlet I had. I even had a partner one time—like the Nicholas Brothers—I'd make the routine. Then after I got stabbed in a gang war when I was eighteen—a very bad wound [left side below the ribs], I was supposed to die but I didn't—and after I lost my fingers [three middle fingers, sliced off midway, on his right hand] at a steel factory, all in two months, I said, Bye, Philly. I did sheeting at a steel factory. It seemed like a bad omen, time to get out of town. So, I came to New York in 1956. I came there to play. I could have boxed; I had an offer to train. I stayed sort of in the streets of New York, the Bowery, thirty-five-cent hotels, worked at the agencies that the bums worked out of for about a year. But I bought books, and every night I would keep studying; nobody would mind.

But you didn't have a set of drums yet.

No, I'd go to jam sessions. And then, at nineteen, a buddy across the street at an after-hours joint said, "Murray, you're a drummer, right. Come over here. I got this set of drums. They got left when the police raided everybody." I went and picked up my first drum set. I pushed it all the way down Third Avenue. I had found a little teeny room, and the first thing I did was I set them up and put on a Max Roach record loud as I could, and practiced. New York don't care if you practice!

And within a few years you were playing with Cecil Taylor and everybody?

Yeah, it's amazing. In four years I was with Cecil, in five and a half or six I was playing with John [Coltrane], with [Sonny] Rollins in between. It blows my mind too, because I used to go to the first Five Spot, at Fifth and Third, and the owner—Joe Termini, a nice man—he thought I was a clothes shark. He had a big stomach, and he'd always walk me out the door with his stomach. He'd be smiling, and I'd go stand back outside. Then finally one day, it was raining a bit. I came in, and he said, "I'm sorry." I said, "That's okay, I'm playing tonight" [*laughs*]. "Playing to-night?" "Yeah! With Cecil!" "Oh," and he moved out of the way.

You said in an interview with Michael Anderson that Bernard Stollman was the one who encouraged Cecil Taylor to go off on his first European tour in 1962, to Norway and Sweden. It was on that trip, in Sweden, that you met Albert Ayler, when he sat in with Cecil and the group. How did that come about?

When we got there, Albert was just about ready to leave. He said to me, when we were playing, that he had stayed over from the army and had been playing in the Black Forest for about a year by himself. He had found some cats he could play with, like Sune [Spångberg], who was a good drummer, but he was brand-new. So, he said he had this vision that he would meet cats like us, his kind of people. I said, Well, we're here. I don't know how the hell we got here. He said, "Can I play?" "Well, you've got to ask Cecil." So, immediately Cecil was like,

"Nah, I don't know." Me and Jimmy understood Cecil, so I told him [*whispers*], "Go home and get your saxophone."

He comes back with this big shiny new Selmer to blow down the walls of Jericho. I said, "Damn, man!" and Jimmy laughed. We told Albert when we give him the signal he should come up and play. So we played and had fun, and we gave him the signal and he came up there, and Cecil must have jumped half out of his chair. But then he was into it, and it was exciting. Albert had never played with cats like us, particularly me. So that was it, and Cecil said our next engagement was in Copenhagen, at the Montmartre, for a week. What was Albert going to do? Cecil said he wasn't going to hire him, because he couldn't afford it. So, Albert hung with me in my room in Copenhagen, and Cecil let him sit in and play.

Albert was a charmer. He had all the broads and people. Then, it came time for Cecil to go. Cecil made a record—that we made at the Montmartre—that was his money to go home, and my money to go home, and Jimmy's, but he didn't use Albert on that date. Probably there wasn't enough money. But Albert made a record right behind that, a holy roly record, traditional stuff, and that got him home. Of course, he didn't know New York from a can of beans. So, he came over to my house, and I took him to meet Archie and all the cats.

Besides all the ESP records under Ayler's name that you worked on, there was one very unique date that included both of you, New York Eye and Ear Control. *Do you recall that session?*

Yeah, but I don't even know why we did that. But Albert played some personal things on there—he could be very melancholy sometimes, and I used to enjoy playing with Albert because I can be melancholy; we could be the same emotion sometimes. I haven't run into too many tenor players like that. Odean [Pope] sometimes, we can be the same emotion. And Jimmy Lyons, he always had a little brush of the Bird in there. I'll never understand why a lot of these great avant-garde cats couldn't hear something in another way too, not just the screaming honking, honking screaming. That shit went on back in Duke Ellington's band in 1931. Lockjaw Davis would put them out of business.

What were your expectations in recording your own date for ESP?

Well, I thought Bernard was somebody who could aid me at that period in my career. I had touched on something from Europe that inspired me to try. It was just a new way to do a date. That's why I used a thirty-six-inch bass drum, because there's something about that instrument that homogenizes the group, if I can say that. The saxophone now is beginning to repeat itself—with a lot of hard trying, and still it's repeating itself. But when you're listening in your inner ear to Albert, he's still somewhere else.

Most of the pieces on the ESP record are your own. Were you writing since playing with Cecil?

No. After I left Cecil I didn't have much choice, because nobody was giving me a job. So I did a small job. Cecil came to it, and I played all of Max Roach's pieces. They were correct, and then I wrote some music, and I asked my children did they like it. They said, "Yeah, Dad." So I found out I could write. My first record, *Sonny's Time Now*, they're all my pieces: "Virtue," "The Lie," "Justice." It's a strange record because Albert and Don [Cherry] are playing like this [*makes screeching sound*].

Was that a working band you had on the ESP record?

Well, I didn't get no gigs with it. Probably if I'd have gotten some work, it would have been. I've had so many nice bands and no gigs. And what happens, the cats come along with the gigs and take my band. I got tired of that.

How did you end up having Jacques Coursil in your group for that date?

He was washing dishes in a restaurant, and a bebop alto player who was a good buddy, Clarence Sharp, said, "There's a cat works in the kitchen. He's pretty good, Murray. You ought to check him out." So I went in the kitchen; he had his apron. I said, "You play trumpet?" "Yes," with that French accent, "I play trumpet." You want to play something with us? He said, "Oh, I'd love to." He dried his hands and came out, and whatever he did it was good. So I gave him a gig, and then the record came up. Bernard had been trying to get me to do a record, so I finally did it, but he didn't really pay me for that record. He made a contract of fifty-fifty, and I never saw my fifty.

Nonetheless, despite the financial problems, you seem to have had a long history with Bernard.

Bernard could have paid everybody. First, he just disappeared. I found out because we had things going on in Woodstock, workshops and stuff with Karl Berger, and one evening around the fire, he said, "You know, Bernard's up here." He was up there on his farm; eventually he lost it to his wife. So I took my Cadillac, me and Khan Jamal—we drove up there to this crazy farm. I parked in front of Bernard's farm, and I put the lights on it. Finally, he came out, and I said, "Don't move! I'll blow your fucking brains out!" Bernard fell down on the porch; his old lady hid behind the couch. Finally, we just started laughing and cut the lights out. I said, "Hey, Bernard, how you doing?" "Sunny!" "See? I can always find you." Anyway, I've had those kinds of feelings, but I never hated Bernard.

I've told him, "You disappeared for a number of years. You didn't have to disappear. You could have stayed here and helped us, and we'd all work together. But you just disappeared. You said there was no money, but if there was you took it and disappeared; and if there wasn't, you disappeared. We could have used you to help us in all kinds of ways." So, I got him to legalize my publication company; that's one sort of thing we can use.

Bernard is an all right guy, but he has to pay me my money. I think I'm his one victim in life. I said, "Bernard, you don't have to break the bank. Just show me your goodwill." Then I sent him *Apple Cores, An Even Break (Never Give a Sucker)*, and another record; Japan sent him *Sonny's Time Now*. He has that now. He said he might want to put it out; he has the tapes. I had sent them because he made me an offer. Me, I'm stupid; I sent them to him.

Has the business side of the music changed much for you over the years? Even to this day, you have often had to negotiate with producers and club managers to get what you think is fair.

The problem of it is, this music has not established many real connoisseurs, men with quality and taste, so we get a lot of meatheads that are in control of the business—if music is a business; so far it's not. When a guy comes up, we're suspicious and he doesn't understand it, but we've been dealt with so many Frankensteins that we want to make sure this guy is not a Frankenstein. Like Michael's not a Frankenstein—Michael Ehlers, Eremite Records—he'll take a chance. And that's what made this business work, guys that took chances. They put down John Hammond, but he gave me a chance. I thought, when he gave me the chance, maybe the old man was too senile. I was with Columbia Records from '67 to '69, a two-year contract. I only made one orchestra thing, and then it's a big long story what happened. Byard Lancaster got drunk and destroyed the studio, attacked John Hammond, stole money out of his pocket—I'm in the toilet, and when I come out, the musicians were all putting their instruments up. I went to the engineer and said, "Where's Mr. Hammond?" "Sunny, he's gone." Did he take the contract? He had a six-year contract. "He took the contract." The name of this record would have been *Love's Last Cry*. It never came out.

How do you feel in retrospect about having made a career as a jazz drummer?

I am proud to be a jazz musician. I'm proud to have spent those years with bebop. Now it's very profound solace when I have problems and feel down: it's not vague, it's not empty, there's something there. It's part of your human support, part of your motivation. You have to be proud of having this history.

Marc Albert-Levin

Journalist, art critic, Dadaist poet, collage artist, Marc Albert-Levin came
to know a number of the musicians who recorded for ESP in the 1960s,
visiting New York several times that decade. He wrote about them in Paris
and reported as well on the Pan-African festival in Algiers and the festival in
Amougies. He also organized a concert in Paris, in September 1969, with
Ornette Coleman, Anthony Braxton's quartet, the Art Ensemble of Chicago,
and François Tusques's quartet. One of his New York friends, photographer
Larry Fink, collaborated on what became his second book, *Tour de farce*
(1970), ostensibly about the Fugs, but as he says, "more about myself at
the time." In recent years, he has added another role to his literary
activities, as translator of Buddhist texts into French.

*You made your first visit to New York for a few months in 1966. How did you meet
people?*

I had translated Dore Ashton, the art historian, and she said I should meet two
friends of hers: one, she said, was an electronic genius, Richard Alderson, and
the other a promising photographer, Larry Fink. Those two people were my
very first guides in New York. When I arrived at Richard's studio, he was recording Marion Brown. I sat through the recording, and after that I met Marion, who was like a brother to me. He took me to Rivington Street, where I
rented a room with paper-thin walls for twenty-three dollars a month.

Marion really encouraged me to write about music. He knew I was a journalist writing about art for a big weekly paper, *Les lettres françaises*, the director
being Louis Aragon, one of the cofounders of surrealism. So, from Richard's
studio I met a lot of musicians. Marion took me to Pharoah Sanders, to Sun Ra.
I was overwhelmed by the openness. That also has something to do with age. I
was twenty-five years old: if you're sincere in your love for the art of older people, they react very positively.

A lot of my articles about the New York scene were published in *Les lettres
françaises* every week, then I made a collage of them and wrote a personal diary

in between the pages. That was how I wrote my first book, *Un printemps à New York* [1969; A Spring in New York].

Didn't you eventually stay in New York for an extended period?

I made a couple of short trips back to New York, and then in 1970 I came to teach a course in art history at Cooper Union—Dore Ashton was the chair of the art department. My son Kimson was born in New York at that time, and I ended up living there until 1977. It gave me plenty of time to understand that all my impressions about New York were pure invention, because there are just as many New Yorks as there are New Yorkers. I was kind of forced to leave, because I stayed the whole time on a three-month visa, but that turned out to be a good thing. In New York, without a legal existence, I ended up doing anything to survive, including being Miles Davis's cook for five months.

How did that happen, working for Miles Davis?

Through women. I had a girlfriend who knew Sheilah Anderson, and Sheilah was just moving in with Miles at the time. She had said she wouldn't cook or clean. So he told her with his raspy voice, "Hire someone!" I had already been a cook in a vegetarian restaurant down on Second Avenue, called The Beautiful Way, near St. Mark's Place. When I arrived at Miles's house on West 77th Street, he was in a bathrobe, and he had those shiny, really incredible diamond eyes, spectacularly good-looking, and that immediately caught me. I had listened to his music since I was fourteen. I was absolutely fascinated by him. So, he looked at me and told me [*in a low raspy voice à la Miles Davis*], "You're a short motherfucker, aren't you?" And I looked at him and realized that he was exactly my size! Instead of feeling insulted, I thought very intensely, "And what about you?" I didn't feel the slightest antagonism. He said, "Go ahead, Indian," because of my look at the time, and he let me in.

You cooked just dinners, or all his meals?

That's the paradox of it. He wouldn't eat anything. I was cooking mainly for myself. Because he was in a phase where his main sustenance was Heineken beer. He wanted to give it up, so he wouldn't allow me to buy more than two at a time. But I would cheat and buy a six-pack, because I knew it wasn't going to happen. I was living there.

Were you doing much writing while you were there?

No, I only wrote two things. A letter from Air France came asking him to be part of some ad, where they had celebrities in fictitious airplanes, and Miles was one of them. So I wrote one page for him, which they reduced to one paragraph, and he received a lot of money—probably more money than he had ever given me, because I was really underpaid. I was making a hundred bucks every two weeks, but with lodging and food, and in order to get that I had to go to his manager's office in midtown. And then I wrote children's stories, and one of them was called "Mitch the Witch" that I dedicated to him. It went, "Once there was the sand / And on the sand was a witch / Which witch? / Mitch, the sand witch."

Miles had a son, Erin, the same age as mine, and with another kid I would gather them together, with my own who was living with his mother, and I'd go pick them up with Miles's limousine. I thought, with all the money he had, it was absurd that he wouldn't do anything for his own son. At the time, Miles would say, "This is not a day care center, you know."

So how did you cross paths with Bernard Stollman?

Richard Alderson told me that Bernard was producing records, and he was working for Bernard. When I left after my first visit, Richard gave me all these records, of Albert Ayler, Marion Brown, Ornette Coleman, Patty Waters, Bob James. . . . Those times were really open and free, not only in the style of music. There was nothing like this before. The music was unheard of, like Bernard's slogan, and he himself was just spending some of his family's money, not making any profit. The fact that he would be accused of having made money on the back of the musicians is a joke. It's really so unfair. He went bankrupt; he had to resume his law practice.

I think maybe the first contact was in about '93 when I went to visit Marion Brown, who was in a nursing home in Brooklyn. Bernard had reissued a record of Marion's, and I discovered that he was actually very friendly—he managed to give a little money to Marion, who was in bad shape. I spoke with him on the phone while I was in New York.

But I didn't meet him until years later, here in Paris, when he was looking for Sunny Murray. In this very room we had a strange evening. I invited them both to dinner. Sunny Murray voiced out all this resentment of an entire generation of musicians who would rather think they've been exploited by Bernard than to face the fact that it doesn't sell; it never did. So, Sunny started telling Bernard, "Where were you when we needed you? What if I come home with no money in my pocket?" He was so insistent that Bernard dug out of his pocket two hundred francs. It was really not so pleasant. It was a long dinner. Sunny rambled on, and then at one point while they were talking, I went across the room where there is a Buddhist altar and started chanting *Nam Myoho Renge Kyo*, because this is the only way I've found to avoid hostility: to chant for peace in my heart, in my immediate environment, and in the entire world.

Didn't you remain friends with Marion Brown for many years?

To this day. He came to Paris in the '80s; we were roommates in '83 to '84, when he was working with Gérard Terronès and Free Lance Records. The thing is, I was at his first recording, and I met him at the time when my first articles were being published, so we were fetishes for each other. He's also a visual artist, and I treasure some of his watercolors that I still have today.

Back in the '60s, he would rehearse on the roof of 27 Cooper Square, where he was living—it should be a famous building, because LeRoi Jones lived there, and Archie Shepp too. Marion Brown would go rehearse on the roof, and I would sit there for hours listening, happy to gorge myself with these sounds never heard before! And with Manhattan all around us, and the traffic below, it was really fascinating.

Weren't you also friendly with Frank Wright?

In 1969 there was a festival in Amougies, and I went there to cover it for *Les lettres françaises* with my wife, who was also a writer, Barbara Summers. It was like a happening, because nobody knew where it would take place: we were guided through the radio to a large meadow in Belgium where tents were installed. That was the first time I met Frank Wright, who was with Noah Howard, Bobby Few, Muhammad Ali, and Alan Silva.

When they came to Paris for the first time, I was living with my wife on the Rue Bergère, near the Boulevard Bonne Nouvelle, and the house was open to these expatriates. Barbara would cook for them, so we started hanging out together with Frank. He was a very lovely person, very warm, very joyful, and his anger was not directed at people. It had to do with what he thought was unfair. He was called the Reverend, and he had a very strong spiritual thing. For instance, he would be possessed by the music, a little bit like people get possessed in voodoo. He would lose all sense of what was really happening in the "real world." He would go off. I remember one concert he gave at the École Spéciale d'Architecture on the Boulevard Raspail, across from the old American Center. It was in the winter, and the room was cold. After five or ten minutes of this music he would be shaking chains and bells, howling like a wolf, and blowing the saxophone in all possible directions, even playing lying on his back. So, we weren't cold; after a while we were taking off our sweaters. It was eerie music really, and you would totally forget where you were and what time it was.

Jacques Coursil

A native of Paris, from a Martinican family, trumpeter Jacques Coursil
came to New York in the mid-1960s and plunged into the free jazz scene.
He recorded on dates led by Sunny Murray as well as Frank Wright, both for
ESP, and even made a record of his own for the label in 1967, which went
unreleased. Visiting Paris in 1969, he made two records as a leader and
appeared on a Burton Greene date, all for the BYG label. Among other
projects in New York, where he remained for the next several years, in
1969–70 he played alongside Sam Rivers in the city-funded Afro-American
Singing Theatre, featuring operatically trained singers in such works as
"The Black Cowboys" (music by Rivers) and performing all over the city.

Then, for the next three decades, he left his music career to the side
and became a university professor, teaching literature and linguistics. In
2004 he made a solo record, *Minimal Brass*, for John Zorn's Tzadik label,
followed by *Clameurs* (2007), recorded in Martinique for Universal France.
That label subsequently released *Trails of Tears* (2010), an oratorio that
commemorates the forced deportation in 1838 of the Cherokee nation
from their native Georgia to reservations in Oklahoma; there he employs
two ensembles, one recorded in Martinique and the other in New York and
Paris, where he was reunited with some old free jazz associates, including
Sunny Murray, Alan Silva, and Perry Robinson. Since retiring from teaching,
he has been living in Achen, Germany.

When did you first arrive in the United States?

In 1965. I came to New York to play music—I was involved with the free scene
at the time. But like many musicians on that scene, I had mentors. Jaki Byard
was one of them. In composition, I was studying with Noel DaCosta, who was
one of the founders of the Society of Black Composers. At the same time, I was
also performing.

How did you learn about the ESP label, and how did you meet Sunny Murray?

We were all living in the same building on Avenue B at the corner of 9th Street, by Tompkins Square Park [substantial legacy within one short block: a few doors up, Charlie Parker had lived at 151 Avenue B for four years in the early '50s; at 143 Avenue B, George Gershwin had given his first public concert]. On every floor there were musicians: Sunny Murray was living there, and many others. Byard Lancaster was around; Perry Robinson was around. So, we were playing improvised music day and night. Things like that happen only once in a lifetime! Next door to me was a blues guy from the South; he played blues guitar, with steel strings and fingerpicks. He made such a sound that the whole building would be shaking, more than from any drummer. Day and night we would visit each other and play.

Didn't that building have other connections as well for you?

It's a funny story. I was playing in a club on St. Mark's Place, the Dom, and I had to leave because I wasn't a member of the union. The owner of the Dom also owned that building, so he was paying me at night and taking the money back at the same time for my rent. He managed to find many other things for me to do there, so that his rent would be paid. At that time, the Dom was a jazz club, next door was a discotheque, and on top was the famous Polski Dom [soon to be the Electric Circus], which had happenings—Andy Warhol was there. St. Mark's Place was great: across the street was the Five Spot Café, with Mingus sometimes, and Monk, and we would catch a set while we were working at the Dom.

Weren't you even washing dishes there?

Yes! Stanley [Tolkin] was the owner of the Dom, and since I couldn't play legally, he made me a bartender. My English was not very good, and to make a Tom Collins and two Pink Ladies, it wasn't easy. But everybody liked the way I was mixing drinks, because I put in more alcohol than usual. They would say, "I want Frenchy to serve me. Let Frenchy mix it." And then I was a waiter, a dishwasher, and even a cook. And I was playing around, making a little money here and there. At the same time, I was going to school. I mean, I was in the kitchen washing dishes and all the musicians were coming in. Philly Joe Jones would say,

"Hey, Frenchy, give me that." Elvin Jones was there; McCoy Tyner was there. Tony Scott was playing there, and he was inviting everybody to play. Roy Haynes was there, a lot of drummers, and Jaki Byard was playing with him. Paul Chambers too, but he was already very ill. Hugh Masakela came often as well. So, I realized that I was pretty lucky to have played in such a place.

When you arrived in New York, you entered pretty quickly into the free music scene. Had you been thinking in that direction in Paris before that?

I was studying music in Paris—first classical, then jazz (bebop), and then atonal contemporary music. But since I didn't want to play contemporary music or bebop, it was very evident that the only direction I should take was free jazz, so-called at that time.

*In New York, you also found your way to Frank Wright. You recorded with him as well for ESP, on his second album [*Your Prayer, *1967]. How did you meet?*

Frank Wright was also in the building; at least I always saw him there. I would play with him practically every day. He'd be blowing by himself in a room for about an hour, and we would ask him, "What are you doing, Frank?" He'd say, "I'm tuning up." For him, tuning up was just playing by himself. And he was doing that every day. We tried to get together as many times as possible, because we wanted to breathe together. That was our concept of unity, breathing.

What about the unreleased date you did for ESP in 1967, which would have been your first record as a leader? Marion Brown was on it, and Eddie Marshall played drums.

Eddie Marshall! Thank you for reminding me. He was the sweetest guy in the world. I don't know what this record is worth, but I remember that the compositions were sophisticated [*laughs*]. I wrote a series of pieces, close to the first Ornette Coleman records, I think. Those were straight. For the [later] BYG records I wrote something very loose (with the help of Bill Dixon), in order to bring musicians together with a nonrhythmical structure. But the pieces on my ESP record were straight tempo.

After that, you played for a time with Sun Ra and especially Bill Dixon [throughout 1968, he was a member of Dixon's University of the Streets orchestra and the Judith Dunn/Bill Dixon Company]. How important were these experiences for you?

I never did any gigs with Sun Ra, though I did a lot of rehearsals with his Arkestra. The saxophone section was so great, the best since Duke Ellington. But I don't like families, tribes, mysticism. So, one day I split. Downstairs in the street, I met Bill Dixon, who said to me, "Jacques, where are you going?" I joined his group, and I learned a lot of things with him—sound, breathing, calm. Bill Dixon is a great musician. With Sun Ra, I was just bewildered by the excellence of the individual musicians.

A number of the musicians you knew in New York, like Sunny Murray and Frank Wright, went off to Paris in 1969 and stayed a while. Didn't you go there around the same time?

I didn't want to stay in Paris. I came for a series of concerts, a tour, with Arthur Jones. Sometimes Burton Greene was there. The Art Ensemble of Chicago was there too—this is the reason why on the second record, *Black Suite*, I invited Anthony Braxton. BYG signed me for two albums, and then I went back to New York.

As a teenager in Paris you had an early interest in New Orleans musicians like Sidney Bechet and Albert Nicholas. In the '60s when you were playing free jazz, did you feel any connection to that earlier interest musically? Did you feel any continuity?

It's difficult to say. I was born into a Martinican family, and in such a family you listen to Martinican music. And when your parents sing, they sing creole songs. I was also going to church and was interested in Gregorian chant. And I was going to music school, studying the classical repertoire. The New Orleans musicians, Albert Nicholas particularly, were the first black guys I had ever seen who were not from Martinique. But the musician who impressed me most was Don Byas. I was fourteen at that time, and there I was in a Parisian club. Don Byas dropped in from I don't know where with a white suit, white shoes, a shiny saxophone, playing so sweetly. I said, Well, we are all miserable compared to that guy! Paris then was full of jazz, full of painting and poetry. It was really the cultural place to be, if you were interested in that. Writers, painters, actors, they were all very nice to young people who were interested. You just had to know three lines of two poets, and you were sure to be in. I was extremely fortunate. Paris was really very kind to me in that respect.

Didn't you find, at least, that the Martinican music you heard at home had a direct relationship to New Orleans styles?

Yes, yes. All that is creole music, as far as I'm concerned.

How did that musical background affect your subsequent interest in free jazz?

Coming to the free jazz scene, I firmly intended to deconstruct the whole apparatus of rhythm. I wanted to "destroy" the beat and harmony too. So, I wanted to play atonal without any rhythmic framework. I also wanted to stop playing scales, to get away from melody. I was clear on that; I didn't want to play with my background. At that time, I was a strong revolutionary. I wanted to break everything down [*laughs*].

Decades later, that rejection of scales and rhythm led to your record Minimal Brass *[2005].*

You're right. *Minimal Brass* was kind of a statement where the music goes into circles, in some way. I wanted to find some point where my hearing finally ended, and it came out like that. John Zorn was really surprised.

For many years the two records you did for BYG were really all you were known by as a musician. What did that mean for you?

Well, it was behind me somehow. I was happy to have done those dates. But I was looking forward to what was new and open.

After your visit back to Paris in 1969, you ended up teaching at the United Nations International School [UNIS] for a couple of years, where John Zorn was your student. How did that happen?

That was a nice time, because I entered the United States with a tourist visa, okay, and I stayed ten years. But in the middle of that, I was caught at Kennedy

Airport by a customs officer, and they decided to deport me back to France. Well, at that time, because of my university degrees, I got a job at the U.N. school, and they gave me an official visa. So, I had to work. I played my double life, working as a musician and working at the U.N. school with my tie on. In this school I was teaching French and sometimes mathematics too. John Zorn was a student there. He was sixteen or seventeen, and he was interested in Schoenberg, Berg, Webern. I gave him some clues on serial writing and things like that—I was a teacher, I was supposed to know. So I told him about Darius Milhaud, Luigi Nono, Stockhausen; he wanted to know them all. Particularly John Cage, whom I met.

Did you remain in contact with Zorn?

No. When he became a big star, I didn't even connect the man with the brilliant kid that I knew before. But he remembered me.

At what point did he find you again?

I was teaching at Cornell University, philosophy and literature. I received an e-mail from him, which he sent to the chair of the department. He said to me, "Well, let's have dinner." So, as we finished dinner together, he said, "Let's do a record." First I tried some things that didn't work too well, so I decided to do the date solo—because I'd been working on sounds and developing new trumpet techniques, circular breathing and so on.

After returning to France in 1975, you earned a PhD in 1977 and taught literature, linguistics, and philosophy of language at the University of Caen [Normandy]. Then in 1995, you earned a second PhD in science and started teaching in Martinique. What took you so long to get around to spending time there?

I don't like identity things. I don't have to claim where I am from; it's so evident. As a young man, I decided to go to Africa. I ended up in Mauritania and Senegal and West Africa. That was really my first step outside of Paris and the whole Rive Gauche. And I lived in the house of [Léopold Sédar] Senghor! Since I ran into some trouble in Mauritania, Senghor brought me to Dakar. I stayed with him for a long time. On his behalf, I visited all the heads of state in West

Africa. I was twenty-one! I had a suitcase, and a little briefcase, and I was carry-ing papers to Modibo Keita [first president of Mali], to Hamani Diory [first president of Niger], to [Ahmed] Sekou Touré [first president of Guinea]. After that, I went back to France and continued my studies—literature, sciences, and music. In 1965 Malcolm X was assassinated and I decided to go to the United States. A young black man like me in Paris had two things to discover: Africa and America. That was clear in my head. So I went to the United States, and ten years later I came back to France, I did a PhD. I taught at the University of Caen in Normandy and was involved in the psychoanalytic scene in Paris. Then at last I got a chair in Martinique. During all this time, I practiced trumpet like a painter trying to find his colors. At the end of 2002, I went to Cornell University as a visiting professor and stayed three years.

How comfortable were you in Martinique? Did you feel like it was not entirely your own?

No, it was totally my own. I never felt foreign there. But I never felt foreign in Africa, nor in the United States.

Did you learn about Senghor and Aimé Césaire, and the Negritude writers, as a natural part of growing up in Paris when you did?

Yeah, from a young age. First of all, because in my family we recited poems, and we were supposed to know those poets by heart. And then, I was fascinated by their writing. Thus, I learned the essential things in literature in my family, be-fore the age of fourteen. Literature, in my family, was the most important thing in the world. To be illiterate was the worst insult you could get.

You went back to Martinique to make your record, Clameurs *[2007]. With texts by Frantz Fanon, Edouard Glissant, and others, it seems to have been like a great* cahier d'un retour au pays natal *[notebook of a return to one's native land], to use Césaire's phrase.*

It's funny, I'm always saying that I'm not attached to identity, and suddenly I cut a record totally involved with Martinique. But precisely this is the difference between identity that is an image and being what you are.

Looking at where you've been, and considering Clameurs, *it's almost as if it took the better part of a lifetime to arrive at doing that record. Or was it a simpler process that you went through?*

Well, since I didn't want to be what I am [*laughs*], I was just trying to do something. Anyway, you cannot be an artist if you don't have one foot on the ground and the other outside the planet.

A couple of years ago in an interview you said, "On ne fait pas de la musique en écoutant de la musique: il faut écouter le monde [*You don't make music by listening to music: you must listen to the world*]." *Where along the line did you come to that understanding?*

I strongly like the noise of the world: cars, planes, people, stones falling down. I'm more interested in sound and timbres than in melody proper. If you listen to *Clameurs*, you see that the melody comes out of the sound: I don't play any phrases there or melodic motifs; I just play the sound, and the sound makes the melody.

Steve Weber

Cofounder of the Holy Modal Rounders, with Peter Stampfel, guitarist Steve Weber rarely gives interviews. From the start he was recognized for the fluency of his technique and the divine spontaneity he brought to old-time music. During their initial period in New York in the mid-1960s, the Rounders recorded in studio as a duo and with the Fugs, as well as the Detroit concert *Live in 65* released by ESP some forty years later. They were already in their first reincarnation on *Indian War Whoop* for ESP in 1967, an album that cross-pollinated popular genres with hearty abandon. By 1970, with the addition of Robin Remailly, Dave Reisch, Richard Tyler, Teddy Deane, and Roger North, the band moved to Boston for a couple of years, playing throughout New England; meanwhile, Stampfel stayed in New York, effectively leaving the group except for occasional reunions. In 1972 the Holy Modal Rounders went off to Stockholm as the house band for Wavy Gravy's Hog Farm commune, which was sent by Stewart Brand as the alternative U.S. delegation to the U.N. Environmental Conference.

After Europe, the expanded ensemble made Portland, Oregon, their base (where they became the house band at the White Eagle) and toured the United States off and on for the next twenty-plus years. Weber moved back east in the mid-1990s—first to his native Pennsylvania and eventually to West Virginia where he lives today—though he returned to Portland annually to play with the band. The original Rounders made one more record in 1999 and performed for the last time together in 2002.

For many musicians coming up in the late 1950s and early 1960s, who were interested in American folk traditions, the Harry Smith anthology was a fundamental source. Was that true for you as well? And how did Joseph Spence shape your perspective?

Yes, the anthology was important to me. I learned a lot from it. Joseph Spence felt incredibly right to me, like a delightful puzzle. I liked his percussive handling of the guitar and the decoding of his words, which was as intriguing as it was difficult due to his thick accent. It was clear that he performed without inhibitions—the mark of a natural-born musician!

What made the Rounders different from all the folk revivalists, in your view?

We took more of a raucous and zany detour. Most folkies were very serious about social reform, which was good. I regret we didn't move more along those lines.

How did you end up joining the Fugs?

I was hanging around the Peace Eye Bookstore on the Lower East Side and met Ed Sanders. The Rounders were not doing much at the time, and Ed invited me to join the yet-to-be-formed Fugs.

How would you describe your contribution to the Fugs' sound?

I guess, Ed and Tuli were more poets than musicians, and vice versa!

Did you write "Boobs a Lot" for the Fugs? Did the life of that song surprise you at all? Did you write other songs for the Fugs?

No, I wrote it when I was still living in Pennsylvania. Did the life of that song surprise me? Yes and no. I didn't think much about it at the time. But folks do seem to like novelty theme songs. I never wrote any songs for the Fugs, per se.

The Rounders hadn't been playing together hardly at all by the time ESP invited you to do a record in 1967. Besides whatever money, why did you accept?

Ed knew Bernard Stollman, and I really didn't care what label at the time. It was just fun making a record, as usual. We did *Virgin Fugs* and *Village Fugs*. Those are the only two Fugs albums that I am on. I'm glad I did the Fugs albums, as I liked the more social comment.

Did you know of ESP before then?

I wasn't aware of the label at the time. I was just young and went with the natural flow of things.

There has been a range of opinion about the ESP record. What do you think of it yourself? How did the radio-theater element come about?

I do like *Indian War Whoop*; it's unusual. The engineer told me to just do whatever comes into my head. I liked the free association concept. I still do. That's my approach to performing, always!!

Stampfel has said you didn't want to work out new songs. But on the ESP album most of the songs had not been recorded before by the Rounders. So, were those songs on the record already in the Rounders' repertoire, or . . . were they new songs?!

Why is recording onstage repertoire a problem? If he didn't like the songs we were performing, why were we performing them at all?

How would you say your approach to playing and rehearsing might be different from Stampfel's?

I don't like rehearsing much. I like to keep things fresh and natural.

What was your experience of payment and royalties on the ESP record?

I left the business to others. I was trusting and naive at the time. I was really just enjoying the collective music scene.

How did working with Sam Shepard affect the Rounders' approach, on that record and later being part of his play Operation Sidewinder? *Did having a drummer change things much?*

This was not our first drummer: Ken Weaver played drums with the Fugs. Sam has terrific energy and humor, like any great drummer he gave backbone to the Holy Modal Rounders! *Operation Sidewinder* was never recorded, unfortunately. But it was one of our first big time gigs—Lincoln Center. I thoroughly enjoyed working with the theater!

What kind of relations did you have with Bernard and ESP in the decades between the release of Indian War Whoop *and discussions about releasing* Live in 65?

I didn't see Bernard again until a gig at Tonic in New York, where after the show he gave Peter and me each a check for seven hundred dollars, I believe it was. That was around 2000.

How was it that you and Peter got back in contact with ESP after so long, if the results of the Rounders' one record for the label produced such mixed feelings?

It was at one of the Tonic gigs. And I had no feelings one way or the other. I had no problem with *Indian War Whoop.* I was just surprised and happy to see a royalty check!

How did the record Live in 65 *come about?*

A lot of our stage performances were recorded by fans—you know, bootleg recordings. This one was on cassette, long forgotten, and when Peter's mother died it was found in her attic by Peter's brother.

Why did Peter give you a copy of the CD transfer of the tape?

He didn't. I was invited to a party in Brooklyn, and sound engineer Matt Sohn transferred the cassette to CD format. He had made two master copies: one he gave to me and the other to Peter.

Why did you, and Bernard, go ahead with its release if Peter was so much against it?

I didn't know about Peter being against it. He never said anything negative about Bernard to me. That wasn't a topic of discussion. He never said a word to me even when we met up with Bernard after so many years at Tonic.

But weren't the negotiations for that record's release complicated by some prior agreement with Gene Rosenthal and the Adelphi label?

I never signed any agreement to give Adelphi any records. No such paper exists with my signature on it. Gene Rosenthal told me to be at that party and arranged for somebody to pick me up in Bucks County, Pennsylvania, to bring me there "so we could discuss Adelphi possibly releasing *Live in 65*." Neither Peter nor Gene talked at all to me about it. Gene just took a lot of pictures at the party, and then he and Peter left together! I called Peter within a week and asked him if we were going to discuss releasing *Live in 65* with Gene or whoever. Peter then snapped at me saying, "It's MINE. It was found in my mother's attic, it's mine!" I answered him back, "No, Peter, it belongs to both of us. Where it was doesn't matter. It always belonged to both of us." So, since Rosenthal and Peter were going to make a deal without me, I decided to take it to Bernard, and the contract I had drawn up with Bernard states "50 percent of net profits are to be paid to Peter Stampfel." Even though he was not willing to share it, that was not how I thought. I wanted to do what was fair! If Bernard didn't pay him, well, I didn't get any royalties from it either. I did ask Bernard a number of times about the royalties, and he said something about a distributor that went out of business or something to that effect. I still do not understand!

In 2006 a documentary was released about the Holy Modal Rounders, Born to Lose. *Why were you dissatisfied with the film?*

At first, I thought it was some college project. I asked the filmmakers, who originally were a band Peter played with, "What are your intentions?" Then they said they would want to release it to the public. At that point, I told them that I want to see work in progress and reserve artistic control, have a contract written for all parties involved, and get a percent of the profits. They agreed. When I began pressing them for a contract, that's when their true intentions began to show. They told me, "You will get NO money. We are going to make you notorious." At this point, I stopped letting them film me. I was due for my annual gig in Portland, which I always loved doing!! I knew those paparazzi would be there lurking for me. Terribly torn up inside, I was thinking of all my friends and fans; I didn't want to let them down. But I just could not let myself be subjected to those paparazzi after having been lied to and tricked.

When the film was finished, I did ask for a copy to review, and they said that it was "too late to edit, it's already finished"—although they edited it a number of times after!! They stopped pretending to be my friends and lawyered up and tried to make me sign a release before they even sent me a copy to see! Finally, their lawyer had them send me a copy, knowing nobody would sign any release for something they never saw. When I did see it, it literally made me ill. I was completely taken out of context. The film is NOT a documentary of the Rounders (nineteen years of the Rounders on the West Coast were but a footnote!!). I can't think about this anymore; it still makes me ill. That film is the reason I am no longer in the Holy Modal Rounders. Me, blowing the gig . . . Other band members decided to make the best of this tabloid film. But I was the one trashed in it. Enough said. [*Big sigh.*] Silence.

Steve Stollman

Youngest brother, and sixth of the seven siblings, Steve Stollman took on the role of freelance liaison for the label during an extended visit to Europe in the mid-1960s and remained an intermittent associate on his return. Thirteen years younger than Bernard, he subsequently worked as a distributor of underground newspapers and comix, and for more than three decades was proprietor of a nineteenth-century Manhattan storefront at 49 East Houston Street, where he sold antique bars and original Automat machines. He also worked as a community activist out of that space, fighting the city's demolition of newsstands and helping environmental and cyclists' rights groups, while offering them a space to meet.

Where were you when the ESP label started?

I was living on Christopher Street. I had moved into the apartment of Ralph Rinzler, who was one of the Greenbriar Boys, but he was also Alan Lomax's deputy. He'd been called down to Washington, and he left all his instruments hanging on the wall. A girlfriend of mine knew him, so I ended up subletting his apartment. I got out of college in '63, and I was going crazy living back at home. Then I was able to buy the apartment underneath his, and I had that until I left the country in 1965. I was pretty familiar with what Bernard was up to. But I don't know, where was his office at that point?

Around that time he was using your parents' apartment as a sort of office, while he lived up in the maid's room.

I lived in that maid's room too, after he moved out. It was Erich Fromm's maid's room before him. And later after I moved out, Peter Shaffer bought it. So, I was encountering Bernard while he was putting the label together in my parents' apartment. And then, he got me a job at the Village Vanguard. He was Ornette's lawyer, and he got me this job as the headwaiter. I took over from a guy who had been there for years, Hilly Kristal; he later started CBGB on the Bowery. So, part of my job was supposed to be to watch the door, to make sure that Ornette didn't get cheated, allegedly. I had no idea what money they took in. I was there for around six months, and during that time the most incredible succession of musicians came through there, no lightweights. The lightest-weight people were Richard Alpert and Tim Leary. Richard Alpert tried to do a comedy act, which fell on its face, and Timothy Leary brought over a bunch of people who were involved with taking LSD. They called themselves the League of Spiritual Discovery—they lit candles, they wore white robes, they put on projectors; it was bizarre. Meanwhile, Ornette turned me on to LSD. And I got paid for listening to all this music! If I owe Bernard anything, that job alone was worth the price of admission.

What was your arrangement with Bernard when you went to Europe in '65? Where did you go?

I told him as long as I'm going to be there, I might as well try and help him out. He had contacts; the records were more popular in England and France than in the United States. I was there for about eighteen months. I traveled around to different countries: Denmark, France, Germany. I think I did a little better than he was ready to give me credit for, considering the fact that I was totally naive, and I'd never really had any experience in business.

I landed in Paris. The first thing I did for Bernard was I went over to the record store on the Champs-Elysées, which had sold more of his records than anybody in the world, I think. I tried to negotiate a distribution deal for him in Paris, but I was hopelessly inexperienced. And somehow I met Gaït Frogé [who ran the English Bookshop]. I was staying at the Shakespeare and Company bookshop, crashed upstairs. Gaït had done the Burroughs record [*Call Me Burroughs*]. She was friends with him, but she didn't know what to do with it. So, I sent it to Bernard.

Wherever I went, I contacted the people he was doing business with and tried to get them to do something more serious. I don't know that any of the contacts I made resulted in improved relations. One particular mind-blowing encounter was in Germany—at Deutsche Grammophon, I think. It was very bizarre for a company like Deutsche Grammophon to consider selling records like ESP. But I went to a meeting with these people and started playing records. Nobody had turned on the lights because it was daytime when we started, but by the time we finished, the room was almost totally dark, and Sun Ra was playing on the phonograph. These people were not ready for this stuff, but the public was, so they had to be interested. The idea was to get a deal in each country for distribution. You had to do it country by country.

You were most active in London during that trip. What did you get up to there?

I went to Better Books and hooked up with [Barry] Miles and his crew. I fell in with this crowd, and John Hopkins—the guy he started the *International Times* with—and a few others. I arrived there at the same time as Michael Hollingshead did, the man who supposedly turned Timothy Leary on to LSD, so there was a lot going on, a lot of intellectual ferment and questioning.

I ended up doing these happenings. I wanted to figure out how I could promote the record company. The point was, to me, breaking down categories—these definitions were not helpful; they were instead problematic. So, I thought it would be a great idea to have events that took activity from different fields and different points of view. And these people liked the idea. These people all knew each other too well; they needed somebody from the outside to come in to shake things up a little, and I ended up being that person.

I did about five or six of these events at the Marquee Club, and there were also a bunch of them at the ICA. And they were musical; there were some people who ended up being famous who played there, like the Graham Bond Organisation, with Jack Bruce and Ginger Baker. Essentially, the question was, What is the connection between all this liveliness that was happening? What were the possibilities of people breaking out of their conventional definitions of what matters?

Ian Sommerville was part of the crowd that I was hanging with. The concert that Ian recorded as the sound engineer, and then disappeared with the tape, was the first happening. That was the first time that Pink Floyd had played in public; it went on for like three hours. They came back a couple of times.

Peter Lemer, for instance, was one of the people who played at the ICA. He ended up making a record for Bernard [*Local Colour* was Lemer's debut and also the first appearance on record of saxophonist John Surman]. Once the word got around that these things were happening, people just showed up. I was barely part of the scene. I just dropped in from nowhere, but that was good in a way because I didn't have the baggage, the rivalries.

You also did some work for ESP after returning to New York. Didn't you go to the convention of black radio executives in Atlanta with Alan Silva, where they had no interest in ESP artists?

That was hilarious. We got there late, so we missed the announcement that all the white executives should please go home. Bill Cosby was the keynote speaker.

It was one of those very few occasions that we did something in a businesslike way. I remember sharing an elevator with Nicholas Johnson, who was one of the FCC commissioners; he was a speaker at this thing. I said to him, "Do you mind if I ask, we've got this group called the Fugs, and there are people who are telling me they're going to get in trouble by announcing the name of the group on the radio. Would you mind telling me whether you think that's so?" He said, "As far as I'm concerned, it's fine. I don't see any problem with it." I actually got a quasi-official opinion from the FCC!

When were you at ESP, which location? How was it to work for your brother?

I came back and worked for Bernard at 156 Fifth Avenue. I worked for Bernard at West End Avenue and 74th Street. I worked for him all over the place, when he was on 55th Street and Eighth Avenue. I spent many months of my life trying to help him out, to push him in a certain direction. My beef with Bernard is very simple: all he really ever cared about was signing new artists. He just loved the idea of reaching into the universe and discovering some gem, pulling it out from under the ocean, washing it off, and then putting it in a box and up on a shelf.

Unless you had a record, you didn't exist and you couldn't get gigs. There was all this bullshit, these magical gates that you had to be able to go through. So, he helped destroy that, the artificial barrier to people being able to make their way into the real world. And for that I think he deserves a lot of credit. It was difficult to do. But the job was always to take it the rest of the way, and to a certain extent he didn't follow through. He didn't want to do the dirty work.

What sort of work were you doing for him?

I was trying to do selling and promoting and just trying to make the place work in some fashion on the business end. But I could only do so much. The problem was I was always his kid brother, and he just professed to have no interest in that whole area. It was "That doesn't matter, because that part of it is being a merchant." My parents were merchants; there was nothing romantic about that— that's how you put bread on the table. But this other stuff about art, and politics, and breaking through these barriers to experience—that's exciting, that's fun. The mundane shit, anybody could do that.

It was my idea to get Alan Silva to be a salesman, and Becky Friend; that was the sales department: Becky and Alan and me. And I got a WATS line, which he never stopped criticizing me for. It cost eight hundred dollars a month or some huge amount of money, but anybody could call you for free. I thought it was the greatest idea in the world: we could connect to all these salespeople and all these stores, and the radio stations, and they would all call us. We could never quite get up the head of steam to do it. We would talk to people out there in the hinterlands. It was like you had forty distributors, and then you had major stores. You had to really work the territory to make a success in that business.

As the oldest of the seven children, he went to your parents and asked for his inheritance now instead of later, to run the company. How did that play out among the rest of you?

But then he got it later too! He got this money for the company, and they were not rich people. They didn't give him his inheritance; they didn't give him one-seventh of what they had—they gave him a huge chunk of what they had! They didn't have any investment capital; they just ran these stores every day. And so, they eventually came into the business because they were afraid he was going to squander the entire family fortune, such as it was.

He had my parents working in that club on Lafayette Street [the Astor Place Playhouse], where the Fugs were. They were standing there watching the door, selling tickets so people could come in and see Sun Ra or see the Fugs. My poor immigrant parents, they're in this place selling tickets! They didn't care. They were tough; nothing bothered them.

So, with Bernard receiving that windfall, it wasn't a point of contention in the family?

We were not brought up to be materialistic. Perhaps some of my siblings might have been resentful of it, that's possible. I wasn't resentful. I thought that what he was doing was noble—my God, criticizing the CIA to help people who were struggling to have some dignity and health in a society that is determined to keep people from having their dignity and their health. And here's somebody who gives a fuck about that? Thank you, Bernard. I think he largely gave me my social conscience. So, I'm very pleased that Bernard was like that. He got it from somewhere. His parents were people who were peasants, who managed to keep from getting killed and scored big in the United States. They appreciated life every day and thought it was wonderful to be alive, and they instilled in their children an appreciation of life.

Index

Cohen, Michael, 98, 101

Coleman, Ornette, 16–19, 109, 174, 279–80

Coltrane, John, 49, 91, 98–99, 145–46, 174, 196, 255

Columbia Records, 41–42, 194, 259

Connecticut tribe, 240–43, 247

Contemporary Records, 103, 106

Cooper, Jerome, 252

copyright, 14, 41–42, 76–77

Cosby, Bill, 67

Coursil, Jacques, 103, 145, 254, 257, 265–72

Crist, Art, 61

Cromagnon, 240–46

Davidson, Lowell, 109–10, 114–15, 161, 210–16

Davis, Art, 14

Davis, Miles, 261–62

Dexter, Van, 199, 201–3

Dillon, Jay, 53, 95–96

Dixon, Bill, xv, 22, 103, 110, 135, 145, 172–74, 267–68

Dolphy, Eric, 103, 106, 151

Dom, the, 266–67

Donald, Barbara, 99–100, 103–7

Douglas, Alan, 18, 135

Downs, Charles, 210–12

Dufty, Maely, 13

Dylan, Bob, 151–52

East Village Other, 28, 34, 40, 85

Edmiston, Peter, 53, 55, 130–31

Ehlers, Michael, 258–59

Ellington, Duke, 175–76

Elliot, Brian, 240–42, 244–45

Ephron, Michael, 65, 176

Erdman, Jean, 57, 155, 199–203

ESP-Disk': art directors, 24–25, 53; business, 23, 26–28, 31–36, 38–44, 52–56, 60, 75–76; college tour, 29–30, 183, 196; European artists, 32–33, 87–89; failure, 38–44; Global Copyright Administration, 31, 76–77; launch, 27–28; licens-ing, xvi, 36, 42, 69–72, 237; Pier 17 concert, 30–31; politics, 34, 38–40, 60, 86, 157; publishing, 31, 76, 82; record-ing engineers, 24, 30, 43, 46–47, 61–62, 150–59, 177, 244–45; relaunch, xvii–xix, 73–76, 232, 237–39; royalties, xvii, 35–36, 69–71, 76–77, 82–83, 237; Town Hall concert (May 1, 1965), 45

ESP-Disk' catalog: *Balaklava* (Pearls Before Swine), 128–29, 132; *Barrage* (Paul Bley), 112; *Bells* (Albert Ayler), 45, 150–51, 204; *Black Beings* (Frank Lowe), 217–19; *Burton Greene Quartet*, 194–95; *Call Me Burroughs*, 57, 280; *Closer* (Paul Bley), 154; *The Coach with the Six Insides*, 31, 57, 155, 199–203; *College Tour* (Patty Waters), 51; *Concert for the Comet Kohoutek* (Sun Ra), 48–49; *Contact High with the Godz*, 54; *East Village Other*, 34, 40, 85–86, 157; *The Forest and the Zoo* (Steve Lacy), 58; *The Fugs*, 52, 83, 155–56; *The Giuseppi Logan Quartet*, 47, 112, 181; *Gold* (Lindha Kallerdahl), 247; *Helio-centric Worlds* (Sun Ra), 48, 152–54; *Indian War Whoop* (Holy Modal Rounders), 158, 185, 188–90, 275–76; *In Search of the Mystery* (Gato Barb-ieri), 224–26, 250; *Live at the Blue Note in Paris, 1961* (Bud Powell), 18; *Live in 65* (Holy Modal Rounders), 185, 191, 276–77; *Marion Brown Quar-tet*, 145–47; *Movement Soul*, 58; *Music from Europe* (Gunter Hampel), 87–90; *Music from the Orthodox Liturgy* (Slavonic Cappella Ensemble), 59; *Music from the Spheres* (Sonny Sim-mons), 98, 100, 103–5; *New York Art Quartet*, 48, 91–93, 110–12, 160–63, 228–29; *New York Eye and Ear Con-trol*, 91–92, 141–43, 163–64, 256; *Ni Kantu en Esperanto*, xv, 20; *One Nation Underground* (Pearls Before

Rapp, Tom (Pearls Before Swine), 26, 38–40, 53–55, 67, 126–33, 136, 157–58
Reed, Ishmael, 85–86
Revolutionary Ensemble, 248, 250–53
Ribback, Alan, 58
Rivers, Sam, 103, 194, 265
Robinson, Perry, 51, 192, 196–97, 265–66
Rose, Boris, 41, 239
Rudd, Roswell, 48, 91–93, 110–12, 141, 143, 160–65

Salgado, Sal, 240–46
Sam Goody's (record store), 94, 217, 234
Sanders, Ed, 39, 52–53, 82, 155–56, 274
Sanders, Pharoah, 46, 146, 196, 229
Sarser, Dave, 17
Scholtze, Onno, 43, 62, 177, 245–46
Scott, Calo, 225, 249–50
Senghor, Léopold Sédar, 270
Shepard, Sam, 185, 188, 190–91, 275–76
Shepp, Archie, 22, 145–46, 164, 228–29
Silva, Alan, 65, 172–79, 192–93, 209, 254, 265, 281–82
Silver, Roy, 67
Simmons, Sonny, 98–101, 103–9
Sinatra, Frank, 155–56
Singleton, Charlie, 15
Sirone, 147, 225, 248–53
Smith, Harry, 185–86
Smith, Warren, 127–28, 134–39, 180
Smith, W. Eugene, 45
Smithsonian, 71
Snow, Michael, 91, 141–44, 163–64
Sommerville, Ian, 57, 281
Sondheim, Alan, 119–25, 180
Spence, Joseph, 273–74
Stampfel, Peter, 185–91, 273, 275–77
Stollman, Bernard: Catskills farm (Acorn Hill House), 42–43, 65, 72, 208, 258; college, 8–9; Esperanto, xv–xvi, 20; Jewish background of, 3–5, 7; law practice, 13–18, 22–23, 41–44, 46, 72; law school, 9; MIDEM,

33–34, 64–65; military service, 9–12; musical education, 7–8; and Norman Stollman (brother), 41, 73; parents of (David and Julia), 3–8, 16, 23, 26, 43–44, 54, 73–74, 103, 118, 279, 283; parents' dress shops, 4–6, 8; Paris, 11–12, 46, 59; Plattsburgh (NY), 4–8, 12; political activism, 9–11, 283; and Solomon Stollman (brother), 5; textile business, 12; wife of, 41–43, 71–72, 258
Stollman, Sandra, x, 73, 105
Stollman, Steve, 18, 57, 73, 119, 178, 279–83
Strata-East Records, 138
Streisand, Barbra, 63–64
Studio Rivbea, 66, 217
Sultan, Juma, 65
Sumac, Yma, 55–56
Summers, Barbara, 263–64
Sun Ra, 22, 29–30, 48–49, 52, 146, 152–54, 173–75, 232–36, 268

Taylor, Cecil, 16, 45, 113, 176, 254–57; Café Montmartre (Copenhagen), 45, 256
Taylor, James, 67
Tchicai, John, 91–93, 110–12, 141, 160–61
Termini, Joe, 255
Terronès, Gérard, 148, 263
Thiele, Bob, 17, 46
Thornton, Paul, 53, 94–97
Tiger Tiger, 43–44
Tolkin, Stanley (Stanley's bar), 85, 266
27 Cooper Square, 51, 111, 146, 228–29, 263

Vandermark, Ken, 220–23
Variety Arts Studio, 21
Velebny, Karel, 32–33
Velvet Underground, 157
Village Theater, 67, 248–49
Vision Festival, 48, 51, 217, 254

Warhol, Andy, 157
Warner Brothers, 38–40, 53, 67, 130–31

About the Author

Jason Weiss is a freelance writer, editor, and translator. He is the editor of *Steve Lacy: Conversations* (2006) and *Back in No Time: The Brion Gysin Reader* (2001), and the author of *The Lights of Home: A Century of Latin American Writers in Paris* (2003). He lives in Brooklyn, New York.